JOSÉ VELÁSQUEZ:
SAGA OF A
BORDERLAND SOLDIER
(Northwestern New Spain
in the 18th Century)

by
Ronald L. Ives

Southwestern Mission Research Center
Tucson, Arizona
1984

ISBN 0-915076-10-1

Library of Congress Catalog Card Number 84-050008

Cover drawing of José Velásquez:
Artist conception by Paul Rossi, Santa Fe, New Mexico

DEDICADO

A la memoria
de los tres viejos amigos

Alberto Celaya
Rev. Dr. Bonaventure Oblasser, O.F.M.
Ygnacio Quiroz

TABLE OF CONTENTS

LIST OF ILLUSTRATIONS

FOREWORD

hose who knew Ronald Ives remember him as a prolific writer of scientific and technical articles. His personal bibliography reached over 800 separate titles before increasing ill health slowed his productivity in his retirement years. Ron was known to most as a meteorologist and cartographer; but he was also an electronic and instrument specialist, an accomplished instructor in survival in difficult environments, and more than an amateur historian.

José Velásquez: Saga of a Borderland Soldier was Ron's only book length manuscript. In his last years, when this book was offered to various presses for consideration, he learned that some wanted shorter treatment, some wanted more biography, and some shied away from a book on the wastelands of the West. Ron remained steadfast about the lowly soldier he learned to respect from the archival record. He saw in José Velásquez a kindred spirit who could survive and conquer life-threatening wilderness. He saw in him the strength of loyalty and the stability of genuine dedication. These were Ron's own qualities because he had participated in some of the U.S. Army's most awesome experiments in chemical warfare. He knew more than he would ever admit even to his closest friends. In many ways the burden of his knowledge forced him to be a semi-recluse, and in that self-imposed seclusion he grew to know the great men of desert exploration like Kino, Ugarte, and Garcés. He was fascinated by Pedro Fages and was introduced to José Velásquez, an obscure but vital frontiersman.

When José Velásquez died, surely no important Spanish official of the time would have ever imagined that centuries later a quiet, keenly observant scientist-professor would write a book about him. But that's exactly what Ron did, and perhaps the generations to come will now know something about the greatness of ordinary life. Time will honor both the humble soldier from New Spain and the scientist who loved the desert skies.

When staff members of the Southwestern Mission Research Center read this manuscript, the impression was unanimous — it was a book that deserved to be made available to the general public. It is in itself a piece of Ronald Ives' life. It is his expression about the mystery of life — told in unemotional understatement. When the decision was made to publish the book, Ron was still alive but greatly weakened. He worked on proofing the first chapter, but the sands of time ran out. This book is presented as Ron wrote it. The text is his; the photos are his; the maps are his. In a way Ron was saying "This is José Velásquez in context, and here am I."

Charles W. Polzer, S.J.

PREFACE

his short book is a biography of José Velásquez, soldier of Spain, who lived from 1717 to 1785 and who served his king with rank slowly advancing from private to alférez from 1751 to 1785.[1] Primary information sources have been his own writings, all available official reports, and various letters. Secondary sources have been his service record *(cf. Appendix A)* and a very few mentions of him and his work in other records and documents. Numerous hiatuses in the record give clues to documents which once must have existed, but which if still extant remain to be found.

Itineraries of José Velásquez' major journeys, as described in available documents, have been verified in the field; all major routes were followed afoot or by jeep. All of the area has been overflown in fixed-wing aircraft, and small sectors, all in Alta California, by helicopter.

Prior to the writing of this work, a considerable amount of research was done on the life of José Velásquez by Charles N. Rudkin, John W. Robinson, and Froy Tiscarena. After careful checking, major portions of this ''inherited'' work were found reliable and have been incorporated. Site and trail descriptions by others who travelled over approximately the same routes helped to clarify many points unspecified in Velásquez's narratives.

The major source for documents was the Bancroft Library, Berkeley, California, which over a period of years has been most helpful — not only in supplying data from its own voluminous collections, but also in indicating actual or probable sources of information elsewhere.

During the preparation of this work discussion of documentary problems and general ''note swapping'' was done with Rev. Dr. Ernest J. Burrus, S.J., of El Paso, Texas; Rev. Dr. Charles W. Polzer, S.J., of Kino House, Tucson, Arizona; and with the late Rev. Dr. Maynard Geiger, O.F.M. of Old Mission Santa Barbara, Santa Barbara, California. These exchanges were found most profitable. Geographical data to augment field work was supplied by the U.S. Geological Survey, the U.S. Coast and Geodetic Survey, the National Aeronautics and Space Administration, the U.S. Weather Bureau, the Servicio Geológico de México and the Servicio Meterológico de México. Access to unpublished

---

[1]His name is variously spelled; the first being written as Josef, Joseph, and José. The last is seen as Velásques, Velázques and Velásquez.

"Color Infra-Red" and "Color Enhanced" aerial photographs of parts of Baja California was provided by several governmental agencies, which helped to clear up a number of geographical uncertainties.

Assistance and information in the field was furnished by a wide variety of Mexican citizens, ranging in station from high government officials to sandaled road-menders. All is here gratefully acknowledged. Similarly appreciated are the assistance and information furnished by the staffs of the Cleveland National Forest and of Anza-Borrego State Park in (Alta) California.

† x †

ACKNOWLEDGEMENTS

he preface to this book includes the acknowledgements of the author to the several people who played a part in its composition. These acknowledgements, however, are gratefully made to certain other persons who have made the publication of this book possible. Ronald Ives we feel certain would have included them in his own remarks had he lived to witness their role in this book's final preparation. First on the list is Julian Hayden of Tucson. Throughout Ron's vital years, Julian was protagonist, antagonist, foil and crutch in the struggle to understand the awesome area at the head of the Gulf of California. In Ron's last days when the altitudes of Flagstaff were too unhealthful, Julian shared his home and offered unexcelled hospitality. Second on the list was Jane Harrison Ivancovich also of Tucson who sat on the Board of Directors of the Southwestern Mission Research Center with Ron. It was she who recognized and championed the cause of this book's publication. Third on the list is Ron's natural sister Mrs. Charles Beyer of Williamsville, New York. When she learned that the SMRC was already planning on the publication of José Velásquez, she directed a portion of Ron's estate to help defray some of the costs of publication. Hardly known to Ronald Ives or the other principal parties in the publication of this book were dedicated typists and editors. Martha O. Martin seemed ceasely to type the manuscript into the SMRC's computers. Thomas H. Naylor read, critiqued and polished points in the text. And Carmen V. Prezelski bolstered the author's spirits by fielding long telephone calls to search out information or to arrange critical consultations. Like José Velásquez before him, Ron was surrounded by scores of silent coworkers whose contributions Ron would be the first to recognize. Thanks to each and all.

HISTORICAL SUMMARY

hen the biography of a king, viceroy, governor, or an important military leader is written, there is relatively little need for an historical background because such high ranking authorities by their very acts make history. However, when the biography of a common soldier or a low-ranking officer is written, an historical summary is much more appropriate because those of lower rank do not make policies or issue major orders. Instead, they follow the policies and orders made and given by their superiors in rank. Moreover, to evaluate the work of those relatively low in the table of organization, it is important to distinguish between acts performed under firm orders from above and those performed when the individual had a free choice.

During the life of José Velásquez great changes occurred in northern New Spain — in Sonora, Baja California, and, later, in Alta California. Although these three provinces are commonly regarded as separate governmental entities, their interrelations were close and complex not only politically, but also militarily and economically. Many outstanding officers served in two or even three of these provinces during their careers.

Sonora, after the death of Padre Eusebio Kino in 1711, suffered for a prolonged period from a shortage of missionaries and soldiers. Probably in consequence of these shortages Indian unrest also grew. Increasing numbers of settlers — ranchers, farmers, and miners — complicated the situation and brought about pressure for the secularization of the missions. The principal Indian uprisings that affected this history include the Pima Revolt of 1751[1] and the extended Seri wars of 1766 and after.[2]

---

[1]Russell C. Ewing, "The Pima Uprising of 1751-1752: a Study in Spain's Indian Policy," unpublished doctoral dissertation, University of California, 1934; Russell C. Ewing, "The Pima Uprising of 1751," in *Greater America, Essays in Honor of Herbert Eugene Bolton* (Berkeley: University of California Press, 1945) pp. 259-280.

[2]Donald W. Rowland, "The Elizondo Expedition Against the Indian Rebels of Sonora, 1765-1771," unpublished doctoral dissertation, University of California, 1931.

Frequent raids by one or another of numerous Apache bands in Sonora assured that the local garrisons did not suffer from ennui or idleness. Many of the soldiers who served in the Sonoran Indian campaigns later played an important part in the exploration, settlement, and government of Alta California. Among these were Juan Bautista de Anza, José Joaquín Moraga, Pedro Fages and Joseph Romeu.

Although poorly publicized and documented, Sonora during this period became an important mineral producer; many of today's active mines were discovered prior to 1800. Spectacular mineral bonanzas included the "Bolas de Plata" find at Arizonac in 1736[3] and the Cieneguilla placers in 1771.[4] Apparently many Sonoran mines at this time were worked secretly to avoid payment of the "King's Fifth" among other taxes.

After 1745 a new group of Jesuit missionaries, mostly from northern Europe, arrived in Sonora to replace the pioneers on the northern frontier, whose ranks had been thinned by death, transfer, and retirement. Among these newcomers were Jacob Sedelmayr[5] and Juan Nentvig.[6] Mission plans at this time included expansion of the mission chain to extend northeastward into New Mexico, northward into the unknown lands *(Tierra Incognita)*, and northwestward to Alta California. Diligent efforts were made to realize these plans, but definitve results were not obtained due to lack of missionaries, soldiers, and funds.[7]

In mid-1767 by the royal edict of Charles III the Jesuits were expelled from all Spanish domains in the New World. The Sonoran *expulsados*, forty-nine in all, were gathered first in Mátape in south central Sonora and marched to San José de Guaymas where they were imprisoned in a windowless warehouse for ten months. When a French packet boat commandeered by the Spaniards finally arrived at Guaymas in 1768, the exiles were blown across the Gulf to Baja California. Dangerously weakened and ill, the men reached port at San Blas. From there they travelled overland across Mexico, stopping for a time at

---

[3]R. L. Ives, "The Bolas de Plata Discovery of 1736," *Rocks and Minerals*, Vol. 10, 1935, 183-184.

[4]Kieran McCarty, *Desert Documentary*, (Tucson: Arizona Historical Society, 1976) pp. 19-24.

[5]R. L. Ives "Sedelmayr's Relación of 1746," *Bureau of American Ethnology*, Bul. 123, 1939, pp. 99-117: Peter M, Dunne, *Jacobo Sedelmayr*.

[6]Juan Nentvig, *Rudo Ensayo*, Translated and edited by Eusebio Gutieras, Records American Catholic Historical Society of Philadelphia, Vol. 5, No. 2, 1784, pp. 99-264.

[7]John A. Donohue, *After Kino, Jesuit Missions in Northwestern New Spain, 1711-1767*.

Guadalajara. Twenty-five survivors from the original group reached Veracruz; they sailed for Spain aboard the *Princess Ulrica* and the *Adventurer*. Once arrived, most were imprisoned for varying periods.[8]

Although all Jesuit possessions and property were carefully inventoried or otherwise accounted for at the time of the expulsion, stories of a vast "Jesuit treasure" immediately gained currency and survive to this day. Rather thorough and repeated checking of records indicates that the "Jesuit treasure" had about as much real existence as anhydride of water. Despite great masses of evidence to the contrary, tales of this "Jesuit treasure" are still heard, even in places where the Jesuits never went. The value of this mythical hoard seems to increase by one order of magnitude with the passing of each generation.

Almost immediately the expelled Jesuits were replaced by Franciscans, for the most part from the College of Santa Cruz de Querétaro. They carried on the work of the Jesuits with a minimum of trouble and friction. Comparison of Kino's Plan of 1703 with the well documented achievements of the Franciscans amply demonstrates that, although the field personnel changed, the general mission pattern did not.[9]

Historically important Sonoran Franciscans at this time included Francisco Hermenegildo Garcés[10] and Pedro Font,[11] both very closely

---

[8]Many volumes have been written about the Jesuit expulsion. One is particularly pertinent here; it is the report of Joseph Och, S.J., a Sonoran Jesuit. His report was translated and edited by Theodore E. Treutlein, *Missionary in Sonora*, pp. 49-115.

[9]Ernest J. Burrus, *Kino's Plan*.

[10]Francisco Tomás Hermenegildo Garcés, O.F.M., was born on April 12, 1738, at Monte del Conde, Aragon. He was ordained as a priest in 1763. After missionary studies at the Colegio de la Santa Cruz, Querétaro in Mexico, he was assigned to Mission San Xavier del Bac near modern Tucson, Arizona, in 1768. During the ensuing years he made extensive explorations in Sonora, Baja and Alta California; many were in support of the Anza expeditions. In 1779 he was assigned to the new missions at the Yuma crossing, and there in July, 1781, he and his three companions, Fathers Juan Antonio Barreneche, Juan Marcelo Diaz, and José Matías Moreno were murdered during the Yuma massacre. Cf. Elliott Coues, *On The Trail of a Spanish Pioneer;* John Galvin, *A Record of Travels in Arizona and California.*

[11]Father Pedro Font was born in Catalonia, and his name first appears in New World records at the Colegio de la Santa Cruz, Querétaro, Mexico. He was assigned in 1773 to mission San José de los Pimas thirty-eight miles ESE of Hermosillo. An excellent navigator and chronicler, he was "drafted" to accompany the second Anza expedition to California and to write the journal of the expedition (1775-76). He later served at various Sonoran missions and died at Pitiquito east of Caborca, September 6, 1781. His magnum opus is now known as *Font's Complete Diary*. Herbert H. Bolton, *Anza's California Expeditions;* Vol. III, pp. 205-307 and all of Vol. IV are Font's work.

associated with Juan Bautista de Anza,[12] finder of the overland route to California, and Lieutenant José Joaquín Moraga[13] who became the first commandante of Yerba Buena, now San Francisco. Many of the Sonoran leaders after 1770 also played an important part in the history of Alta California; regardless of their nominal "home base" they travelled extensively and served in both of the frontier provinces.

Shortly after his assignment to mission San Xavier del Bac in 1768, Father Garcés began a series of explorations north and west of his station, retraversing and extending the trails explored and mapped by Kino almost three quarters of a century earlier and reestablishing friendly

[12]Juan Bautista de Anza was the name of two important Sonoran military leaders — father and son. Juan Bautista de Anza, the elder, was born in Spain in 1694 and came to the New World at an early age. He spent most of his very active life as a frontier soldier, much of it as captain of the presidio of Fronteras. In addition to extensive campaigns against Indian rebels he administered the very troublesome "Bolas de Plata" silver discovery; at his own expense he cared for Father Agustín de Campos, S.J., during his declining years. Captain Anza was killed on active duty during an Apache ambush in 1737. Juan Bautista de Anza, the younger, who was born at Fronteras in 1734, began military service as a lieutenant, July 1, 1755, becoming captain December 12, 1759. After extensive service in the Seri Wars, he was assigned captain of the presidio of San Ignacio at Tubac, now in Arizona, in 1760. After serving again on special assignment in the Seri Wars, he spent most of 1774, 1775, and 1776 exploring the overland route to Alta California and took the first settlers to Yerba Buena, now San Francisco. Immediately thereafter, he personally reported his findings to the viceroy in Mexico City. On that return journey he took with him Salvador Palma, chief of the Yumas and two Indian companions. Subsequently, he was appointed Governor of New Mexico where he spent a decade battling Comanche and Apache raiders and struggled with crop failures and smallpox epidemics. Juan Bautista de Anza, the younger, died suddenly in Arizpe, Sonora, on December 19, 1788. See Herbert E. Bolton, *Anza's California Expeditions*.

[13]José Joaquín Moraga was born at Fronteras, Sonora, perhaps in 1735, the son of a soldier of that presidio who died in battle. By 1774 he had served eighteen years and held the rank of alférez. "Because of his ability to write," he was recommended for promotion to a lieutenancy by Juan Bautista de Anza and appointed on December 30, 1774. Accompanying the second Anza expedition to Alta California as second-in-command, he arrived in what later became San Francisco June 27, 1776. As commandante of San Francisco he made several explorations inland; he supervised the building of the mission of San Francisco de Asís, now usually known as Mission Dolores, and the presidio of San Francisco. He is also credited with the founding of mission Santa Clara and the pueblo of San José. Lt. Moraga became very deaf in his later years as a result of exposure in the Yuha Desert in mid-December, 1775. He died in 1785 and is buried beneath the crossing of the nave and the transept in Mission Dolores. His son, Gabriel (ca. 1770-1823), was a prominent military leader in Spanish Alta California; his many descendants still live in that area.

relations with the Indians along these trails. Eventually, his travels took
him to the mouth of the Colorado, the west coast of California (mission
San Gabriel), the headwaters of the Kern River, the depths of Havasu
Canyon (he was probably the first white man to see it), and the hostile
pueblo of Oraibi.[14]

Using his own extensive geographical knowledge of the Sonoran
frontier, augmented by the Kino and Sedelmayr records, and by the new
findings of Father Garcés, Juan Bautista de Anza revived the old idea of
an overland route to California. By 1774 he had obtained viceregal
approval for the journey. Guided in the eastern portion of the route by
Father Garcés, and in the western portion by Sebastián Tarabal, a
California mission Indian who had survived the journey afoot from San
Gabriel to Yuma.[15] Anza and his party journeyed from Tubac westward
across the deserts to Caborca, thence over the Camino del Diablo from
Sonoyta via the Tinajas Altas (Arizona) to Yuma. There, with the
assistance of Salvador Palma, the Yuma chief, they crossed the Colorado

[14]The extensive travels, dependable maps, realized plans, and missionary dreams
of Father Eusebio Francisco Kino, S.J., are detailed in Herbert E. Bolton, *Kino's
Historical Memoir of Pimería Alta*; Herbert E. Bolton, *Rim of Christendom*; Ernest J.
Burrus, *Kino's Plan*; Ernest J. Burrus, *Kino and the Cartography of Northwestern New
Spain*; Fay J. Smith, John L. Kessell, and Francis J. Fox, *Father Kino in Arizona*;
Charles W. Polzer, *Kino Guide II*; Ernest J. Burrus, *Kino and Manje, Explorers of
Sonora and Arizona*. A complete Kino bibliography would contain very considerably
more than 1,000 entries, in a minimum of six languages. A definitive biography of Father
Garcés is still awaited. Bancroft, Coues, and Bolton are all somewhat vague and
occasionally in error regarding some of Garcés' trails. Best information available to date
(1976) is in John Galvin, *A Record of Travels in Arizona and California*.

[15]Sebastián Tarabal, also known as "El Peregrino," was a lower California
mission Indian who had come north to San Gabriel. Finding conditions there not to his
liking, he deserted the mission in late 1773. Accompanied by his wife and a relative
(brother?), he travelled southeastward to the summit of the sierra, descended Coyote
canyon, crossed the Borrego flats, arriving at San Felipe Creek. From there he travelled
directly across the desert toward Yuma. In the Algodones Dunes on the east side of the
Salton Sink (now the Imperial Valley) his wife and companion died of thirst.

Sebastián eventually reached the Yuma settlements, where he was nursed back to
health and taken to Sonora by Chief Palma. At Altar Sonora, he met Anza who recruited
him as a guide for the first expedition to California. For him is named San Sebastián
Marsh near the junction of Carrizo Wash and San Felipe Creek. From this point, he
guided the party westward to mission San Gabriel. On the second Anza Expedition
Sebastián Tarabal remained at Yuma crossing, later accompanying Father Garcés on his
extensive explorations between the Colorado River and the Great Valley of California.
He did not accompany Garcés on his memorable journey to Oraibi, July, 1776; he
disappears from the historical record shortly after May 30, 1776.

and travelled westward across the then-arid Colorado delta lands.[16] When they passed beyond the western limit of Father Garcés' explorations, they were considerably south of Sebastián Tarabal's eastward trail. They had many difficult days of wandering largely due to lack of water and forage for the animals. Eventually, after a return to Yuma to redeploy, they found a workable course around the south side of Volcano Lake (Baja California) and Cerro Prieto. Crossing the Cocopah Mountains, they found water at the north end of Laguna Mecuata and in Pinto Canyon at the base of the Sierra Juárez.

From this barren watering place on the east side of the Sierra Juárez near the foot of the "snaketrack" grade by which modern Mexican Route 2 climbs westward toward La Rumorosa, the Anza party travelled northward into the Yuha desert, making a stop for water at the spring of Santa Rosa de las Lajas (now dry) northwest of modern Yuha Well. Travelling northwestward over loose sand and coarse gravel, they entered Carrizo Wash and after more miles of northerly travel they came to a swampy, spring-fed basin which was recognized by their guide, Sebastián Tarabal, as a stopping place on his eastward journey. This they named San Sebastián in his honor. Water is still present here at about 100 feet below sea level on San Felipe Creek about one and half miles northwest of modern Harper's Well. From San Sebastián the route went up San Felipe Creek, across the Borrego Flats, and up Coyote Creek to the summit with a stop about midway at Santa Catarina Spring, which still flows plentiful sweet water. Route from the summit to San Gabriel was via Bautista Canyon, the upper San Jacinto Valley, and Bernasconi Hot Springs — all over relatively easy terrain compared to the hardships of the deserts to the east. Arriving at the old site of San Gabriel on March

---

[16]Salvador Palma, whose tribal name was Olleyquotequiebe, was the left-handed, probably asthmatic, leader of the Yuma people who controlled the strategic Yuma crossing. From 1774 he became a friend and associate of the Spaniards — ferrying their expeditions across the Colorado, guarding equipment, furnishing supplies, and aiding the missionaries. In the late summer and fall of 1776 he was taken to Mexico City. He was introduced to the viceroy, instructed in Christianity, and baptized in the Cathedral of Mexico with Licenciado Don Agustín de Echeverría y Orcolaga, prebendary of Durango, officiating. Lieutenant Colonel Don Juan Bautista de Anza stood as sponsor and godfather. Returning to Yuma early in 1777 with a new uniform and a host of glittering promises, Palma later aided in establishing the missions and settlements near the Yuma crossing. When the Yumas revolted in the summer of 1781, as a result of broken promises, which was exacerbated by Spanish arrogance and ineptitude, Salvador Palma tried vainly to save the lives of the missionaries. Later, as a consequence of this revolt, he became a hunted fugitive.

22, 1774, the Anza party attended a mass of celebration, but they then faced a shortage of supplies because the ships from Mexico had been delayed, as usual.

While on the California coast, Anza visited San Diego and Monterey. En route he took time to confer with Father Junípero Serra, president of the California Missions; with Pedro Fages, military commander of Alta California; and with Father Francisco Palou, second-in-command of the missions of Alta California. Fathers Garcés and Serra also conferred at length while riding from San Diego to San Gabriel. Although no summaries of these conferences have been found — they probably were never written down, subsequent statements and acts by the various principals indicate that the Californians had received an excellent briefing on the overland route from Sonora. The Sonorans gained much understanding of the California settlements and their problems.

Because of food shortages at San Gabriel the Anza expedition returned east in several separate groups. Using substantially the westbound trail from San Gabriel to the San Sebastián water hole, they took a short cut via San Anselmo Spring (modern Kane Springs) southeastward to the vicinity of modern Mexicali and thence over known trails to Yuma.

Accompanying the expedition as far as the Colorado River were six soldiers from Monterey sent by their commander, Pedro Fages, "in order that they might learn the road." At Yuma it was found that Salvador Palma had taken good care of the supplies and livestock left with him; a good raft was ready to ferry the expedition across the Colorado. At Yuma crossing the California soldiers began their return to Monterey. The main expedition returned to Tubac via the Gila Valley.

Juan Bautista Valdés, the viceroy's courier, departed southward for Mexico City apparently via the Camino del Diablo, Caborca, and Altar. Leaving Yuma after April 25, he arrived in Mexico City before June 14, 1774, and personally delivered the report of Anza's success to the viceroy. As Valdés had brought Anza's original orders from Mexico City to Tubac and had accompanied the expedition to San Gabriel, he became the first man in recorded history to make the round trip on horseback between Mexico City and San Gabriel.

Immediately upon his return to Tubac Anza was assigned to duty at Terrenate, the result of an administrative blunder by Antonio Bonilla, adjutant military inspector. Soon, however, Anza was ordered to Mexico City and reported in person to the viceroy, Antonio María Bucareli.

Within a short time he was promoted to lieutenant colonel and his soldiers were awarded a lifetime bonus of one extra escudo per month. Plans were started for a second overland California expedition with Anza as leader. The second Anza expedition to California was one of the most carefully planned, skillfully executed, and thoroughly documented migrations in American history. It was specifically designed to colonize the San Francisco Bay area, insuring Spain's title to one of the world's best harbors. Settlers were recruited mostly from poverty-stricken areas of southern Sonora (now Sinaloa) and were completely outfitted "from shoes to hair ribbons" for the journey of approximately 1500 miles. With the viceroy's approval many of the soldiers were personally selected by Anza mostly from the frontier presidios of Sonora. Surviving records indicate that these men were veterans of a variety of Indian campaigns with long and honorable service. The soldiers personally selected by Anza performed well on the expedition, and afterwards. Some raw recruits, later assigned to the expedition to fill out the table of organization, did not fare as well.

José Joaquín Moraga, alférez of the presidio of Fronteras at the time, was promoted to lieutenant and became second-in-command of the expedition. He was later appointed commandante of San Francisco. For the expedition's sergeant, Anza selected Pablo Grijalva from Terrenate.[17]

To measure latitudes en route and to keep records of the journey, Fray Pedro Font, missionary at San José de Pimas, was chosen. Father Font's latitudes were carefully measured, and his diary of the expedition is one of the best travel accounts in American history (see Reference #11).

During the spring and summer of 1775 supplies and settlers for the planned expedition were assembled at Horcasitas, Sonora; a start was planned for early September. An Apache raid at Tubac and a stampede at Horcasitas deprived the expedition of much of its livestock and delayed the start until September 29. As a result of these misfortunes the expedi-

---

[17](Juan) Pablo Grijalva was second corporal of the presidio of Terrenate when appointed as Sergeant of the California expedition. The record shows that he had served honorably for ten years up to that time (1775) and that he could read and write. He served capably on the expedition to San Francisco where he served for ten years when he was transferred to San Diego with the rank of alférez to fill the vacancy caused by the death of Alférez José Velásquez in late 1785. He served in that rank for ten years and retired as a lieutenant. He died in 1806. His two daughers became Mesdames Antonio Yorba and Pedro Peralta.

tion set out with too few pack and saddle animals, and some of these were replacements of poor quality. Route was roughly northward, passing through Magdalena (now Magdalena de Kino), Tumacácori, Tubac, and San Xavier del Bac, over trails blazed three quarters of a century earlier by Father Kino.

On leaving Tubac, the expedition consisted of 240 persons, 695 horses and mules, and 255 beeves. Baggage was contained in 165 mule loads; some of it was expedition property and some, private. Unlike most other migrations, this expedition grew as it travelled. There were three births along the trail and only one death en route due to complications of childbirth. Unfortunately, the expedition's livestock did not fare as well because they suffered continual attrition from hunger, thirst, exhaustion, straying, stampedes, and Indian depredations.

Northward from San Xavier del Bac the party passed through Tuquison (modern Tucson) and marched along the valley of the Santa Cruz River to the small lake of Comari near the Gila River. While the main party rested here, the leaders visited the "Casa Grande de Moctezuma," modern Casa Grande National Monument. Father Font measured the latitude here and found it to be 33°3′30″ (modern value 32°59′30″ approximately). Both Font and Anza wrote descriptions of the ruins which were in mutual agreement and closely resembled earlier descriptions by Kino, Manje, and Sedelmayr. From Comari, near modern Blackwater, the course swung westward through the country of the friendly Gila Pimas, who still farm and irrigate the area diligently.

Near the Pima villages the Gila River swung northward, joining the Salt, then goes westward to its junction with the Hassayampa. It then turns southward for many miles, eventually resuming its westward course near modern Gila Bend. To save leagues and days, Anza went directly westward across the desert from the Pima villages, re-entering the Gila Valley at San Simon y Júdas de Uparsoitac, which is near modern Gila Bend. Proceeding down the Gila, the party reached Agua Caliente where a day of rest was taken so that the animals could graze on the fair local pasture, and the families could wash in the water of the hot springs. Westward from Agua Caliente the expedition travelled slowly down the brushy Gila Valley. The animals suffered from exhaustion, scanty forage, and cold. At Laguna Salobre, west of modern Wellton, Arizona, the party was met by a friendly Yuma delegation led by Chief Salvador Palma. Aided by the Yumas, the expedition forded the Colorado on November 30, 1775, and made camp on the far (California) side.

While at Yuma Anza delivered to Chief Palma a spectacular uniform sent him as a present by the viceroy. He supervised and encouraged the establishment of several intertribal peace treaties and saw to the building of a small cabin for Fathers Garcés and Eixarch who were to stay at the Yuma crossing with two servants, three interpreters, and two muleteers.[18] One of them was Sebastián Tarabal who had guided the first Anza Expedition from what is now known as the Imperial Valley to San Gabriel. During this busy halt a small advance party checked trails and water holes to the west and found few changes in conditions since the first Anza expedition.

On December 4, 1775, the march was resumed, travel being west and southwest from the crossing and passing south of the Algondones Dunes. A halt was made at Santa Olaya, the last good campsite for many miles. From this point, the expedition marched in three sections: the first headed by Anza, the second by Sergeant Pablo Grijalva, and the third by Lieutenant José Joaquín Moraga. These parties left Santa Olaya a day apart so that the scanty water holes would not be exhausted. Route was very roughly along the present international boundary over country that was desert then, but is now highly productive, irrigated farmland. The three divisions all watered on separate days at Santa Rosa de las Lajas, near modern Yuha Well, on the northwest side of Signal Mountain, known in Mexico as Cerro de la Centinela. Despite extreme cold and a snowstorm, they proceeded northwest to Carrizo Wash and then north to San Sebastián where the three groups rejoined and rested. The animals caught up on their grazing and drinking. Being the rainy season, pasturage at San Sebastián was better than during the first expedition. Troubles were experienced with animals dying of cold, and there was some difficulty with the "taking ways" of the local Indians.

Passage westward from San Sebastián was delayed by lack of water, a cattle stampede in which fifty head were lost, and the condition of the animals which were acclimated to southern Sonora and unaccustomed to suffering from cold. On reaching Santa Catarina Spring in Coyote Canyon the water problem decreased, but forage was still minimal. A day's march up the canyon brought the party to Los Danzantes,

[18]Father Tomás Eixarch, O.F.M., was missionary at Tumacácori in 1775 when he was selected to go to Yuma with the second Anza expedition, apparently at the request of Father Garcés. He spent five months at the Yuma crossing as a missionary, writing an excellent diary of his experiences. See H.E. Bolton, *Anza's California Expeditions*, Vol. III, pp. 311-381. He built the first structure atop what is now known as Mission Hill. In 1776 he returned to Tumacácori. Later he served at Atil and Oquitoa.

modern Upper Willows, where Christmas was spent — and where Salvador Ignacio Linares was born. The day after Christmas, the march was resumed over the same general trail as the first expedition. Progress was good despite tired mounts, snow on the Sierra, and high water in the rivers. New Year's Day was spent in crossing the swollen Santa Ana River, and the expedition reached San Gabriel on January 4, 1776. This was the new, and now present, site which had been moved several miles north since the first Anza expedition.

At San Gabriel, plans for an immediate northward march were changed, because there had been an Indian uprising at San Diego. Roads north were also muddy due to the winter rains, and supplies were inadequate as was almost standard in California at the time. Anza, Font, and seventeen soldiers went south to the relief of San Diego, while the colonists camped on half rations at San Gabriel under the care of Lieutenant Moraga. Anza returned to San Gabriel on February 12, 1776, leading a pack train loaded with badly needed supplies. But now he faced a new problem. The night before his arrival five men, some of whom had been looting the scarce supplies at San Gabriel, deserted and took with them some twenty-five or thirty horses and mules as well as an assortment of other items. Riding in pursuit, Lieutenant Moraga caught up with the deserters near Santa Olaya. He brought them and the surviving horses and mules back to San Gabriel, recovering on the return march some of the cattle that had stampeded on the earlier eastward journey.

While Lieutenant Moraga was chasing deserters in the deserts of southeastern California, Anza, who was suffering from annoying stomach trouble (bad food?), started the northward march toward Monterey with most of the colonists. Twelve families together with the cattle herd were left at San Gabriel under the care of Sergeant Grijalva. They were instructed to follow on when Lieutenant Moraga returned from his search for the deserters. The northern route was already a familiar trail, which quite closely followed the route later known as the Camino Real, now the famous Highway 101.

Passing along the Santa Barbara coast, they found the channel Indians somewhat timorous because of misconduct by soldiers on previous visits. They experienced only the usual minor problems with thievery. They rested for a day at the growing mission of San Luis Obispo; then, the party climbed the steep grades to the north and descended into the valley of the Río de Monterey, today's Salinas River. Detouring west, up the valleys of the Nacimiento and San Antonio Rivers, the tired colonists stopped for a day of rest at mission San

Antonio de Padua, now sometimes known as San Antonio de los Robles. Here Lieutenant Moraga rejoined the expedition and reported the successful capture of the deserters from San Gabriel and the recovery of some of the cattle. Sergeant Grijalva with the remaining colonists followed at a slower pace, bringing with him the rest of the animals.

Three days travel northward from San Antonio, with the last in a heavy rain, brought the party to Monterey where they were welcomed immediately by "three volleys of artillery." Next day they were visited by Fathers Serra and Palou, and three other friars who came from nearby Carmelo. Father Font preached a sermon of thanksgiving. Despite suffering a painfull illness at Monterey, Anza, who was accompanied by Father Font, Lieutenant Moraga and various soldiers, set out on March 23, 1776, to pick sites for the mission and presidio on San Francisco Bay. Travel from Monterey to San Francisco was approximately due north, more or less along the route of the modern main road; it was excellently documented by Father Font with prominent landmarks clearly cited. Some of these landmarks, such as the Palo Alto at the north boundary of the modern city of the same name, are still extant. Suitable presidio and mission sites were chosen — indeed, well chosen because both are still at the original sites two centuries later.

Completing this work, Anza travelled around the south side of San Francisco Bay and along the south shore of the puzzling Río Grande de San Francisco, which connected the bay with a swampy jungle of tulares some miles inland. This area, now known as Carquínez Strait, was determined to be a "mass of water which might better be called a fresh-water sea than a river for it has neither floods nor currents like a river; like the sea its water is clear and verging on blue, and it has ebb and flow and little waves on the beach." Leaving the puzzling area of Carquínez Strait and Suisun Bay, which we now regard as the drowned mouths of the Sacramento and San Joaquín Rivers, Anza turned southward passing through the Livermore Valley, east of Mount Hamilton, and thence, through the Gilroy Valley to Monterey again. On his return to far distant Tubutama in the Pimería Alta, Father Font drew a rather good map of their travels between Monterey and San Francisco.[19]

After four days at Carmel Anza rode to the presidio of Monterey and turned over command of the expedition to Lieutenant Moraga. Following the usual administrative delays, the land expedition set out

[19]Reproduced in Herbert E. Bolton, *Outpost of Empire*, opp. p. 266.

again to the north with Lieutenant Moraga in command and Fray Francisco Palou as chief missionary and chaplain. To transport some of the needed supplies from Monterey to the new settlements, the colonists were aided by the supply ship *San Carlos* with Fernando Quiroz as captain and José de Canizares and Cristóbal Revilla as pilots. In the previous year (1775) the same vessel, captained by Juan Manuel de Ayala with José de Canizares and Juan Bautista Aguierre as pilots, made the first known Spanish entry into San Francisco Bay.[20] Construction of the new settlement on San Francisco Bay went forward rapidly with the help of the sailors and ship's carpenter from the *San Carlos*. The presidio of San Francisco was dedicated on September 17, 1776, and the mission of San Francisco de Asís on October 8. Houses for the settlers were built; crops were seeded; and irrigation ditches were dug — and so was established the city of San Francisco.

Meanwhile, Juan Bautista de Anza travelled southward on his return to Sonora, accompanied by Father Font, some soldiers and muleteers, and a pair of colonists who decided to return to Sonora. En route to San Gabriel Anza had several meetings and near-meetings with Francisco Xavier de Rivera y Moncada, military governor of California, who strongly opposed the settlements on San Francisco Bay despite orders to aid them. He was also acting "foolish and crazy." Captain Rivera, who had been recalled from retirement to serve as military governor of California (replacing Pedro Fages at Father Serra's request), found himself in a nearly impossible situation with unclear orders, inadequate supplies, personnel and equipment, and continual troubles with fractious Indians and deserting soldiers. His salary had not been paid for years, and he had recently been excommunicated for removing an Indian fugitive from the sanctuary of the church in San Diego. After what resembled a game of hide-and-seek along the trail south from Monterey, Anza and Rivera finally communicated, this time in writing, at San Gabriel; Anza eventually rode east toward Yuma crossing.

From this important site, the journey southeastward to Horcasitas, Sonora, now accompanied by Chief Palma of the Yumas and several other Indians, was uneventful. Shortly, Anza and his Indian friends moved on to Mexico City, leaving Horcasitas in mid-August and arriving in the capital (1100 miles distant) in late October. Here, Anza made an extensive report to the viceroy. He introduced the Yuma visitors and, at

---

[20]This historic voyage with reproductions and translations of salient documents and maps is excellently described in John Galvin (ed.), *First Spanish Entry*.

Salvador Palma's request, composed a most interesting letter in which Palma gave his life history, stating his hopes for the future and requesting baptism as a Christian.[21] Written in the clear and practiced hand of Anza, it is signed by shaky crosses placed at the end by Salvador Palma and his companions, who were equally illiterate, and then countersigned by Anza. Anza and Palma spent four months in the capital during which Palma was presented at the viceregal court and baptized in the Cathedral of Mexico as he had wished. In late February, 1777, they started the long journey northward, taking with them many gifts and a "book full" of promises most of which were unfortunately never kept.

Beginning shortly after the Jesuit expulsion (1767), it had become apparent that the military forces of New Spain were somewhat over-extended. With the planned settlement of Alta California and the acquisition of Louisiana from France in 1763 the situation became critical. Soon, this problem was recognized, and a series of studies were undertaken to determine the exact situation and to propose remedies thereto. These extensive studies, performed by a variety of officers (some of them competent), disclosed that a few frontier presidio commanders, such as Juan Bautista de Anza, were capable leaders and doing a good job. But they also uncovered many instances of graft, corruption, incompetence, poor siting of presidios, understaffing, and inadequate supplies and equipment. Findings from these inspections and investigations are summarized in the Rubi report of 1769.[22] These findings were later incorporated in the Royal Regulations of 1772.[23] To carry out these royal orders Viceroy Bucareli in 1772 appointed Don Hugo Oconor to the rank of commander and inspector.[24]

Oconor proposed and carried out many reforms and improvements in the northern frontiers, but he encountered serious difficulties with shortages of almost everything as well as political delays. By 1776 the collapse of the northern provinces of Mexico seemed imminent and a

[21]This letter, which is still extant, is in AGN Provincias Internas, Vol. 23, pp. 1-5, dated Nov. 11, 1776.

[22]AGI 103-4-15 Superior Gobierno. Año de 1771, No. 1, Pral. Testimonio de los Dictamenes . . .

[23]Sidney B. Brinckerhoff and Odie B. Faulk, Lancers for the King, pp. 11-67.

[24]Hugo Oconor (O'Connor) was an Irish soldier who had long been in the service of Spain. From 1768 to 1771 he had been captain of the presidio of Los Adais (Texas) and interim governor of the province of Texas. From 1772 to 1776 he served as Commander Inspector of the northern frontier of New Spain, and in 1777 was appointed Governor and Captain General of the Province of Yucatan. He died in Mérida on March 8, 1779.

governmental reorganization ensued.. The entire northern tier of the, provinces of Mexico was partly detached from the viceroyalty, renamed the "Commandancy-General of the Interior Provinces of New Spain" *(Provincias Internas)*, and put under the command of Teodoro de Croix.[25] Despite enormous efforts by Croix and his subordinates the situation on the northern frontiers of New Spain improved only slightly. Many historians attribute the lack of progress to incompetence on the part of Croix. A careful study of the records of the time, however, suggests that most of the trouble was lack of capable subalterns, good soldiers, able settlers, funds, horses and mules, weapons and other supplies. The lines of communication and transportation were too long; most of the areas to be held against Indian attack were not self-supporting. Moreover, Spain was almost continuously involved in European wars; it had little money and few men to spare for the overseas colonies. It should be noted in passing that the Indian troubles prevalent on the northern frontiers of New Spain in 1776 were not solved militarily for more than a century; many of the social, economic and governmental problems are still with us.

Because of the governmental reorganizations incident to the establishment of the Provincias Internas, the planned and promised settlements at the Gila-Colorado junction were not organized until 1779; and the final plan bore little resemblance to the proposal by Anza, Garcés, and others who realized the importance of the Yuma crossing. As finally organized, the settlement was a combination mission-presidio-colony, staffed by two missionaries (Fathers Garcés and Díaz), an ensign (Don Santiago Yslas, who had been first ensign of the presidio of Santa Gertrudis de Altar), a sergeant (José de la Vega), two corporals (Pascual

---

[25]Don Teodoro de Croix, a Caballero of the Teutonic Order, was of French origin, being born June 20, 1730, at Prevote near Lille. At the age of seventeen he entered the Spanish army and served in Italy as an ensign of the Royal Guard. He transferred to the Walloon Guard in 1750, becoming a lieutenant by 1756 and a colonel by 1760. He was decorated in Flanders with the Cross of the Teutonic Order. By 1765 he advanced to captain in the Viceregal Guard. In that capacity he came to Mexico in 1766 and was appointed governor of Acapulco. From 1766 to 1770 he was inspector of all troops in the kingdom of New Spain, holding the rank of brigadier. In 1771 he went to Havana, and five months later to Spain where he stayed until 1776. From 1776 to 1782 Croix served as Commander General of the Provincias Internas. In 1783 he was promoted to lieutenant general and appointed viceroy of Peru where he served five years. He died in Madrid, March 25, 1790, "leaving an estate of 15,000 pesos." His lengthy correspondence and extensive reports are detailed in Alfred B. Thomas, *Teodoro de Croix*. A broader view of the Provincias Internas is given in John F. Bannon, *The Spanish Borderlands Frontier, 1513-1821*, pp. 167-189. See the Lafora map opp. p. 172.

Rivera and Juan Palomino), eighteen soldiers borrowed from the already-thin ranks of the Sonoran presidios, and twenty families of settlers, most of whom were recruited in Sonora. Most, if not all, of these had arrived at Yuma by December 1780, had laid out the settlement, and had started construction of mission La Purísima Concepción on what is now known as Mission Hill, directly across the Colorado from modern Yuma. Soon they were joined by two more missionaries, Fathers Juan Barraneche and Matías Moreno. A second mission, San Pedro y San Pablo Bicuñer, was started southwest of the Gila-Colorado junction, near modern Pilot Knob. A third structure, used for occasional religious instruction, was started northeast of Concepción, near modern Potholes.

Relations between the Yumas and the colonists were somewhat strained from the outset because most of the presents promised Chief Palma in Mexico City in 1777 did not materialize. The colonists paid little attention to Yuman land rights and agricultural customs; they let their livestock graze in the Yuma croplands. When the supplies brought by the colonists were exhausted, the Yumas had little to spare and demanded high prices. Finally, as supplies were not forthcoming from Sonora, Alférez Yslas sent to San Gabriel for aid, and in late June, 1781, received some supplies from their meager store. Although the Fathers made some converts and more friends, these persons were apparently ostracized by the rest of the Yumas; anti-Spanish feeling mounted in the village. The situation was certainly not improved by Alférez Yslas, who had several Indians flogged or put in the stocks for various "offenses," which may well have been caused only by their inability to understand.

The Yuma troubles were exacerbated even later in June when Captain Fernando Xavier Rivera y Moncada, who was then Lieutenant Governor of Baja California, arrived at the Yuma crossing with a convoy of settlers for Los Angeles and the proposed settlements along the Santa Barbara channel and a large herd of livestock. The animals, starved from their long journey across the Sonoran Desert, promptly ate everything green in sight, including Yuma crops. The Sonoran military escort was sent back; the settlers and some of the animals were sent on to Alta California under the command of Alférez Cayetano Limón with Alférez José Dário Arguello assisting.[26] Captain Rivera, accompanied by his soldiers and a small squad from California, recrossed the Colorado, making camp on what is now the Yuma townsite.

On Tuesday, July 17, the Yumas rose in revolt, killing the Fathers and most of the male settlers and soldiers at both mission settlements (La Purísima Concepción and San Pedro y San Pablo Bicuñer). Crossing the river, they murdered the military group headed by Captain Rivera. The women and children of the two settlements were captured and made to work, but were not otherwise molested. There is some suggestion that Salvador Palma interceded for the missionary Fathers, but his influence in the tribe, because of multiple broken promises, was waning and his efforts failed. Shortly after the initial massacre, which apparently extended over three days, a pack train that was bringing supplies from San Gabriel under command of Corporal Pascual Bailón with an escort of nine soldiers arrived at Yuma and was promptly wiped out. Total Spanish casualities in the Yuma massacre approximated 150.[27] As a result of this massacre, the Yuma crossing, so important in the planned settlement, supply, and defense of Alta California, became economically worthless, and could only be used by large, well-armed military expeditions, of which there were few in Spanish or Mexican times.

Despite the isolation of Yuma from the settled California coast, and from the missions and presidios of Sonora, news of the Yuma massacre reached both relatively quickly. After delivering his convoy of settlers and livestock at San Gabriel, Alférez Cayetano Limón began his return to Sonora. Advised by local Indians of the massacre, probably at San

---

[26]Alférez Cayetano Limón was an experienced soldier from the presidio of Altar, where he had served most of the time since 1760, in which year his daughter had been baptized by Father Ignaz Pfefferkorn, S. J. Alférez José Dário Arguello accompanied the settlers from Sonora through Yuma to San Gabriel, arriving July 14, 1781. He took part in the official founding of Los Angeles on September 4. He later served at Santa Barbara, San Francisco and Monterey, becoming acting Governor of California in 1814-1815 and Governor of Baja California from 1815 to 1822. He died in Guadalajara in 1828. His wife was Ignacia Moraga, a niece of José Joaquín Moraga of San Francisco; she bore several children among whom was the later María de la Concepción Marcela Arguello (1790-1857). Her ill-fated engagement to Baron Nikolai Petrovich de Rezanov (1806) has been the subject of many romantic tales, some of them true. See Charles E. Chapman, *History of California*, pp. 413-417.

[27]Primary information source for the Yuma colony and the Yuma massacre is Juan D. Arricivita, *Crónica Serfica y Apostólica del Colegio de Propaganda Fide de la Santa Cruz de Querétaro en la Nueva España*, pp. 529-554. See also H. H. Bancroft, *Early California Annals*, pp. 353-371. An eyewitness account of the Yuma massacre by María Ana Montielo, widow of Alférez Santiago Yslas, is given in Kieran McCarty, *Desert Documentary*, pp. 35-41. A general history of Yuma crossing is Douglas F. Martin, *Yuma Crossing*. See also a summary of the culture and history of the Yuma people in Jack D. Forbes, *Warriors of the Colorado*. It is somewhat ironic to note that Captain Rivera planned to retire on completion of this assignment, as indicated in Alfred B. Thomas, *Teodoro de Croix*, p.238, item #596. Rivera, however, was not the seventy years of age stated in Croix's report, but about fifty-eight (birth ca. 1725).

Sebastián water hole, he pushed forward toward Yuma to make a personal inspection. The massacre was confirmed; two men were killed during the reconnaissance and both Limón and his son were wounded. On his return to San Gabriel, he was sent back to Sonora with the news via Loreto in Baja California. Meanwhile, word of the massacre reached Sonora via the "Indian telegraph" and was confirmed by a captive who found his way to Altar. On receipt of this bad news, General Croix sent an account to Governor Felipe de Neve of California, August 26, 1781, probably via Loreto, warning him to take military precautions. Unknown to Croix, Governor Neve was already well aware of the massacre through the findings of Alférez Cayetano Limón. Because of the news he was soon en route to Arizpe (by September 1). The two messages probably passed each other somewhere along the Camino Real of Baja California. On September 9 a council of war was held by Croix at Arispe; the Yumas were declared to be "apostates and rebels," and a military campaign against them was planned. To head this, Pedro Fages, a veteran frontier officer, was dispatched northward from the presidio of Pitic on September 16.[28] Marching north through hostile Indian attacks, they came to the royal presidio of Santa Gertrudis de Altar. Here they delivered nineteen prisoners and rescued captives, rested for two days, and augmented their supplies. At Altar the company was joined by Captain Don Pedro de Tueros, presidio commander, and by Father Joseph Enrique Cenizo, chaplain. On Monday, October 1, the small

---

[28]Pedro Fages was born in 1734 at Guisona, Catalonia, Spain. No record of his education has been found, but, judged from his extensive writings, it was good and thorough although not classical. Fages' military career began some time before 1762, at which time he was *alférez del segundo regimento de infantería ligera de Cataluña*, based in Barcelona. From this unit in 1767, the Compañía Franca de Voluntarios de Cataluña was formed with Agustín Callis as captain and Pedro Fages as lieutenant. Callis later had extensive honorable service in Sonora, largely at Pitic and about 1776 became Fages' father-in-law. Fages' promotion from alférez to lieutenant was dated May 12, 1767. On May 27, the Catalonian Volunteers sailed from Cádiz originally destined for service in Havana; but plans were changed and they arrived in Veracruz late in August of that year. After a short rest in Mexico City, they were sent north to Pitic (modern Hermosillo) to serve in the Elizondo Campaigns against the Seri. After short service in Sonora Pedro Fages with twenty-five men sailed from Guaymas to La Paz, and thence aboard the *San Carlos*, Vicente Vila commanding, to Alta California. They arrived in San Diego Bay on April 29, 1779, after a voyage of 110 days. Half or more of the ship's company died of scurvy, either during the voyage or very shortly after landing. By mid-July of 1779, Fages, as military commander of Alta California, began five years of intensive exploration and pacification of his area. He accomplished much despite runaway Indians, deserting soldiers, inadequate supplies, stubborn missionaries and unclear orders. In May of 1774,

troop, which now numbered about 100, set forth to the northwest to make war on more than 3,000 rebellious Yumas. Course was directly across the Papaguería from Altar to near modern Gila Bend, using a trail previously travelled by Fathers Kino and Sedelmayr, then down the Gila to the Yuma crossing.

While reconnoitering the east bank of the Colorado, a messenger, "a captive soldier of Buenavista named Miguel Antonio Romero," brought a letter from Salvador Palma stating that if the soldiers came in peace, "he was also thus inclined."[29] Subsequent negotiations resulted in the ransoming of some forty-eight captives. The bodies of Captain Rivera y Moncada and his companions were found — that of Rivera being "unmistakably" identified by "the break in one of the shin-bones." The next day fourteen more captives were ransomed, and the bones of Rivera y Moncada were gathered up and buried.[30]

On Saturday, October 20, the Fages troop somewhat unwillingly, because several captives remained to be ransomed, joined a coalition of Indians. Some 600 Halchedunes, Pimas Gileños, and Cocomaricopas were, at least for the time being, enemies of the Yumas and friends of the Spaniards. Together they mounted a massive attack on the Yumas. This battle lasted from daybreak nearly to noon. The action wreaked havoc on the Yumas, making any immediate rescue of captives unlikely. After a council to determine possible actions "agreeable to the service of God

---

Pedro Fages was replaced as military commander of Alta California by Fernando Xavier de Rivera y Moncada, largely at the request of Father Serra. Fages with his few surviving Catalonian Volunteers returned to Mexico City. After an illness there, he served for a time at Real de Pachuca, north of Mexico City. Soon again ordered to Sonora, he served at Pitic for about five years. He married Doña Eulália Callis there and also became a lieutenant colonel. In 1781 he was put in charge of the Sonoran part of the punitive campaign against the Yumas, and in 1782, while still busy with Yuma troubles, was appointed Governor of Alta California. Serving well in this capacity until 1791, despite the combined problems of an isolated frontier and a fractious wife, he retired to Mexico City and disappears from available records in 1794. See Donald A. Nuttall, "Pedro Fages and the Advance of the the Nothern Frontier of New Spain, 1767-1782," unpublished doctoral dissertation, University of Southern California, Los Angeles, 1964. Joseph P. Sanchez, "The Catalonian Volunteers and the Defense of Northern New Spain, 1767-1803," unpublished doctoral dissertation, University of New Mexico, Albuquerque, 1974. H. H. Bancroft, *Early California Annals*.

[29]The original manuscript specifically reads *carta*. As Salvador Palma was illiterate, this letter must have been written for him by one of the Spanish captives.

[30]As nearly as can be determined, this burial took place somewhere in the older part of the Yuma townsite. The grave, never identified, was probably obliterated perhaps more than a century ago by local urban construction.

and the King and to the welfare of all,'' the troop retreated eastward to Sonoyta with the captives they had managed to rescue, travelling over the Camino del Diablo, so often traversed by Kino more than three quarters of a century earlier. Arriving in Sonoyta on Saturday, October 27, the rescued captives were sent south to the royal presidio of Altar; the remainder of the troop rested in Sonoyta while awaiting supplies for a new advance against the Yumas.

The second Yuma campaign started westward from Sonoyta on November 23, over the Camino del Diablo toward Yuma with very rapid progress and some record-breaking rides — ''all this day, the night, and the following day (30 leagues or about 75 miles) — over the Lechuguilla Desert. At Yuma there were numerous skirmishes and one concerted attack on the horse-herd which was successfully repulsed by Sergeant Juan Noriega and his men. After somewhat lengthy and difficult negotiations, the few remaining captives were rescued from the Yumas, the last being Doña Juliana Sambrano and her new-born child. Continuing search of the ruined villages of Concepción and Bicuñer led to the discovery of the remains of the four Franciscan martyrs — Fathers Francisco Garcés, Juan Barraneche, Juan Díaz, and Joseph Moreno. The bones of the martyrs were deposited on the altar of the ruined church of San Pedro y San Pablo Bicuñer. This church ''although burned, still had its walls almost intact, especially those of the high altar. Upon this altar candles were lighted, and the troop and the rest of the people being gathered together, except the guard; we recited the Holy Rosary in concert with the Reverend Father Cenizo.'' Later the bones were packed ''in a great cigarette case,'' which was wrapped ''with jute cloth'' for transportation to Sonora. Searches of the ruined villages disclosed a variety of other objects, and in the sporadic skirmishing with the Yumas Salvador Palma was saved from death because a soldier's pistol misfired three times in succession. The baptismal font was searched for, but not found ''since the Yumas must have taken it somewhere else to cook squash and things in.'' Three of the mission bells were recovered at this time. Another, the fourth and last, which was probably the great bell of mission La Purísima Concepción, still remains to be found.[31] Accompanied by the remaining rescued captives and carrying the bones of the four martyrs and a variety of recovered articles, the troop left Yuma crossing on Thursday, December 13, travelling east to Sonora via the Camino del Diablo, over which they made some phenomenally long rides. Leaving some exhausted animals at Sonoyta in the care of the native captain, the party proceeded south, roughly along the course of modern Mexican Route 2, to Aribaipa (Sonora), where they rested. The presidial troop was sent ahead on December 22 to Santa Gertrudis de Altar with the rescued captives and the bones of the martyrs.[32] Leaving Aribaipa on December 26, the reduced troop proceeded without event through Caborca to Pitic de Caborca (modern Pitiquito) where they rested while the exhausted animals recovered from their long desert journeys.

Although these two lengthy military operations resulted in the rescue of the captives, recovery of the remains of the four martyrs, and the salvage of some of the mission material, the Yuma tribe had not been sufficiently punished for their outbreak according to the Spanish authorities. Another campaign was ordered, consisting of a joint attack on the Yumas from California and the Pimería Alta. To carry these new orders to Governor Don Felipe de Neve of California, Pedro Fages set out from Pitic del Altar with thirty-nine soldiers (ten Catalonian Volunteers, one sergeant, and twenty-eight presidial soldiers, some from Tucson), all "badly mounted," on February 27, 1782. Route was over the Camino del Diablo to the Yuma crossing, where they arrived and forded the Colorado on March 11, 1782. Experiencing no difficulties with the Yumas, they crossed the Algodones Dunes through a pass which now lies north of modern Route 8. They reached the familiar water hole of San Sebastián on March 15 and rested there for one day. Then accompanied by Pachula, chief of the settlement, and several of his tribesmen, the Fages contingent followed the Anza trail to San Gabriel where they arrived March 26.

---

[31]A bell, inscribed *San Luis Gonzaga, Anno 1719* was offered for sale by a "desert rat" in the early 1960s with a story of its finding that suggested that it might be the missing Yuma bell. After lengthy travels and several changes of ownership, it was determined that this bell had been illegally acquired and imported, and it was returned to Mexico by U.S. authorities. The San Luis Gonzaga bell may be the missing great bell of Yuma. It certainly is not one of the bells stolen from mission San Borja in the early 1960's.

[32]The bones were sent shortly from Altar to the mission of San Pedro y San Pablo de Tubutama for burial. Some time between 1782 and 1784 the bones were exhumed and transported south by "the muleteer, Félix" to the Colegio de Santa Cruz de Querétaro. Excerpts from the memorial sermon preached there by Father Bringas de Manzaneda are contained in John Galvin, *A Record of Travels in Arizona and California*, pp. 106-110. Recent studies indicate that the bones are still there and still packed in "the great cigarette case" where they were placed by Pedro Fages on December 12, 1781. Clarence Cullimore, *The Martyrdom and Interment of Padre Francisco Garcés*.

Figure 1. Modern historical marker at the Yuma Crossing. Most of the original crossing site has been altered and obscured by a modern bridge and other construction. First recorded crossing at this approximate site was by Captain Melchor Díaz, in late 1540. Photo by R.L. Ives.

Governor Neve was not at San Gabriel when Fages arrived with his soldiers because he was still en route to the new settlements on the Santa Barbara channel. A special messenger was sent to recall the governor, and he soon decided that, as the Colorado was in flood, the campaign against the Yumas should be postponed until September when the river should hopefully be lower. It now became necessary to send the Sonoran troop back as it approached the Yuma crossing from the east. Pedro Fages volunteered for this ''messenger journey'' and left San Gabriel on April 2, 1782, in the company of ten soldiers from Sonora and ten from Monterey. Travelling over the now familiar trail, they arrived at the crossing without event on April 13 and promptly communicated with the Sonoran troop, commanded by Captains Joseph Romeu and Pedro Tueros. Later, Fages crossed the river on a raft to have a lengthy conference with the officers of the Sonoran contingent. Recrossing the river, Fages and his small troop rode west the next day and crossed the Algodones Dunes by their previous route, arriving at San Sebastián water hole on April 17.

Reports of Indian unrest in the San Diego area were rife, so Fages changed his plans about returning to San Gabriel and turned south from San Sebastián, following Carrizo Wash. Here he encountered a small problem because Chief Pachula of San Sebastián wanted to go with the Fages party together with more than thirty of his tribesmen. Dissuading Pachula took some time and patience. Route westward was up Carrizo Wash to Three Palms, then up Vallecito Creek to San Felipe which Fages named and described.[33] This is the site of modern Vallecito. A short march west brought them to Mason Valley; an arduous climb up Oriflamme Canyon led to Cuyamaca on the summit. Cuyamaca Reservoir is man-made and was not there in 1782. A short downhill march west from Cuyamaca over rather rough terrain brought the troop to the San Diego River, then called the Río San Luis in the vicinity of modern El Capitán Reservoir. Another short and relatively easy march downstream brought them to mission San Diego de Alcalá where they arrived April 20, 1782. After attending mass the next morning at the mission, the troop rode downvalley to the presidio of San Diego, where ''the lieutenant in command, Don Joseph de Zúñiga and his Alférez (José) Velásquez''

---

[33]Fages mentioned San Felipe as a good site for a presidio. Although none was ever established there, it later became an army sub-depot on the trail from San Diego to Yuma, and still later as the Vallecito stage station. Today it is a county park.

came out to meet them. This completed the first recorded journey from Yuma directly to San Diego.

The march northward from San Diego was over the already well worn Camino Real with a stop at mission San Juan Capistrano. The troop arrived at mission San Gabriel late in the day on April 25, and a special messenger was immediately sent north to inform Governor Felipe de Neve of their safe arrival. Neve was still at the settlements along the Santa Barbara channel.[34]

The last major expedition against the rebellious Yumas got under way in late August, 1782. Governor Felipe de Neve led one contingent from California, proceeding east from San Gabriel toward Yuma *(Cf. Appendix B, Note 10)*. Captain Joseph Romeu led the other from Altar, travelling west over the Camino del Diablo toward Yuma *(Cf. Appendix B, Note 15)*. Initially Pedro Fages was second-in-command of the California contingent. But before the California troops reached the Colorado River, both leaders received promotions. Neve was made Inspector General of the Provincias Internas and Fages became Governor of California. This campaign, in which Alférez José Velásquez took an active part both militarily and as an official witness, will be detailed later in this work.

After this expedition, Spanish use of the Yuma crossing ceased to all intents and purposes; this considerably increased the already serious settlement and supply problem of Alta California. Although several Spanish leaders — Anza, Garcés, and Fages among them — took an active part in the establishment and defense of the Yuma crossing.

---

[34]The major Colorado River campaigns of 1781-1782 are described in the complete, accurate, and excellently written diaries of Pedro Fages. Original documents are in the Bancroft Library. A scholarly translation of these was published by H.I. Priestly, *The Colorado River Campaigns, 1781-1782: Diary of Pedro Fages*, pp. 135-233.

A very slightly improved translation, annotated and with complete route maps with site photographs has been published by R.L. Ives, "Retracing the Route of the Fages Expedition of 1781," *Arizona and the West*, Vol. VIII (Spring and Summer, 1966) pp. 49-70 and 157-170; "From Pitic to San Gabriel in 1782: The Journey of Don Pedro Fages," *Journal of Arizona History*, Vol IX (Winter, 1968) pp 222-244; "Retracing Fages' Route from San Gabriel to Yuma, April, 1782," *Arizona and the West*, Vol 17, No. 2 (Summer, 1975) pp. 141-160. The foregoing matieral augments and partially supplants the material in H.H. Bancroft, *Early California Annals*, pp. 366-370. Because Fages, unlike many military commanders of his time, mentioned his subordinates and associates in his diaries, and because many of these persons are mentioned in other accounts and records, a "Dramatis Personae" of the expedition with references is provided in Appendix B.

The key figure, however, was a left-handed, asthmatic, and illiterate Indian, Olleyquotequiebe, known to the Spaniards as Salvador Palma. Whether he was a "traitor, rebel, and apostate," as some of the Spaniards called him, or the victim of circumstances not of his making and largely beyond his control, still remains to be determined.[35]

Today, the site of mission La Purísima Concepción, of the Yuma massacre, and of many of the military operations, is occupied by Saint Thomas' Indian School on Mission Hill on the California side directly across the Colorado River (north) from the Yuma Territorial Prison. At that site, facing Yuma, a statue in memory of Father Garcés has been erected (Cf. Appendix C).

Earlier during this general time interval California had experienced slow settlement, largely by Jesuit missionaries and the few soldiers who accompanied them. Settlement began in the southern part of the peninsula, now the State of Baja California Sur, and very slowly over the next three quarters of a century crept northward into what is now the State of California. Missionary activities in the arid and sterile peninsula of Baja California were constantly inhibited by lack of missionaries and soldiers, insufficient funds, shortages of all sorts of supplies and manufactured goods, and very serious transportation difficulties inherent to the use of sailing ships in an area of undependable or contrary winds. These conditions led Father Johann Jakob Baegert, S.J., of mission San Luis Gonzaga to comment that California "of all the countries of the globe is one of the poorest."[36]

Because of the aridity and sterility of the peninsula of Baja California, the missions there were never economically self-sufficient and help from "outside" was needed during the entire mission period. Each mission had a garden which produced some fruit and vegetables, and a few also produced grain in good years. The area of the garden was determined by the amount of level land near the mission; the output of the garden was limited by the amount of irrigation water available. At some of the missions there was considerable crop "shrinkage" because of the "taking ways" of the natives, who apparently learned what was good to eat rather rapidly, but assimilated the commandments much more slowly. The missions also had herds of livestock — horses, mules, cattle, sheep

---

[35]Further Sonoran history, beyond the scope of this summary, can be found in E. W. Villa, Historia del Estado de Sonora.

[36]M. M. Brandenburg and C. L. Baumann, Observations in Lower California by Joahnn Jakob Baegert, S.J., p. 48.

Figure 2. The Father Garcés memorial statue at St. Thomas' Indian Mission, on Mission Hill, directly across the Colorado River from modern Yuma, Arizona. Photo by R.L. Ives.

and goats — which supplied some of the needed meat, leather, and wool. Because of poor forage and native depredations these herds were not as productive in Baja California as similar herds were in Sonora. Deficiencies of meat and grain were normally made up by generous donations from the relatively prosperous missions of Sonora.[37] Manufactured goods and comestibles not available from Sonora, such as chocolate, were purchased in Mexico and shipped by land and sea to Baja California. Payment for these goods was usually made through the Pious Fund, although few royal grants assisted in their shipping.[38] Transportation costs of goods purchased in Mexico commonly exceeded the purchase price, and many cargoes destined for the missions were lost at sea or spoiled in transit. In consequence, Baja California prices were more than double those on the mainland.

Although there were sporadic attempts to colonize Baja California from the time of Hernán Cortés (1533), none accomplished much of lasting importance until the time of the Kino-Atondo expedition of 1683-1685. This expedition, with Admiral Don Isidro Atondo y Antillón as military commander and Father Eusebio Francisco Kino, S.J. (see n. 14) as chief missionary, was organized to make a lasting settlement on the peninsula.[39] It almost succeeded. Father Kino was appointed *juez eclesiastico vicario* as representative of the Bishop of Durango whose jurisdiction was a bit uncertain, and also royal cosmographer as a representative of the king whose jurisdiction was clear. Sailing from Chacala, Sinaloa, on January 17, 1683, the expedition arrived in two

---

[37]Although a complete tally has never been made, these donations amounted to many hundreds of head of livestock and some thousands of tons of grain. To facilitate these shipments from Sonora to Baja California, the seaport settlement of Guaymas was established by Father Juan María Salvatierra, S.J., in 1701. This mission settlement, although physically in Sonora, was under the administration of the California Jesuits. Cf. H. E. Bolton, *Rim of Christendom*, pp. 448, 462, 628, 445-447.

[38]The Pious Fund was established in 1697 by Fathers Juan de Ugarte, S.J. and Juan María Salvatierra, S.J. to finance the Jesuit missionary efforts in Baja California because no royal funds were then available for the purpose. This fund, made up entirely of private donations and bequests and the income therefrom, aided in the support of the missions of California from their establishment until the end of Spanish rule in Mexico. P.M. Dunne, *Black Robes in Lower California*, pp. 41-44, 354-374; Zephyrin Engelhardt, *The Missions and Missionaries of California*, Vol. I, Second Edition, pp. 497-502, 675-677; C. E. Chapman, *A History of California*, pp. 174-183, 253, 290-291, 469-472.

[39]Admiral Don Isidro Atondo y Antillón, born in Navarre (Spain), was already an experienced soldier and seaman when appointed governor of Sinaloa in 1678. His assignment ''in addition to his regular duties'' was to fortify and settle California. After the expedition of 1683-1685, he disappears from available records.

ships in the harbor of La Paz, Baja California on April 1, several stops
having been made en route.

The site chosen for the settlement was in a palm grove with a well of
good water nearby; it is now occupied by the modern city of La Paz.
Formal possession of the country was taken on April 5 by Admiral
Atondo, acting in the name of King Carlos II. Immediately thereafter,
Father Kino, assisted by his companion Father Goni, took spiritual
possession of California in the name of Bishop Juan Garbabito of
Guadalajara. Formalities concluded, a church and fort were begun;
fields were plowed and planted; and the *capitana* was careened to
prepare for a voyage to the Río Yaqui for more supplies. The environs of
La Paz were explored during this time, and the fathers began to learn the
local Indian language. Initially, the outlook for the La Paz colony
seemed promising.

By June trouble with Indians began to break out. There were two
local tribes, the Guaicuras and Coras, who were not on the best of terms.
In attempting to deal equally with both, the missionaries gained the
confidence of neither. The soldiers, likewise, had their difficulties.
Although willing to accept presents, the Guaicuras tended to be belligerent
and intractable and were not overly impressed by the lethality of firearms
— despite several adequate demonstrations. Then Zavala, the drummer
boy, disappeared in the company of some Guaicuras; the Coras reported
that he had been killed by them.[40] Shortly after, while the colony was
still worried about the disappearance of Zavala, a Guaicura shot a dart at
a soldier. Although it did little harm, the offending Indian was placed in
the stocks and later confined in bilboes (leg-irons) on the ship. The
Guaicuras protested loudly and vehemently. Early in July, a party of
Guaicuras came into the settlement, making signs of peace. Fearing that
this was either an attack on the colony, or an attempt to rescue their

------

[40]This report, which was believed at the time, was completely untrue. The
drummer, Zavala, had not been killed by the Guaicuras but had deserted the La Paz
colony. Going to the coast, he came upon a ship (probably an illegal pearl fisher), traded
a pearl for a canoe, and paddled across the Gulf of California to the mainland of Mexico.
Many years later in Oculma, at the hacienda of Guadalupe del Valle de Acoman
administered by the Pious Fund (near modern Acolman about sixty miles northeast of
Mexico City), Zavala met Father Juan de Ugarte, S.J., and told him the story. The
account later reached Father Juan María Salvatierra in Loreto and is recounted in a letter
of Salvatierra to Miranda October 10, 1716. This is summarized in Miguel Venegas,
Empressas Apostólicas, Bancroft Library ms. 1739, p. 826.

imprisoned tribesman, Atondo ordered them fed. While they were eating, a cannon was fired into their midst, killing three and wounding others, who (most understandably) fled the scene. With "public relations" at a nadir, military morale low, and the supply ships long overdue, the La Paz colony was in a bad way.

On July 15, 1683, the eighty-three colonists boarded the *almiranta* and sailed across the Gulf of California to San Lucas on Agiabampo Bay, Sonora, where they arrived six days later. The La Paz colonization attempt was definitely a failure.

Neither Atondo nor Kino were ready to give up the idea of colonizing California despite the dismal failure of the La Paz attempt. Two hot and damp months were spent at San Lucas while equipment was gathered and repaired. Supplies were collected from Atondo's capital of San Felipe, Sinaloa, and from the Jesuit missions of both Sonora and Sinaloa. During this time, Blas de Guzmán, captain of the capitana, sailed into San Lucas with a long, sad tale of misfortunes at sea due in large part to contrary winds and high seas. However, he also told of a certain Río Grande where he had gone ashore and found the Indians friendly. After many conferences and discussions, this became the objective of the second colonization attempt.

When all equipment and supplies were readied, the expedition, again in two ships, set sail from San Lucas on September 29, 1683. With the usual fickle winds of the Gulf of California in the fall of the year, it took until October 5 to reach the mouth of the Río Grande. Many unwanted detours from the straight-line course of about 125 nautical miles had been required by the winds. Landing on October 6, formal possession of the land was taken with civil and religious ceremonies. Being the feast-day of San Bruno, that saint's name was applied to the area. Consequently, the Río Grande of Guzmán's original report became and remains today the Arroyo de San Bruno. Good water was found about a league up the arroyo; friendly contacts were immediately made with local Indians. Soon a mission and fort were constructed on a low mesa northeast of the arroyo about two miles inland from the river's mouth. The ruins are still visible. While this work was in progress, the missionaries preached to the Indians, and the capitana was readied for a voyage to Yaqui to get supplies, which included "eighteen pack mules and two dozen wrought-iron mule shoes, with their nails and a thousand nails extra." That voyage of about ninety nautical miles each way was quick and successful.

By December 1 of 1683, the San Bruno settlement was firmly established, and extensive exploration of the surrounding lands began. Several journeys were made up and down the coastal plain, reaching south to the area later known as Loreto. In these explorations, the plain of Londó inland from San Bruno was found, and near a good water hole crops were planted there. The site called San Isidro, later became the site of San Juan Londó, an important visita of Loreto. The facade of the ruined mission building still stood in 1968. Initially, the high mountain barrier of the Sierra La Giganta prevented travel to the west. Eventually passes were discovered and soldiers and missionaries crossed the range with much labor. They reached the great plateau to the west — a relatively flat, slightly dissected area considerably larger than the state of Rhode Island. More than 1,000 feet above sea level, this plateau has a number of shallow (temporary) lakes on the surface. These were full in 1684 as plainly stated in Father Kino's descriptions. With strenuous and extensive field work, aided by Indian friends, Father Kino eventually found a pass by which a mounted expedition could cross the Sierra de la Giganta. He learned of a river on the far west side that flowed west to the South Sea (Pacific Ocean). Soon, Kino and Atondo made plans for an expedition to that area.

The summer of 1684 was spent in preaching to the Indians, tending crops that didn't grow very well, improving the fort and church at San Bruno, constructing fortifications and guard quarters at San Isidro, and gathering supplies and equipment for the planned trip to the shore of the South Sea. The supply ships were late, as usual, and fear of starvation at San Bruno was growing very real. Late in the summer, the almiranta (officially known as the *San Jose*) returned to San Bruno, bringing badly needed supplies and twenty additional men, who were ill-trained and poorly equipped. On board was Father Juan Bautista Copart, S.J., a Belgian missionary who had served in the Tarahumara. On August 15, shorty after the arrival of the almiranta, Father Kino made his final vows before Father Copart.[41]

After discharging its cargo, the almiranta was dispatched to Yaqui for more supplies. It made four round-trip voyages in rapid succession, bringing to San Bruno supplies, horses, mules, shoe iron, and the myriad other items needed to keep the isolated colony going. The almiranta was

---

[41] Facsimile of this famous document is included in E.J. Burrus, *Kino Escribe a la Duquesa*, p. 274.

badly in need of repairs after these voyages, so it was sent to Matanchel, a former seaport about three miles east of modern San Blas, Nayarit. On the return to the mainland it carried numerous reports for the viceroy and Father Copart as a passenger. While the ship was being refitted at Matanchel, Captain Guzmán went overland to Guadalajara to get more supplies and some much wanted pearl-divers. Alonso de Zavallos, President of the Audiencia of Guadalajara, furnished the supplies promptly, but had some difficulty finding pearl-divers. Four were eventually located, and in describing them Zavallos wrote "they will set forth within two or three days, for I have kept them in jail in this city in order that they might not flee; they will be escorted to Matanchel under careful guard and custody . . ." By March 28, 1685, the ship had returned to San Bruno and brought the much needed supplies together with the apparently unwilling pearl-divers.

While the shipyard at Matanchel was busy with repair work, the colony at San Bruno was also busy. Some of the personnel were at San Isidro where they were trying to raise food crops in poorly watered fields. Many others were away on the long-planned expedition to the coast of the South Sea. Still others were busy with the "house-keeping" tasks at the San Bruno fort and settlement.

The expedition to the South Sea was one of the major explorations in the history of Baja California. Personnel included Admiral Atondo, Father Kino, Dr. Castro (the surgeon), twenty-nine soldiers, two mule-teers, and nine Christian Indians from the mainland. A varying number of California Indians accompanied to act as guides. The cavalcade included five horses in metal armor, thirty-two horses with bullhide *cueras* (leather armor), thirty pack mules loaded with provisions, two mules ridden by the arrieros, and twenty-two relay animals.

Leaving San Isidro on December 15, 1684, the party travelled northwest to the foot of the pass previously discovered by Father Kino. Here, after much labor spent in improving the trail, they climbed westward to the summit of the Sierra La Giganta, reaching the far side near modern Canípole. Travelling southwest, they came to a canyon and descended into it. This was the Arroyo Comondú in which some years later old mission San José de Comondú was founded. Travelling northwest again, with much labor, they came to the main canyon, then called the Cadegomó and now the Arroyo La Purísima. Down this canyon they rode, mostly westward, struggling over loose boulders and through dense growths of reeds. En route they came to an excellent water hole which they called Ojo de Agua. It is still there and bearing the same name and delivering the same dependable flow. Below and to the west of Ojo de Agua, the party entered the country of the Guimes who tried to turn the Spaniards back. The Indians from San Bruno deserted the party at this point in fear. But Father Kino not only eventually pacified the Guimes, he enlisted their help as guides. Struggling through two more leagues in a maze of boulders and reeds, they emerged at a place they named *Noche Buena* because it was Christmas Eve. It was only a short distance upstream from modern San Isidro. Christmas Day was spent in searching out a better trail, but none was found. More struggles on the day after Christmas brought them into more passable country, and that night they camped at a place they called San Estevan. This was near modern La Purísima. On the 27th, while the main expedition rested and the farriers retreaded the pack and saddle animals, Father Kino with two soldiers climbed a nearby peak to survey the terrain ahead. This they called El Sombrerete ''because it had the shape of a sombrero.'' Today it is known as El Pilón. It is a high butte separated from the main Comondú upland by faulting and erosion. From this summit Father Kino hoped to see the Pacific ocean, but his observations were made uncertain by the fog and haze common in the area during the winter season.

Many of the tired animals were left under guard at San Estevan where the pasture was good and water was plentiful. A smaller party travelled down the canyon to the west by easy stages, eventually coming to the place where the Río Cadegomó joined another river coming in from the northeast. This was named the Río Santiago, now the modern Arroyo San Gregorio. Crossing both rivers, the expedition travelled westward along the north shore of the great embayment at their combined mouths and reached the shore of the Pacific Ocean, which they called the South Sea. This completed the first recorded crossing by Europeans of the peninsula of Baja California. Along the shore, they met some Indians, who were at first timid but eventually accepted gifts. Father Kino especially noted the profusion of shells along the beaches, specifically including the blue abalone, which he later used as biological tracers to demonstrate the possibility of a land passage from California, then thought by many to be an island, to the mainland of Mexico.[42]

Returning to the bay at the combined mouths of the rivers, Atondo wrote a careful description of the harbor on January 1, 1685, and named it La Bahía de Año Nuevo.[43] Today it is known as the Laguna de San

[42] R. L. Ives, ''The Quest of the Blue Shells,'' *Arizoniana*, Vol. 2, No. 1, Spring, 1961, pp. 3-7.

Gregorio. After measuring the latitude of the mouth of the estuary which he found to be twenty-five and a half degrees, Father Kino with the rest of the party began the return journey over the outgoing route.[44] Most of the trip was uneventful, but one of the armored horses fell into the Río Cadegomó and drowned; several other horses succumbed to exhaustion. The explorers reached San Bruno on January 13, 1685.[45]

Not long after their return, Atondo, who was disappointed at not reaching Magdalena Bay, some distance south of Bahía de Año Nuevo, went on another exploring expedition, accompanied this time by Father Goni who had become expert in the Edu language, spoken to the south of San Bruno.[46] Journeying south along the east shore of the peninsula,

[43]Atondo's description is translated in W. M. Mathes, *First from the Gulf to the Pacific*, pp. 49-51. Bolton, writing in 1934, comments that "it all looks now just as they described it two hundred and fifty years ago, so accurate were their observations" (H. E. Bolton, *Rim of Christendom*, pp. 189). Comparison of Atondo's description with any good modern description, such as H.O. Publication 84, *Sailing Directions for the West Coasts of Mexico and Central America*, pp. 54-55, shows that the inland or eastern end has filled with a considerable volume of sediments from the river and that the bay has shoaled considerably since 1685. Since the founding of San Isidro in the mid-1930s, much of the flow of the Río Cadegomó has been diverted for irrigation purposes.

[44]This measurement was made with an instrument designated as a sesente. The sextant, as we know it today, had not yet been invented, and Kino in other works refers to his astrolabe, it is probable that this measurement was made with an astrolabe of which one sixth of the circle was calibrated in degrees. Modern latitude of the mouth of Boca de San Gregorio is 26°30′25″ N. — the slight error in Kino's determination probably being due to abnormal refraction, common in this area.

[45]For more detail see R. L. Ives, "Kino's Route Across Baja California," *Kiva*, Vol. 26, No. 4, April, 1961, pp. 17-29, and W.M. Mathes, *First from the Gulf to the Pacific*. These two publications, based on the diaries of Kino and Atondo, respectively, are in close agreement. The basic contemporary documents, internally cited, give detailed and laudably accurate terrain descriptions.

[46]Father Pedro Matías Goñi (rendered as Gogni in some accounts), Father Kino's missionary companion at San Bruno, was born in Navarra in 1648 and first appears in Mexican missionary records at San Ignacio in Sinaloa in 1677. Shortly thereafter, he went to Yécora. He was chosen as one of the Jesuits to accompany Atondo to California and sailed from Nío on the Río Sinaloa, January 17, 1683. At the conclusion of the San Bruno effort, he returned to Yaqui in May, 1685. He was stationed at Guadalajara from 1690 to 1693, then at San Luis Potosi in 1696. He returned to Guadalajara in 1708 and died in Mexico City on February 12, 1712. Cf. F.J. Alegre, *Historia de la Provincia de la Compañía de Jesús de Nueva España*, Vol. IV, p. 17. J. Ortiz Zapata, *Relación de las misiones que la Compañía de Jesús tiene en el Reino y Provincia de la Nueva Vizcaya en la Nueva España, hecho en el año 1768*, AGN, Mexico, Misiones, Vol. 26, folios 241-269; printed in *Documentos para La Historia de México*, Cuarta Serie, Vol. 3, pp. 309-419.

they searched for a pass over the Sierra La Giganta but found none. Although they travelled roughly 100 miles south of San Bruno, they found no way over the mountains and eventually turned back to San Bruno where they arrived on March 6, 1685.

Slightly more than two weeks later, the capitana arrived at the isolated outpost, bringing badly needed supplies and the long hoped for pearl-divers. With its repeated crop failures, the colony was in a bad way. Several soldiers had died of scurvy, and many more were sick. At one roll call, when sixty-nine soldiers should have reported, only fifteen appeared. Thirty-nine were too sick to appear, and four were reported dead. After a long conference, it was decided to abandon San Bruno, at least temporarily. The sick were to be taken to the Yaqui missions for care. Admiral Atondo and Father Goni were to take some of the able-bodied men in the balandra to hunt for pearls. Captain Guzmán and Father Kino were to sail in the capitana to look for a better mission site. On May 8, 1685, San Bruno was abandoned.[47]

In accord with previous plans, the sick were taken to the Yaqui missions on the mainland where most of them recovered. Admiral Atondo and Father Goni hunted for pearls with little success — the total catch being "two ounces and two drachms." Captain Guzmán and Father Kino explored the upper gulf visiting, among other places, Tiburón Island, then and now the home of the Seri people. In September, 1685, the two ships rejoined and sailed for Matanchel; both were badly in need of supplies. Promptly, Father Kino went to Guadalajara to arrange for further missionary efforts in California, and soon Admiral Atondo journeyed inland for the same purpose. Both achieved apparent success. Returning to Matanchel, the principals prepared for further missionary exploration, but suddenly they were diverted by orders from the viceroy, who dispatched them to sea to intercept the Manila galleon and warn it of pirates along the coast.

Leaving Matanchel on November 29, they intercepted the galleon a day later. Sailing out of sight of land, they convoyed the galleon to Acapulco, successfully evading the pirates, who were ashore raiding coastal settlements for provisions.[48] After this successful rescue, Kino and Atondo went to Mexico City where further plans for California were made. The needed funds were promised and seemed available. Then, troubles began. A revolt was threatening in Nueva Vizcaya which would require funds and soldiers. Spain urgently needed half a million pesos from Mexico to help pay a French indemnity. So the funds for California were no longer available, and the carefully planned enterprise ground to a halt. No more efforts to colonize California were made for more than a decade. Father Kino was assigned to Sonora where he labored effectively for the rest of his productive life. Admiral Atondo disappears from the field of our interest.

Although the Kino-Atondo expeditions did not achieve their planned objective — the founding of a permanent settlement in California — the work done by the party was of inestimable value to later workers there. Friendly relations were established with several tribes on the eastern side of Baja California; the vocabularies of the Cochimí language prepared by Father Kino and of the Monqui language prepared by Father Copart were of inestimable value to those who came later to the barren peninsula. The maps prepared by Father Kino and his developing ideas regarding an overland passage from the mainland of Mexico to California influenced geographical thinking and exploration plans for more than three-quarters of a century.[49] Thus, although the expedition might be rated a failure, it actually laid the foundations for later missionary successes and led to the eventual settlement of the Californias, both Alta and Baja.

For slightly more than a decade the California mission field was entirely deserted because no funds or workers were available. The civil authorities had correctly determined that California, as then known, could not produce enough pearls, metals, or agricultural products to pay for its occupation. During this time Father Kino, who had now been assigned to the Pimería Alta, had founded several missions which became relatively prosperous. The surplus products of these missions, according to Father Kino's reasoning, could be used to help the conversion of California. In 1691, by order of the Father Provincial, Ambrosio Oddón, Father Juan María Salvatierra was sent from his mission at Chínipas to make an inspection of Pimería Alta where Father Kino was

---

[47]For additional details of the Kino-Atondo efforts to colonize Baja California see H. E. Bolton, *Rim of Christendom*, pp. 37-228: R. L. Ives, *"Exploraciones del Padre Kino en Baja California,"* *Caláfia*, Vol. II, No. 3, December 1973, pp. 31-35, map p. 54. Source documents are indexed in these works.

[48]Bolton, *Rim of Christendom*, pp. 220-223; E.J. Burrus, *Kino Writes to the Duchess*, pp. 189-190, 193-194, 199; Peter Gerhard, *Pirates on the West Coast of New Spain, 1575-1742*, pp. 166-172; William Dampier, *A New Voyage Round The World*, pp. 177-181.

[49]Excellent reproductions of the Kino maps of this area which are good even by 1977 standards are contained in E.J. Burrus, *La Obra Cartográfica de la Provincia Mexicana de la Compañía de Jesus*. Vol. II, maps 8, 9, 10, 11 and 12.

working. During their travels together Father Kino "sold" Father Salvatierra on the need for reestablishing the California missionary effort, and thenceforth, despite years of apparently fruitless endeavors, both worked toward that end. In late 1696 and early 1697 plans were made for another California expedition to be financed by private gifts, as no funds were available from the royal treasury. Eventually these private gifts became the famous Pious Fund, which apparently started with the donation of one peso, but grew until it became the major support of the California missions.

At this time Kino and Salvatierra were joined by Father Juan de Ugarte, S.J., of whom we shall hear much more later. Soon, an agreement was worked out with the viceroy by which, so long as no public funds were spent, the Jesuits could make another attempt to colonize California, even to the extent of hiring their own soldiers (provided the Jesuits met the payroll). This agreement with only very minor changes prevailed throughout the Jesuit occupation of California, and, in general, worked very well. This lasting rapport between the Jesuits and the military may stem, in part, from the early military experience of St. Ignatius Loyola, founder of the Jesuit Order.

The viceroy's permission and agreement were dated February 5, 1697. The next day Father Salvatierra started for the west coast. En route, he visited Father Juan Bautista Copart to obtain the information which he had collected during the Kino-Atondo expedition of the previous decade and the grammars of the Indian languages he so carefully prepared. While awaiting the arrival of ships, supplies, and Father Kino on the Sinaloa coast, Father Salvatierra made a quick trip inland to Chínipas, where he became involved in a minor Indian uprising. Returning to the west coast, he made contact with the ships, gathered supplies, recruited soldiers, and finally sailed from Yaqui on October 10. Father Kino, however, was not with him. Because of unsettled conditions in Sonora, he was ordered to remain there because his presence was "considered to be worth a thousand soldiers." In his place, another hard working and successful missionary, Father Francisco María Píccolo, S.J., was chosen.[50]

[50]A full description of the Kino-Salvatierra-Ugarte efforts to reinstate the California enterprise would fill a very large volume. For further information see Gerard Decorme, *La Obra de los Jesuitas Mexicanos*, Vol. 2, pp. 482-484; P.M. Dunne, *Black Robes in Lower California*, pp. 38-45; H. E. Bolton, *Kino's Historical Memoir of Pimería Alta*, pp. I, 89, 90, 117, 159, 215-217, 367 and II, 47, 55; Zephyrin Engelhardt, *Missions and Missionaries of California*, Vol. 1, pp. 98-104.

The tiny expedition suffered the customary problems in attempting to cross the Gulf. Adverse winds blew the ships aground and created repeated delays. Finally, however, the miniscule fleet reached the eastern shore of the peninsula and undertook some limited coastal exploration. They visited the ruined site of Kino's mission San Bruno and then decided on going ashore at the Bay of San Dionisio, where they were greeted by Indians who had known Kino and Atondo. On October 19, 1697, they started clearing the mesa; animals and supplies were unloaded and a corral was built. Even an Indian attack was repulsed. Chief Dionisius, who was suffering from an apparent cancer, was instructed and baptized. Work was begun on the mission and camp of Loreto, which would later become the military and mission center of Baja California.

Pioneer Jesuits associated with the permanent settlement of Baja California were Fathers Juan María Salvatierra, Francisco María Píccolo, and Juan de Ugarte.[51] Military leaders were several, some able, others

---

[51]Juan María Salvatierra was born in Milan, Italy, on November 15, 1648. His baptismal name was Giovanni Salvatierra, María being added when he joined the Society of Jesus on July 10, 1668. Volunteering for service in the foreign missions, Father Salvatierra sailed from Genoa on May 25, 1675, and after only minor delays arrived in Veracruz on September 13, 1675. After studies in Mexico City, during which he perfected his "respectable" Spanish and also learned the "jailbird" version of the same language, he also acquired a working knowledge of Nahuatl, the intertribal tongue of much of Central Mexico. Early in 1680, Father Salvatierra was sent to the Tarahumara missions at Chínipas, in modern Chihuahua near the present Sonoran boundary and north of the Río Fuerte. Here, he founded several missions, explored the Barranca de Uríque which is deeper than the Grand Canyon of Arizona; he may have been the first European to visit the gorge. He made his solemn profession, August 15, 1684, at the mission church of Santa Inés de los Chínipas. Surviving the bloody revolt of early 1690 in which two of his co-workers (Fathers Juan Ortiz Foronda and Manuel Sánchez) were martyred, Father Salvatierra recommended remedies for the Indian grievances. Having pacified the rebels, he soon was riding north as official visitor to inspect the missions of Pimería Alta. Here, he met Father Kino for the first time and travelling with him in the field, he discussed plans for the reactivation of the Baja California missionary efforts.

In January of 1693, Father Salvatierra was appointed rector of the Jesuit College in Guadalajara. Although this was a promotion, he regarded it as an obstacle to his plans for California. After three years as rector Salvatierra was appointed master of novices at Tepotzotlán. While rector and master of novices, he worked strongly for official support of the California enterprise and solicited funds for that effort. These funds eventually became part of the famous Pious Fund which substantially aided the missions of California for many decades. When the enabling order from the viceroy finally arrived on February 5, 1697, Salvatierra wasted no time but set out for his new mission field in

California on February 7. There he spent the major part of the last twenty years of his life, building missions, exploring the peninsula and the Gulf of California, and setting up essential services for the missions of the peninsula (mail, shipping, and supply services). This long period of missionary activity was interrupted for about two years from October 21, 1704 to September 17, 1706 while Father Salvatierra served as Provincial of Mexico. Returning to California, he continued his labors until March 31, 1717. Then, in obedience to orders, he set forth from Loreto to Mexico City, to confer with the Provincial. En route, becoming too ill to ride a horse, he travelled from Tepic to Guadalajara in a litter. There, on July 18, 1717, he died at the age of sixty-eight years eight months. A fuller biography of Father Salvatierra and an extensive collection of his letters (reports) is found in E.J. Burrus, *Juan María Salvatierra*, 1971, 279 pp. 18, 1717, he died at the age of sixty-eight years eight months.

Father Francisco María Píccolo was born in Palermo, Sicily, on March 25, 1654. After studies at the local Jesuit college, he stated his desire to enter the Jesuit Order, eventually won parental consent, and continued his training at Marsala and Modica, both in Sicily. Returning to Palermo in 1680, he began his two years of theology, and toward their end, he requested service in foreign missions. Soon, travelling via Rome, Cartagena and Seville, he was on his way to the New World, where he arrived in Mexico in February, 1684. Almost immediately, he was assigned to Jesús Carichíc in the Tarahumara country where he promptly learned the difficult native language and served effectively as a missionary from 1684 to 1697. Following Salvatierra to Baja California, where he arrived November 27, 1697, Píccolo immediately began an intensive program of exploration and mission-founding that lasted, with a few interruptions by other duties, for more than thirty years. With enormous labor, he built a trail southwest from Loreto to Viggé in the Sierra de la Giganta, and there founded mission San Javier Viggé, November 1, 1699. From this site he also explored westward to the Pacific coast, seeking but never finding, a port of call for the Manila galleons.

In 1702, Father Píccolo went to Mexico, on what may best be described as a "begging trip," and returned with two additional missionaries, Father Geronimo Minutuli and Juan Basaldúa. The years of 1705-1706 found him assigned to Guaymas, the seaport established in Sonora for storing and shipping supplies to California. From 1705 to 1709 Father Píccolo served as visitor to Sonora where he had many contacts with Father Kino, an ardent supporter of the California missions. Returning to California, Father Píccolo was assigned to Santa Rosalía de Mulegé from where he went on many missionary and exploring trips. In 1720 he was appointed superior of all the California missions with his base at Loreto, a position which he held until his death at the age of seventy-five, February 22, 1729. A more extensive biography of Father Píccolo, and a collection of his letters and reports, will be found in E.J. Burrus, editor, *Informe del Estado de la Nueva Cristianidad de California*.

Father Juan de Ugarte, the third "founding father" of the Baja California missions, was born in Tegucigalpa, Honduras, on July 22, 1662. He entered the Jesuit Order at Tepotozolán on August 14, 1679. After teaching at Zacatecas and Mexico City he was appointed rector of the San Gregorio College for Indians in Mexico City. Later, in addition to his regular duties, he became treasurer and representative of the peninsular missions as administrator of the Pious Fund. On December 3, 1700, he left Mexico City for Baja California where he labored mightily for almost thirty years. A list of his verified accomplishments reads like a modernized version of the Labors of Hercules. Among his

not so able. First captain was Don Luis de Torres de Tortolero who did serve ably during the first year of the mission effort but was disabled by an eye infection; he resigned and retired to Mexico. He was replaced in the late summer of 1699 by Don Antonio García de Mendoza who was what we would now call a "sorehead." Apparently nothing satisfied him, and he eventually resigned, probably late in 1700. Next appointee was Lieutenant Isidro de Figueroa. If he ever did anything right, the record does not show it. Soon, because of his total incompetence, the soldiers objected to serving under him. In September of 1701, Father Salvatierra held an election, and Don Estevan Rodríguez de Lorenzo, a native of Algarve, Portugal, who had come to the peninsula in 1697, became the new captain. Unlike his predecessors in office, he served well and faithfully, finally retiring because of blindness in 1744. Not only was Don Estevan an excellent leader, but his wife, a mainland woman whom he married in 1711, also received the praise and approval of the missionaries.[52] Rodríguez died November 1, 1746, after forty-nine

---

works are the relocation and rebuilding of mission San Javier Viggé (1709 and 1717); filling the Cañada de Aranjuéz with 160,000 mule loads of earth to create the agricultural area at San Miguel Comondú; building California's first ship, the *Triunfo de la Cruz*, (about 1719) at Mulegé with timbers cut near San Sebastián some forty miles distant by a very rough trail; and a careful exploration of the Gulf of California in this ship which demonstrated that the Gulf was a closed sea, just as Father Kino had determined twenty years before. Blessed with enormous strength and almost unlimited energy, Father Ugarte is reported to have killed a mountain-lion with his bare hands and to have pacified fractious Indians by picking them up and banging their heads together. Late in 1730, he journeyed to Puebla where he died December 29, 1730, at the age of sixty-eight. A modern definitive biography of Father Ugarte is still awaited. See J. J. Villavincencio, *Vida y virtudes del venerable y apostólico Padre Juan de Ugarte de la Compañía de Jesús, missionero de las Islas Californias, y uno de sus primeros conquistadores*; P.M. Dunne, *Black Robes in Lower California*; T. H. Hittell, *El Triunfo de la Cruz*.

[52]Father Píccolo frequently praised the work of Captain Rodríguez. In a letter from Loreto, dated July 17, 1721, to Alexander Romano, the Father Provincial, he requests what amounts to a scholarship for Rodríguez' two sons, in these words: *Tambien se ha de suplicar que el Padre Rector de San Ildefonso se encomienda de la tutoría y que el Padre Procurador Echeverría de a dicho Padre Rector lo necesario para el gasto de los dos niños. De este empeño, pues, me a de sacar V. R. como lo espero de la mucha caridad y amor que tiene a esta se California, mi Padre Provincial. Y para que los niños puedan salir con seguridad de acá, a dicho fin espero la respuesta de V.R.*

He also adds, as a note, high praise of the Captain's wife: *Mi Padre Provincial, tengo escrupulo no añadir a la súplica un punto, es que aúnque no tubiera meritos (que son muchos) los que tiene el Señor Capitán, merecen ser acomodados estos dos niños,*

years of arduous service on the peninsula. He was succeeded in 1744 by his son, Bernardo Rodríguez de Larrea, who "inherited all the Christian virtues and military qualifications of his noble father, except robust health." He served well and faithfully until his death at Loreto on December 10, 1750.

Last military commander under the Jesuits was Don Fernando Javier de Rivera y Moncada, who was promoted to the captaincy in 1751. He had been a soldier in Baja California since 1742 and served in one capacity or another, except for a short and interrupted "retirement," until his death in the Yuma massacre of 1781.[53] During the Jesuit period his services received and merited high praise from the missionaries.

Even though he was never a captain, another soldier, whose work deserves a lasting place in the history of Baja California, was Juan Bautista Mugazabal. Born in Alava, Spain, about 1682, he came to the peninsula as a soldier in 1704 and was soon promoted to alférez. He spent much time in charge at Santa Rosalía de Mulegé. Highly regarded by the missionaries, he eventually petitioned to be admitted to the Jesuit Order as a brother. This request was granted in 1719, and under the guidance of Father Juan de Ugarte he "became as perfect a religious as he was a soldier." During much of his long religious career, he was stationed at Loreto where he served as procurator (quartermaster, paymaster, auditor). He apparently had and merited the confidence of both the soldiers and the missionaries; his difficult office ran smoothly, and hence he is seldom mentioned in surviving contemporary reports. He died in Loreto late in 1761 at the age of seventy-nine after fifty-seven years on the peninsula, forty-two of which were spent as a Jesuit brother.

It is most difficult to reconcile the high praise given some of the soldiers by some of the missionaries with the blanket denunciations of

solo por la Señora su Madre, esposa del Señor Capitán, que, desde que puso los pies en esta tierra, hasta aora, esta exercitandose en el officio de enfermera, curando a los Indios e Indias en sus rancherías. Su casa es un ospitál donde concurren los infermos de nuestras Missiones, con mucha Caridad u edificacion, ensenando no solo a coser y bordar a las Indias, mas aun a leer. Haec satis. This letter is quoted in full in E.J. Burrus (ed) *Informe del Estado de la Nueva Cristianidad de California*, pp. 217-218.

[53]The appointment of Don Fernando de Rivera y Moncada as Captain of Baja California is made official, and the reasons for it are outlined in a letter dated March 27, 1751, from the viceroy, the Conde de Revilla Gigedo, to the Jesuit Procurador, Juan de Armesto, S.J. See Amado Aguierre, *Documentos Para La Historia de Baja California*, p. 7.

the soldiers pronounced by other missionaries.[54] Study of the available records indicates that most of the soldiers, most of the time, performed their assigned duties rather well, despite conditions of service that were far from ideal.

During the fifty-three years following Salvatierra's landing in 1697 the Jesuit mission system in Baja California expanded from a tenuous foothold at Loreto to a network of fourteen missions, occupying most of the southern portion of the peninsula. These were connected by trails; many had outlying secondary stations *(visitas)* and most were partly self-supporting from local fields, gardens, and pastures. In a few, simple manufactures, such as spinning and weaving, were carried on. A list of the active missionaries and missions in 1751 is given in *Appendix D*. In addition to their efforts at converting and "civilizing" the Indians, the missions of the extreme south (Todos Santos and San José del Cabo) also served as ports of call for the Manila galleons, where the scurvy-stricken passengers and crew members could be given fresh foods and nursed back to a semblance of health before proceeding to Acapulco. Effective use of cactus fruits *(tunas, pitahayas)* as antiscorbutics is repeatedly mentioned in mission accounts.[55]

Growth of the Baja California mission system was slowed in the 1730s by growing Indian unrest, particularly in the south. This culminated in a bloody revolt late in 1734 in which Fathers Lorenzo Carranco was martyred at Santiago, October 1, and Nicolás Tamaral, at San José del Cabo, October 3. Also massacred were a number of soldiers and many Indian converts. In January, 1735, the Manila galleon *San Cristóbal* put in at Bahía San Bernabé, near Cabo San Lucas at the southern tip of the

---

[54]Perhaps the strongest of these is by Father Johann Jakob Baegert, S.J. See Brandenburg and Baumann, *Observations in Lower California*, pp. 145-147. Here, mixed with a store of accurate and factual information, is some wry Germanic humor which does not translate too well. Consequently, although Father Baegert was most certainly not an ardent admirer of the soldiers, his description, in translation, perhaps paints a darker picture than the good Father intended.

[55]For references to local antiscorbutics see: Miguel Venegas, *Noticia de la California*, Vol. II, pp. 284-285; P. M. Dunne, *Black Robes in Lower California*, p. 259, p. 281 n. 5; R. L. Ives, "The Lost Discovery of Corporal Antonio Luis," *Journal Arizona History*, Vol. 12, No. 3, Summer, 1970, pp. 101-115. The Manila galleons are described in Mariano Cuevas, *Monje y Marinero — La Vida y Tiempos de Fray Andrés de Urdañeta*; W. L. Schurz, *The Manila Galleons*; R.L. Ives "The Manila Galleons," *Journal of Geography*, Vol. 43, No. 1, (January, 1964) pp. 5-19.

peninsula, in hopes of obtaining fresh food and water before continuing the voyage to Acapulco. A boat was sent ashore to make contact with Father Tamaral at mission San José del Cabo, but the prearranged signals were not evident. Captain Don Mateo Zumalde of the *San Cristóbal*, having been at sea for many months, had no way of knowing that Father Tamaral was dead or that mission San José del Cabo was in ruins, or that the local Indians were in revolt. Eight men went ashore and set out for the missions. They were ambushed and killed by the Indian rebels who then went to the beach where they attempted to break up the boat and recover the iron aboard. They killed five more Spanish guards. Unaware of these attacks, Captain Zumalde, who found the San Bernabé anchorage unsatisfactory because of adverse winds, sailed some nine leagues westward where he anchored in the sheltering lee of Cabo San Lucas.

At the new anchorage Captain Zumalde sent the sick ashore and began replenishing the ship's water supply. Contact was soon made with local Indians, and as their stories were not consistent, the captain sent soldiers ashore as a precaution. The next day six hundred Indians armed with bows and arrows appeared at the beach. The sick were hurriedly taken aboard the galleon; eight Indians were invited aboard, including one of the rebel leaders, Gerónimo by name. The Indians sensed that their plot had been discovered and showered the retreating Spaniards with arrows. Four Indians aboard the galleon escaped and swam ashore; the other four, including Gerónimo, were seized and placed in chains. Captain Zumalde immediately raised anchor, set sail for Acapulco, and on landing went posthaste to Mexico City to report the incident to the viceroy, delivering his prisoners for suitable treatment. Subsequent investigation indicated that the Indian rebels had planned to capture the Manila galleon, to kill all Spaniards aboard, and to loot the valuable cargo. Only Captain Zumalde's alertness prevented it.

Military action against the Indian rebels began late in 1734 under the able direction of Captain Estevan Rodríguez with the twenty soldiers regularly assigned to Baja California and perhaps 100 dependable Indian allies. Fifty Yaqui archers were sent from the mainland to assist the regular troops, and more loyal Indians from the northern missions joined in the pacification. Assisting Captain Rodríguez was his son, Lieutenant Bernardo Rodríguez who was also an able frontier soldier. Joining the troop early in 1735 was Don Francisco Cortés y Monroi, a competent cavalryman, who was made a lieutenant by Captain Rodríguez. This small force attempted to reoccupy the ruined missions. Fighting many skirmishes with the rebels despite their being hopelessly outnumbered, they kept the hostile Indians "off balance." Some soldiers were detached from the southern campaign for a short time because of reports of pending revolts in the north, but these proved false. The converts of the northern missions remained loyal to the Spaniards. This regionally divided loyalty seems to have followed tribal lines quite closely. The northern Indians, most of whom remained loyal to the Spaniards, were largely of the Cochimí tribe; whereas the southern Indians, some of whom revolted, were members of the Guaicura tribe or of the closely related Pericúes.

While the local garrison with some outside aid was busily trying to quiet the revolt, the viceroy was collecting mountains of testimony. Eventually, at the viceroy's orders, General Manuel Bernardo Huidobro, Governor of Sinaloa, was dispatched to Loreto with fifty soldiers and one hundred Yaquis. They arrived in December, 1735, more than a year after the outbreak of the revolt. General Huidobro seems to have been well supplied with rank and arrogance, but sadly lacking in common sense, military competence, and diplomacy. In consequence, the pacification of the southern part of Baja California required more than two years. Late in 1737 General Huidobro and his Yaqui allies returned to the mainland, probably to the relief of all concerned, and the tasks of rebuilding the southern missions began. Huidobro soon became involved in the Yaqui revolt of 1740, when he again demonstrated his galloping ineptitude that eventually led to his removal from office.[56] As a result of the revolt the long-requested second presidio in Lower California was authorized for San José del Cabo. At first, it was independent of the command at Loreto, but later the commands were unified.

During this entire period, extensive explorations of the peninsula were undertaken by missionaries, usually accompanied by soldiers. Much of this exploration was undertaken to locate new areas for missionary activity, but other efforts were being made to find possible ports of call for the Manila galleons. Attempts were again being made to

---

[56]The Guaicura revolt is detailed in Miguel Venegas, *Noticia de la California*, Vol. II, pp. 289-317; Gerard Decorme, *La Obra de los Jesuitas Mexicanos*, Vol. 2, pp. 523-526; P.M. Dunne, *Black Robes in Lower California*, pp. 257-281. A Jesuit "statement of charges" against General Huidobro — one of many — is found in *De las clausulas injuriosas contra los Jesuitas missioneros, que constan de los escriptos y alegados del gobernador don Manuel de Huidobro*, Holliday Collection, Arizona Historical Society, Tucson.

determine the situation of the Gulf of California and its supposed relation to the mythical Strait of Anián. Reports of these explorations fill several hundred pages in surviving mission documents. They range in content from brief mentions-in-passing to complete day-by-day trip reports, full of detailed and verifiable geographical data. Two of these explorations, the voyages of Juan de Ugarte and of Ferdinand Consag, are worthy of note here.

Juan de Ugarte's voyage began at Loreto on May 15, 1721. He and Guillermo Estrafort (William Strafford or Stratford) were the leaders. His fleet consisted of the *Triunfo de la Cruz* built at Mulegé, a smaller boat the *Santa Bárbara* also built at Mulegé, and a canoe. On this voyage, the Gulf was criss-crossed several times; visits were made to Tiburón Island on the Sonoran side and to a point on the mainland near the mouth of the Río Concepción where supplies were obtained from Caborca. The mouth of the Colorado was visited, the great tidal range at the head of the Gulf was noted, and the tricky currents on the California side of the Gulf near Angel de la Guarda Island were encountered and clearly described. Return to Loreto was on September 15, 1721. From this voyage, Ugarte quite correctly concluded that the Gulf of California was a closed sea that ended at the mouth of the Colorado.[57]

The last great exploration, prior to the end of 1750, was the lengthy and difficult voyage of Father Ferdinand Consag to the head of the Gulf of California in 1746. Once again the objective was to determine whether California was an island or a peninsula. Starting by sea from Loreto in late spring of 1746, Father Consag, accompanied by Captain Bernardo Rodríguez de Larrea, journeyed north to Puerto San Carlos at 28° N. latitude (actually about 27°52' N.) where his fleet, consisting of four small open sailboats *(canoas)*, awaited him. Here his crew of Christian

---

[57]Ugarte's account of this voyage, prepared at San Pablo de Viggé and dated January 12, 1722, was sent to Procurador Joseph de Echeverría, and is titled *Relación de descubrimiento del Golfo de Californias o Mar Lauretano*. Original is in the Biblioteca Nacional Mexico, Archivo Franciscano, leg. 53. Guillermo Estrafort's narrative, prepared at Pitique and dated January 18, 1746, is titled *Descripción de las Californias desde el cauo de Sn. Lucas que esta al sur de sus misiones puertos, baías, plazeres, naciones reduzidas y gentiles que se tiene noticia la abitan y demas necesario para benir en cabal comprehensión y de la Contra Costa para la parte del norte que es como sigui*. Two copies of this, not entirely in agreement, were located in the Biblioteca Nacional by Dunne. Copies of both Ugarte's and Estrafort's reports are in the Bolton Collection of the Bancroft Library.

Indians and six soldiers was assembled. Departing northward on June 9 without Captain Rodríguez, who had returned to Loreto, the expedition made a thorough and detailed exploration of the east coast of Baja California as far as the mouth of the Colorado. Included in the diary of this expedition is a report of an eruption of the Tres Virgenes volcano near Santa Rosalía, a very clear description of the hot sulfur spring on the beach of Puertecitos (July 5), and details of the currents and islands at the mouth of the Colorado. When the expedition was finished, he reported that the Gulf "really ends at the mouth of the Colorado, just as Father Kino reported." Father Consag's map of the Gulf of California is reproduced here as Figure 3.[58] Many of the place names applied by Father Consag are still in general use. To this busy, growing, barren and poverty-stricken mission field came a common soldier one José Velásquez, a native of Ostímuri; his military service began at Loreto on January 1, 1751. In the armies of the Californias he was destined to spend the rest of his long and arduous life.

[58]Ferdinand Consag (Fernando Konsag, Konschak) was born at Varasardia, Croatia, on December 2, 1703, and entered the Society of Jesus on October 22, 1719. He was sent to Mexico at his own request about 1730. He travelled to California in 1733 and served much of the time at mission San Ignacio, until his death on September 10, 1759, at mission Santa Gertrudis of what was probably appendicitis. Three biographies of Father Consag, all overly pietistic, have been published. These are: Francisco Zevallos, *Carta del Padre Provincial, Francisco Zevallos, Sobre la Apostólica Vida y Virtudes del P. Fernando Konsag, Insigne Misionero De La California*; Martin Krmpotic, *Life and Works of the Reverend Ferdinand Konschak, S.J., 1703-1750*; M. P. Servin, *The Apostolic Life of Fernando Consag*. Consag's diary of his 1746 voyage is printed in full in Miguel Venegas, *Noticia de la California*, Vol. 3, pp. 91-120.

Tres Virgenes volcano is at Lat. 27°29⅔ N., Long. 112°35' W. with a summit elevation of 6547 feet. See R. L. Ives, "Dating of the 1746 Eruption of Tres Virgenes Volcano, Baja California del Sur, Mexico," *Bulletin of the Geological Society of America*, Vol. 73, no. 5, May 1962. pp. 647-648.

Puertecitos is located on the east shore of Baja California, about 50 miles south of San Felipe, at Lat. 30°21' N., Long. 113°39'30" W. The area is clearly shown on DETENAL Map H 11 B 77, "Puertecitos," 1/50,000, 1974.

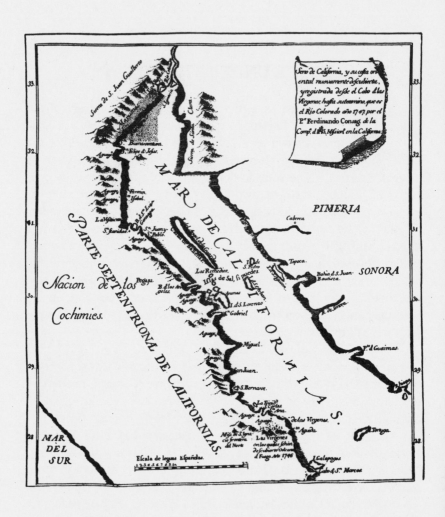

Figure 3. An early printed version of Father Consag's map of the Gulf of California, based on his voyage during the summer of 1746. Map courtesy Jesuit Historical Institute.

SERVICE UNDER THE JESUITS

uly enrolled as a private in the cavalry company of the presidio of Loreto, José Velásquez became what was commonly known as a *soldado de cuera,* so named for the knee-length, sleeveless, multi-ply leather jacket worn as protective armor.[1] The soldado de cuera's weapons theoretically consisted of a lance, a sword, two pistols, and a smooth bore carbine. Because of shortages, the poor quality of both firearms and gunpowder, the chronic lack of skilled gunsmiths, and the usual problem of getting musket balls of the same caliber as the muskets, firearms were not too commonly used, and the soldados de cuera became most skilled with the lance. When properly led and equipped, these soldiers were a most effective fighting force on the frontiers of New Spain. They were able to hold their own, or even win battles against bellicose Indians when the odds were thirty to one or worse.

The soldiers assigned to Baja California during the Jesuit period (1697-1768) were under the orders of the Jesuit rector of Loreto, except for a short period during the bungling campaigns of General Huidobro in the late 1730s. Any or all of them, including their captain, could be reassigned or dismissed at the pleasure of the Jesuit superior. Because of a succession of superior captains — Estevan Rodríguez Lorenzo, Bernardo Rodríguez de Larrea, and Fernando Javier de Rivera y Moncada, this non-standard arrangement worked very smoothly. Some soldiers were transferred from one mission to another and a few were returned to the mainland, but many served in the barren peninsula for a decade or more with no record of trouble, and sometimes with a word of praise in the missionaries' records.

---

[1]Complete description of the arms of the soldados de cuera can be found in S. B. Brinkerhoff and O. B. Faulk, Lancers for the King. The metal cuirass, shown in so many imaginative paintings, was seldom owned and even more seldom used by soldiers on the frontiers of New Spain for the simple reason that it heated up to about 160° F. under the desert sun and became unwearable.

Duties of the Baja California soldiers were many, varied, and arduous. Service at the California missions was rendered more difficult than usual by recurrent food shortages, scarcity of good drinking water, and climatic extremes. Primary duty of the soldiers was to serve as guards at the missions, where one missionary was frequently surrounded by as many as 1,000 semi-civilized Indians, not all of whom were friendly. A soldier usually accompanied the missionary on his parochial travels, acting as guard, companion, and muleteer. While the father was away from the mission, a soldier usually stayed there to maintain order, prevent theft, and to solve minor problems as the father's representative. Soldiers also supervised the transportation of supplies from Loreto to the various missions and accompanied the fathers as guards and muleteers on their exploring expeditions. Between journeys, they were kept busy caring for the livestock of the missions. When a new mission was founded, soldiers assisted in its construction, supervised the labor of the converts, and sometimes instructed them in the practical arts, like the making of adobes. At many missions one or more of the soldiers supervised the distribution of rations when there were any to distribute. Most of the time, the mission guard also acted as civil police, maintaining order among the converts, and meting out such punishments as the missionary father directed. In their spare time, if any, the soldiers acted as sponsors for Indian converts; they tried to augment their scanty rations with small gardens. A few of the soldiers had side-lines of pearl-hunting, which was illegal, and prospecting, usually unprofitable.

Although we have no direct record of José Velásquez' duty assignments while serving as a private soldier under Jesuit orders, we also have no records of disciplinary actions against him, indicating that he performed his duties in a reasonably satisfactory manner. His performance at a later date indicates that during this period he acquired an excellent knowledge of the geography of the peninsula and excellent "survival skills" in the barren area.

At the time of José Velásquez' enlistment (January 1, 1751), the northernmost mission in Baja California was San Ignacio de Kadakaaman (27°18' N., 112°56' W.); the site was found by Father Francisco Píccolo in 1716, and the mission established by Father Juan Luyando in 1728. Missionary in charge in 1751 was Father Ferdinand Consag. All major Jesuit explorations after this time were to the north and into an especially barren area now known as the Central Desert.[2]

By 1751 Father Consag, then stationed at San Ignacio, had made so many converts in the unsettled lands to the north that a new mission was needed. Acting under orders from Father Juan Antonio Balthasar, who was then Provincial of New Spain, Father Consag, accompanied by Captain Fernando Javier de Rivera y Moncada and unnamed soldiers, launched new explorations. Starting from La Piedad, twenty-seven leagues north of San Ignacio and later the site of mission Santa Gertrudis, Father Consag journeyed northwest, via modern Calmalli Viejo, across the southern slopes of the Sierra de Calmalli, eventually reaching the Pacific Ocean. Going inland, he travelled north to a point not far south of the later site of mission San Fernando de Velicatá. On the outward journey he passed by and noted some "white transparent marble" (Mexican onyx) which pinpoints the site beyond any reasonable doubt as El Marmolito.[3] Near his "turn around" point on the return journey, Consag travelled to the ocean again, noting on this side trip some remarkable fossil shells which were probably the amonites in the Arroyo Santa Catarina.[4] Consag's measured latitudes on this journey as on other expeditions are almost universally too high, often by a degree or more. This consistent error, common to most Spanish maps made before 1769, was apparently due to the use of the meridian altitude method of measuring latitudes — the meridian being determined by the use of a compass-oriented sundial which was not corrected for local magnetic declination.[5]

The return journey was a slow one, and it was plagued by fogs which hindered observations. Return to La Piedad was on July 8, 1751, after a month and a half on the trail. Returning to San Ignacio, Father

---

[2]See Homer Aschmann, *The Central Desert of Baja California*, updated and revised edition.

[3]This is on the west side of the Sierra Calmalli on the north side of Arroyo El Salinito at Lat. 28°31'40" N., Long. 113°55' W. and is reachable by a much used and rutted, but little maintained, wheel track from Rosarito on the main peninsular highway (Route 1). In this area are a number of highly mineralized springs, the probable source of the onyx. Local residents report that drinking this water causes kidney and bladder stones, among other discomforts.

[4]These are on the south side of the Arroyo Santa Catarina at and near the base of Mesa El Cerrito at Lat. 29°35'30" N., Long. 115°14' W. This is close to the point where the wheel track from the town of Santa Catarina to Puerto Catarina reenters the Arroyo Santa Catarina from the south. Many of the better ammonite specimens have been removed from the area by unknown persons since 1938. Here, a fossiliferous reef in the Rosario formation (Cretaceous) has been exposed by erosion.

[5]R. L. Ives, "The High Latitudes of Early Spanish Maps," *Kiva*, Vol. 41, No. 2 Winter, 1975, pp. 161-184.

Consag prepared his report of the expedition which is a mine of information.[6]

Efforts to care for the numerous converts at La Piedad were assisted greatly by the work of Andrés Comeneji Sistiaga, a blind Indian *temastián* (catechist) of notable competence and fidelity. Mission Santa Gertrudis was finally opened at this site (28°05′ N., 113°06′ W.) in 1752 with Father George Retz in charge.[7] He had been assistant to Father Consag at San Ignacio while he learned the local dialects.

In the early summer of 1753 Father Consag, accompanied by Captain Fernando Xavier de Rivera y Moncada and some soldiers and Indian allies, set out northward from Santa Gertrudis on another journey of exploration. Although Consag's report of the journey has not been found, secondary and tertiary sources (which are not in perfect agreement) indicate that the course was roughly north-northwest along the east side of the Sierra de Calmalli, from Santa Gertrudis to Bahía de los Angeles, where the Indians were most friendly. Thence, the course was west-northwest into the interior, gradually turning to north, with the "turn around" point being at the latitude of Bahía San Luis Gonzaga, or somewhere between the later sites of Calamajué and Santa María. Consag definitely visited Calamajué with its mineralized water, probably saw the important natural tank at Yubay (east of modern Desengaño), but definitely did not visit the springs at Adak which was later the site of mission San Francisco Borja. Consag commended the services of Captain Rivera highly, but made no mention, good or bad, of the accompanying soldiers.[8]

---

[6]Text of Consag's report is included in José Ortega and J.A. Balthasar, *Apostolicos Afanes de la Compañia de Jesús escritos por un padre de la misma sagrada religion de su provincia de Mexico*, Vol. III, pp. 385-422. A rather rough English translation is contained in M. D. Krmpotic, *Life and Works of Reverend Ferdinand Konschak, S. J.* pp. 83-134.

[7]Father George Retz was born in Dusseldorf, Germany, April 28, 1717. He joined the Jesuit order in 1733, studied at Vienna and Cologne and taught at Vienna, Muenster-Eifel and Osnabrueck. He left Spain on June 16, 1750, and journeyed through mainland Mexico to Baja California the same year. He first served as assistant to Father Consag at San Ignacio, then became missionary at Santa Gertrudis where he continued until the Jesuit expulsion. Father Retz probably died at Trier, Germany, April 8, 1773. It is certain that he did extensive exploration north of mission Santa Gertrudis which is only hinted at in available documents.

[8]Salient information is contained in M. D. Krmpotic, *Life and Works of the Reverend Ferdinand Konschak, S.J.*, pp. 147-148.

With an advanced base at Santa Gertrudis, explorations were continued northward. These involved Father George Retz, Father Ferdinand Consag, a number of Indian converts, and some unknown soldiers. Soon, the somewhat sulphurous warm springs at Adak became known and a "road" (mule trail) was opened to the site. Funds were provided by the estate of Doña Mariana de Borja, Duquesa de Béjar y Gandia, to found the mission of San Francisco Borja in 1752 with Father Wenceslaus Linck in charge.[9] Father Linck, as clearly shown by surviving records, was not only a diligent and effective missionary, but also a competent and energetic explorer. When Father Linck had pacified the Indian *hechiceros* (medicine men) in 1764, he received Father Victoriano Arnes as assistant.[10] He still found time for exploration and soon began a series of expeditions that merit him more fame than he has received to date.

Father Linck's first major exploration was an expedition to La Isla del Angel de la Guarda in the Gulf of California, opposite Bahía de los Angeles. This expedition was undertaken to investigate lights seen on the island which were believed to be evidence of inhabitants who might become converts if properly approached. Accompanied by Lieutenant Don Blás Fernández y Somera, some soldiers, and some Indian allies, Father Linck crossed the Canal de Ballenas to the island, searching diligently for inhabitants. But he found neither people nor water and

---

[9] Wenceslaus Linck was born in Nudek, Bohemia, March 29, 1736, and entered the Jesuit Order at Brno May 18, 1754. After brief studies at Prague he volunteered for missionary service overseas, and set out for Mexico in 1755. There he completed his studies and was ordained. He came to Baja California in 1762, assisting briefly at Santa Gertrudis, then took command of mission San Borja in August, 1762. Here, he expanded the mission area by establishing a number of visitas and ranches and explored extensively north and west of his mission. He was removed from Baja California in 1768 in the Jesuit expulsion, reached his homeland in mid-1769, and was still living and working in Olmuetz, Bohemia, in 1790. Linck's work is excellently described in E.J. Burrus, *Wencheslaus Linck's Diary of His 1766 Expedition to Northern Baja California*, and *Wenceslaus Linck's Reports and Letters 1762-1778*.

[10] Victoriano Arnes was born in Villa de Graus, Aragon, Spain, September 4, 1736. He entered the Jesuit Order in the province of Aragon April 13, 1754, and studied at Granada and Córdoba. Volunteering for missionary service overseas, he sailed for Mexico in 1760. After further studies in Mexico, he went to Baja California in 1764 where for two years he assisted Father Linck. Later, he founded the shortlived mission of Calamajué, discovered the site of Santa María, and founded the mission there. Father Arnes was returned to Spain as a result of the Jesuit expulsion, was imprisoned there for a time, and then deported to Italy where he died in Rome on June 8, 1788.

Figure 4. Bahía de los Angeles, visited by sea by Father Consag in 1746, and by land by him in 1753. This bay later became the seaport from which mission San Francisco Borja was supplied. The long ridge on the far horizon is Isla Angel de la Guarda explored by Father Wenceslaus Link in 1765. Photo by R.L. Ives.

returned to the mainland, having much difficulty with adverse winds and currents.

The second of Father Linck's major explorations lasted from August 1 until after November 18, 1765. Accompanying Father Linck on this expedition were Captain Fernando Javier de Rivera y Moncada, two soldiers, two Germans who had escaped from the English and had reached Baja California on the Manila galleon, and perhaps sixteen Indian aides. The exploration covered the poorly known lands north and west of mission San Borja. Although the full report of this exploration has not been published, it is certain that the party "grid-ironed" the area between Consag's 1751 and 1753 routes.[11] They made friendly contacts with many Indian groups and collected a vast store of geographical information, much of which cannot be surely identified from the fragmentary, "third hand" reports currently (1977) available.

The third, last, and most important of Father Linck's major explorations took place between February 20 and April 18 of 1766. It involved perhaps 1,000 miles of equestrian travel in a "region destitute of just about everything." Unlike Linck's other explorations, for which we have only summary letters and secondary accounts, the original diary of this expedition exists in the Bancroft Library. Although water-damaged, the information it contained was retrieved by ultra-violet light techniques.[12] Personnel in this party included Lieutenant Don Blás Fernández y Somera who had also commanded the soldiers on the 1765 expedition to Isla Angel de la Guarda, thirteen soldiers (who were they?), and a number of Indian allies. Route was roughly north from mission San Borja for some distance, passing through the same general region as the 1765 journey but which followed "a different route from the present one." North of Laguna Seca Chapala the course swung to the northwest, as far as Velicatá which later became the site of the only mission founded by the Franciscans in Baja California. Later course was to San Juan de Dios, thence along the west flank of the Sierra de San Pedro Mártir for about a week. The expedition crossed the sierra with understandable difficulties and entered the Valle de San Felipe by Arroyo Agua Caliente where the adjacent hot and cold springs were noted. A side trip was made to San Felipe on the Gulf; then the party

[11]Rev. Dr. Ernest J. Burrus, S.J., reports that he has recently located additional Linck documents, which are currently being prepared for publication (personal communication, October 22, 1977).

[12]Original condition of this manuscript and the methods by which it was made legible are described in E. J. Burrus, *Linck's Diary*, pp. 10-11.

Figure 5. Mission San Francisco de Borja (1977). This structure was completed by the Dominicans, about 1801, replacing earlier adobe churches built by the Jesuits and Franciscans. Photo by R.L. Ives.

travelled along the west side of the Valle de San Felipe to a point somewhere roughly twenty miles west of modern El Chinero. There, because of exhausted animals some of which were unshod and suffered from worn-down hooves and lack of water, the expedition turned back, returning by a slightly different route bypassing Velicatá. They arrived at mission San Borja in fairly good condition despite a horseback journey of perhaps 1,000 miles.

Hints and vague references in mission accounts and letters indicate that Father Linck made other explorations in the vicinity of his mission, presumably accompanied by soldiers, but specific details are lacking. After his return from the 1766 journey to the north, the need for another mission north of San Borja became apparent. On October 14, 1766, Fathers Victoriano Arnes and Juan José Diez, ten soldiers, and fifty Indian converts from San Borja (including the able leader, Juan Nepomuceno) journeyed north to the deep valley of Calamajué, where the mission was started above the mineralized waters of the Arroyo Calamajué.[13] The settlement at Calamajué soon ran into serious trouble because of bad water and poor soil. Both the soldiers and the missionaries became ill — Father Diez seriously so. When the water was used to irrigate the crops, the plants died. The sheep "starved to death."[14] Father Arnes searched diligently to the north for a new mission site with better water and eventually found one in the arroyo Cabujakaamung thirty-one miles air line to the northwest.

To this site Father Arnes moved the mission in May, 1767, naming it Santa María de Los Angeles. This new mission, near the head of an

---

[13]Juan José Diez was born in Mexico City October 17, 1735, and joined the Jesuits at Tepotzotlán December 23, 1752. After the usual thorough training in Mexico City and Puebla, he worked for a time in the Casa Profesa in Mexico City; then he was assigned to the missions of Baja California where he arrived at San Borja late in 1765 or early in 1766. Later, at Calamajué he became seriously ill and was transported to San Borja, and later to Guadalupe. After his recovery, he was sent to La Purísima. Along with fellow Jesuits, he was expelled in 1768, long detained in Spain, and finally allowed to travel to Italy where he died in Ferrara November 5, 1809.

[14]The water at Calamajué is a chemist's nightmare. Analyses show that in a wet year it contains excessive amounts of salts, mixed metallic sulfates (iron and copper), a high fluorine content, and traces of arsenic, in addition to suspended asbestos fibers, and a variety of dissolved gases. Soil is a mixture of quartz, feldspar, talc, and asbestos fibers, with practically no humus. Additionally, the valley of Calamajué is a natural reflector oven so that some areas within it have very much higher daytime temperatures than the surrounding deserts.

Figure 6a. Calcareous tufa deposits surrounding one of the better springs on the west wall of the Calamajué Arroyo. In dry years, the valley floor is covered with crusts of salt. Photo by R.L. Ives.

Figure 6b. The Calamajué Valley (1977) as viewed from the north. Knee-high mission wall remnants are concealed in waist-high brush on the bench across the valley at left. Photo by R.L. Ives.

arroyo draining east to the Gulf of California, had a moderate supply of fairly good water, a few palm trees, little local vegetation, and very little agriculturally useful land. Fish, however, were plentiful at Bahía San Luis Gonzaga, a day's walk of about fifteen trail miles to the east. Although the soldiers apparently disliked the desolate site, Father Arnes had considerable success in his missionary efforts, and even planted a small field in wheat and cotton. Unfortunately, when these crops matured, the Jesuits were no longer there to harvest them.

In early 1768 came the Jesuit expulsion which put an end to almost three quarters of a century of continuous, dedicated, and successful Jesuit missionary effort on the peninsula of Baja California. Reasons for the Jesuit expulsion were never explained by Charles III of Spain, who signed the expulsion order *(Yo, El Rey)* on February 27, 1767. The expulsion seems to have been prompted by a series of unsubstantiated charges against the Jesuits, which were all later disproved, and augmented by forged documents. Contributing factors were undoubtedly the growing anti-clerical feeling in western Europe at the time and the fact that the Jesuits who in receiving their orders from the Pope resisted the political pressures of various corrupt, hereditary, monarchical courts.[15]

Chosen to carry out the expulsion order in Baja California was Don Gaspar de Portolá, a Catalan, who two years later discovered San Francisco Bay. He was also named Governor of California at this time. Accompanied by twenty-five cavalrymen, twenty-five Catalonian musketeers, and fourteen Franciscans, who were to replace the expelled Jesuits, he travelled westward in accord with his orders, arriving at Matanchel on the west coast of the mainland in the early summer of 1767. Here, he prepared to cross the Gulf of California to the peninsula. Serious but unsuccessful attempts were made in July and August. Finally in September a small party of five dragoons, according to most accounts, managed to cross the Gulf in eleven days and landed at Puerto Escondido just south of Loreto. When, after a considerable wait, they were not joined by the governor, they returned to the mainland. Portolá tried again in mid-October. After a voyage of forty-four days (the staight-line distance from Matanchel to Loreto approximates 500 miles!), they made landfall, not at Loreto as planned, but at San José del Cabo nearly 225

---

[15]A lengthy and somewhat biased discussion of the Jesuit expulsion and its probable causes is contained in Zephyrin Engelhardt, *Missions and Missionaries of California*, Vol. 1, pp. 304-320. A later written account, substantially devoid of bias, is contained in P. M. Dunne, *Black Robes in Lower California*, pp. 416-427.

miles to the south-southeast! The Franciscans in a separate vessel required eighty days for the same journey.

Don Gaspar de Portolá embarked for California, apparently expecting to find a land of milk and honey, with pearls easily available to all, and rich veins of silver everywhere. On his march northward from San José del Cabo to Loreto, he underwent considerable disillusionment because the lands were not only lacking in milk and honey but also in drinkable water and forage. The Ocio silver mines near Santa Ana were reportedly the richest on the peninsula. Portolá found them not only primitive but also only marginally profitable. Pearls apparently were not found. Don Gaspar later reported to the viceroy that ''the greater part of the country is a sandy waste sown with thorns and thistles.'' He was to see even more barren lands later.

Arriving at Loreto on December 17, 1767, Portolá summoned Father Benno Ducrue, who was then superior of the missions of Baja California, from Guadalupe to Loreto. On Ducrue's arrival, Christmas day, Portolá read to him and to the others assembled there his appointment as governor. The following day he communicated to the Jesuits the royal decree of expulsion. Shortly thereafter the other missionaries were summoned to Loreto, whence, after putting their mission establishments in the best order possible, they travelled by boat, mule, and litter. On February 3, 1768, the sixteen California Jesuits embarked, sailing across the Gulf to Matanchel. Thence, they crossed the mainland of Mexico to Vera Cruz, and then the Atlantic with a brief layover at Havana. The Spanish Jesuits arrived in Cádiz July 8, 1768; the Germans, in Ostend, April 13.

We have two good, independent contemporary accounts of the expulsion of the Lower California Jesuits — one by Johan Jakob Baegert and one by Benno Ducrue.[16] Both stress the tact and consideration with which Governor Portolá carried out his difficult and probably distasteful orders; both clearly indicate that the Jesuits, despite royal disfavor, were still esteemed by the general public.

The use of relatively large military forces to expel small bands of Jesuits — fifty armed soldiers against sixteen Jesuits in the case of Baja California — may be interpreted as evidence that Charles III was ''running scared'' or may only be another example of Bourbon over-

[16]Brandenburg and Baumann, *Observations in Lower California,* pp. 165-172; E.J. Burrus, *Ducrue's Account of the Expulsion.*

reaction. This unnecessary use of military force was noted by Governor Portolá, who commented in a letter to Croix "that a simple letter from the viceroy making known the royal order to the superiors would have been sufficient to make the Jesuits abandon all their missions, colleges, and possessions."[17]

During the period of transition brought about by the Jesuit expulsion, the soldiers were kept overbusy. First they had to summon the Jesuit missionaries to Loreto, then they had to guard and administer the missions, maintaining a semblance of order and preventing looting. Subsequently they were required to inventory the mission settlements and their contents to satisfy royal orders. Still later, they also had the task of guiding the Franciscans replacements to their mission assignments and seeing that they had adequate supplies. Much of this work devolved upon the Loreto garrison because the soldiers brought in by Governor Portolá did not know the country and could function only as aides. Although we have no direct record of José Velásquez' assignments at this time, his seventeen years of experience on the peninsula and his literacy assured that he was kept busy, probably acquiring not only saddle sores, but also writers' cramp, in the fulfillment of his military duties.

[17]Loreto, December 20, 1767, AGN Californias, Vol. 76.

José Velásquez — THE EARLY YEARS

osé Velásquez, according to his service record prepared by Lieutenant José de Zúñiga in 1783, was born in San Ildefonso de Ostímuri (Cf. Appendix A). By subtracting his stated age from the date of the report, we find that Velásquez was probably born in 1717. From this same record we find that he was a widower. As no record has been found in the annals of California regarding his wife, it is assumed that he had been married and that his wife had died prior to the beginning of his military service at Loreto in January, 1751. As far as can be determined, there is no record of José Velásquez' education. That he was literate there is plentiful evidence in his reports and letters. The extent of his education is somewhat hard to determine from his surviving writings. However, as many of these reach us as copies, or even copies of copies, we must not attribute all of any literary heresies to Don José himself. His handwriting, in the few originals that have come to light, is that of a practiced writer and strongly suggests that more writings by him once existed. Some may possibly come to light at a future date.

San Ildefonso de Ostímuri is one of the least known and most inaccessible places in northwestern Mexico. According to the latest surveys, San Ildefonso is in the southeastern part of modern Sonora in a deep canyon between Iglesia and Mulatos; the area is drained by a branch (often dry) of the Río Sahuaripa, a tributary of the Yaqui.[1]

---

[1]Approximate geographical location is 28°41' N., 108°55' W.; Alt. 4800 feet MSL. It is theoretically reachable by a seven mile horse trail going east from the Yécora-Tarachi road; the turnoff is about two miles north of Iglesia. Access to Yécora is by improved road from Ciudad Obregon to Nuri; then by a rough but passable road (used by mine and lumber trucks) to Tayopa; thence by either of two very rough roads (Hobson's choice) to Yécora. The Yécora-Tarachi road despite much work is washed out most of the time. Gasoline supplies are undependable east of Tayopa. San Ildefonso was earlier on a mule trail, perhaps used by Father Salvatierra in 1690 and 1691, which went from Chínipas in the Tarahumara north through Santa Ana, Macoiba to Ostimuri and thence to Mulatos, San Ildefonso, Tarachi and northwest into Sonora. Parts of this trail have been obliterated or parallelled by modern "roads" (four-wheel drive recommended; gasoline supplies problematic). Other segments which follow ridges are impassible for four-wheeled vehicles.

San Ildefonso became an important mining camp in the early 1670s, producing gold, silver, and copper (and also zinc, lead, and cadmium which were not then exploited). By 1676, Ostímuri had become the capital of a province of the same name. This was intermediate between Sonora and Sinaloa and included parts of the Río Yaqui watershed, the exact boundaries varying from time to time. Construction of the church of San Ildefonso de Ostímuri apparently began after 1678, when the first priest was assigned there, and stopped before 1723 when the town became a visita of Onapa. In 1687 Don Juan Francisco de Goyeneche became justicia mayor of San Ildefonso. He was apparently succeeded in 1691 by General Marcos Fernández de Castañeda who bore the title of alcalde mayor and served until 1694. Some time after 1695 the tenor of the ore at and near San Ildefonso decreased, and the area went into an economic decline, undoubtedly hastened by repeated Apache raids, shortages of Tarahumara mine laborers, and governmental neglect. Certainly before 1747, and probably even before 1730, the provincial capital was moved forty-nine miles southwest from San Ildefonso to Río Chico; San Ildefonso became completely deserted, remaining that way today "because of exhaustion of the ore." During the Yaqui wars of 1737-1741 most, and some accounts say all, of Ostímuri was abandoned by missionaries and settlers alike.[2]

Ostímuri continued to exist largely as a "phantom province" until about 1815. After Mexican independence Ostímuri's territory which was never very clearly defined was absorbed by Sonora and Sinaloa with a very small eastern part being appended to Chihuahua. Original industries in Ostímuri were mining, subsistence agriculture, and cattle raising. The latter industry profited the Apache raiders greatly but did not pay the ranchers well. Today, the same general area produces cattle with some profit in most years. It still engages in some subsistence agriculture in the higher lands and has recently developed productive commercial agriculture in areas watered by modern irrigation projects, mostly along the

[2]J.A. Donohue, *After Kino: Jesuit Missions in Northwestern New Spain*, pp. 19-20, 36, 54, 70, 87-88; Juan Nentvig, *Rudo Ensayo*, Vol. V, No. 2, June, 1894, p. 242; V.A. Robles, editor, *Diario y Derrotero de lo caminando, visto y observado en la visita que hizo a los presidios de la Nueva España septentrional*, pp. 45-58; Paul Roca, *Paths of the Padres Through Sonora*, pp. 303-307. This work is a mine of geographical and historical information regarding the Sonoran missions. Its usefulness is greatly enhanced by the included maps, the work of Don Bufkin of Tucson.

lower course of the Río Yaqui. Mining is carried on sporadically in many parts of old Ostímuri, usually at little profit, due to scarcity of water for milling in many locations and high transportation costs. In recent years illegal crops of *cannabis* and *papaverum* have been grown in selected hidden locations, sometimes at great profit.

Following José Velásquez' enlistment, the area was disrupted by the Pima Revolt of 1751 and the Seri Wars of 1767-1770 — in addition to Tarahumara unrest, Apache raids, and Yaqui revolts. After the closing of the upland mines the Tarahumara retreated into the deep barrancas of the Sierra Madre and lived in comparative isolation until the middle of the present century.[3] The Apache problem was not resolved until the late 1880s. The Yaqui troubles continued until about 1910. Sonora, always a restive frontier province, was beset with political problems, some so serious that special peace-keeping forces were needed from time to time. The last of these forces, Colonel Emilio Kosterlitzky's rurales, were kept busy maintaining a semblance of order among the gente de razon well past the first decade of the 20th century.

As an understandable consequence of two and a half centuries of economic depression and political unrest, the day-by-day records of Ostímuri — births, marriages, deaths — have not survived to the present, and no local documents concerning the early years of José Velásquez have been found. Despite this lack of direct records, however, the general situation gives us numerous clues to his early years before his enlistment in 1751. At the time of his birth San Ildefonso de Ostímuri was an economically depressed and declining mining camp, afflicted with frequent Apache raids. In 1723 while José Velásquez was still very young, the resident missionary left and San Ildefonso became a visita of Onapa, a difficult day's journey on horseback to the east. Young José was almost certainly taught to read and write by a relative or friend because there is no record or suggestion of a school in or near San Ildefonso.

Population gradually drifted away from San Ildefonso to areas of greater opportunity. In the mid-1730s governmental authority almost vanished from the area while General Huidobro and his soldiers conducted inept and dilatory campaigns against the Guaicura rebels in California. Yaqui and Mayo unrest in the area grew during the general's

---

[3]Karl Lumholtz. *Unknown Mexico*.

absence and broke out into a full-fledged revolt about 1740 shortly after his return. During this series of revolts, inhabitants of the outlying settlements, which could not be defended, were moved to larger places that lacked quarters and subsistence for the refugees. About this time José Velásquez almost certainly became a "displaced person." During the Yaqui revolts Velásquez surely saw some military service because all able-bodied male Spaniards were called upon at one time or another for civil defense duties. It is probable that Velásquez was married during this turbulent period although we lack date and place for the wedding — and name of the bride. It is assumed, from lack of later mention, that his wife died some time before the end of 1750.

In 1741 General Huidobro's incompetence became apparent in Mexico City, and he was replaced as governor by Don Agustín Vildósola who was apparently a good and valiant soldier but a poor administrator. He was given to lengthy and senseless quarrels with the missionaries.[4] Governor Vildósola was succeeded by Don Diego Ortiz Parrilla, whose policies precipitated the Pima Revolt of 1751.

On January 1, 1751, José Velásquez enlisted in the army, officially beginning his service on that date at Loreto, Baja California. In view of the recruiting procedures at the time, it is probable that he "signed on" at some station in Sonora, most likely Pitic or Guaymas, and was sent at government expense to Loreto, his first duty station, on the first available transportation. Thus ended the first half of his life, and his residence in Sonora. So far as can be determined, he never returned to Sonora and never thereafter communicated with anyone in the village of his birth.

---

[4]This period of misrule is outlined from the missionaries' viewpoint in P.M. Dunne, *Juan Antonio Balthasar*.

REDEPLOYMENT ON THE PENINSULA

he Jesuit expulsion was not a simple replacement of one order of missionaries by another. Rather, it involved some complicated changes in the political and social makeup of the California settlements. Most important change was in the status of the soldier. Under Jesuit rule the day-to-day orders came from the missionaries who could and did return misbehaving or incompentent soldiers to Loreto or even to mainland Mexico. The captain at Loreto held office only at the pleasure of the Jesuits. This unusual arrangement gave the missionaries considerable control over the activities of the soldiers and enabled them to enforce definite standards of morality. After the Jesuits had been deported, the soldiers received their orders from the governor and were no longer subject to direct discipline or removal by the missionaries. Not very long after the Jesuit expulsion, reports of the *mal gallico* (syphilis), for which no cure was then known, began appearing in both military and mission records from the Californias. The disease remained a major health problem until well into the 20th century.

This division of command also created two "governments," mutually interdependent, but operating under differing orders with somewhat different objectives and usually with less than perfect liaison. In almost unavoidable consequence, friction developed between the missionaries and the soldiers; the problems were exacerbated by poorly-defined authority and by very slow communications with mainland Mexico where most decisions were made. During the short interval between the departure of the Jesuits and the arrival of the Franciscans, Don Gaspar de Portolá, the newly appointed governor, was in sole charge of the peninsula.[1] The temporalities (supplies, policing, etc.) of

---

[1]Gaspar de Portolá was born in Balaguer, Catalonia, in 1723. After military service in Italy and Portugal he came to the New World, becoming Captain of Dragoons of the "España" Regiment. In 1767 he was appointed civil and military governor of California where he supervised the Jesuit expulsion. Later, he led the northern march to Alta California, helped to found San Diego, discovered San Francisco Bay, and took possession of Alta California for Spain at Monterey, 1770. In 1776 he was appointed governor of Puebla. Retiring to Spain in 1783 with the rank of colonel, he died at Lérida, October 10, 1786.

the missions were administered under his orders by soldiers and *comisionados*.

On April 1, 1768, Father Junípero Serra, O.F.M., disembarked from the *Concepción* that rode at anchor off the barren shores of the peninsula.[2] Governor Portolá met them in a small launch and brought them ashore that evening, Good Friday. And the next morning the rest of the Fernandinos came ashore to celebrate the end of Lent and their arrival in a new apostolate. It was a very different situation because the missionaries were guests in the church's own houses and their expenses were charged against the governor's account. Things had really turned around since the Jesuits were sent scurrying off to exile. Under Serra's personal direction, the reactivation of the missions began. Supplies, as usual, were scanty, and the administration of some of the missions, under soldier *comisionados*, left much to be desired.

On May 1, 1768, José Velásquez was promoted to the rank of corporal. He was then about fifty-one years old and had served seventeen years in Baja California. This promotion brought him a small increase in salary, all paid "in kind," and a great increase in work and responsibilities.

Although Serra labored and travelled extensively to reactivate the missions, the problem of the temporalities remained unsolved. The mission churches proper were under control of the missionaries, but all supply items, even including meal-by-meal rations for the missionary, were controlled by the soldier comisionado who, in some cases at least, was wasteful and incompetent.

On July 5, 1768, Don José de Gálvez, the Inspector-General, who reported directly to the king and was partly independent of the viceroy,

---

[2]Miguel (Junípero) Serra was born in Petra, Majorca, on November 24, 1713. He began religious studies early (September, 1729) and was admitted to the Franciscan Order as a novice on September 14, 1730. A year later (September 15, 1731) he took his final vows, acquiring the name Junípero at the same time. The date of his ordaination is not recorded, but may have been May 31, 1737. Serra acquired a doctorate in theology in 1742 and became professor of theology at the Lullian University at Palma in 1743. After more than five years of teaching, Serra decided on a missionary career and left Palma.

bound for "the Indies" on April 13, 1749. He made the first leg of the journey on an English ship which took him to Malaga, where he arrived on April 27. Four days later he boarded a Spanish vessel bound for Cádiz, where he arrived on May 7. Here, he experienced the usual long wait for transportation across the Atlantic. This was finally provided on August 30, 1749.

The long crossing was broken by a stop-over of seventeen days in Puerto Rico. Serra, accompanied by Francisco Palou, Juan Crespi, and Rafael Verger, arrived in Veracruz, December 6, 1749. From there he walked over the ancient road to Mexico City, arriving before January 1, 1750. On this journey he suffered the first of many attacks of leg trouble (possibly varicose ulcers) which continued intermittently for the rest of his very active life. In the capital Father Serra became affiliated with the College of San Fernando which was his "home" while he was in Mexico City and headquarters for the rest of his life. His first major missionary assignment was in the Sierra Gorda, roughly 130 trail miles north of Mexico City. There he served for more than eight years, part of the time as president of the group of missions. Serra's work here included not only the usual preaching and instruction, but also the building of churches and the establishment of sound agricultural and ranching economies.

Recalled to San Fernando in 1758, Father Serra spent the next nine years in a variety of administrative positions, alternating with preaching assignments in the missions, which took him to Puebla, Tuxpan, and Oaxaca. Although he is nowhere listed or designated as an ecclesiastical trouble-shooter, Serra's assignments during this period suggest that this was his true function from 1758 to 1767. When the Jesuits were expelled from Spanish domains, the guardian and the counsellors of San Fernando selected Junípero Serra to be president of the missions of California with Francisco Palou as his substitute. Setting out promptly for the new mission field, Serra and his companions were delayed on the Pacific coast by lack of ships, storms, and reports of petty squabbles between the Fernandinos, Querétarans and Jaliscans. These reports, which were apparently concocted by an outsider, reached the viceroy and took some time to resolve. Eventually, Father Serra and the rest of the Franciscan company arrived in Loreto on April 12, 1768.

Slightly less than a year was spent in reactivating the missions vacated by the Jesuits, relieving the rather critical supply problem, and combatting the somewhat grandiose resettlement ideas of José de Gálvez. Thereafter, all major efforts were devoted to the march north to occupy Alta California. This led to the founding of mission San Fernando de Velicatá (May 15, 1769) on the northward march of about 300 miles through lands largely unknown. Reaching San Diego, he founded mission San Diego de Alcalá (July 16, 1769). Early in the next year after much exploration, Monterey was found; Serra journeyed there by sea in the spring of 1770. On June 3, 1770, he founded mission San Carlos Borromeo. Headquartered at Monterey, which eventually became the capital of both Californias (Baja and Alta), Serra continued to be active in founding and administering missions in California until his death at Carmel (where mission San Carlos Borromeo had been moved on August 24, 1771) on August 28, 1784. He is buried in the mission. Definitive biography of Junípero Serra is Maynard Geiger, *The Life and Times of Junípero Serra*.

arrived on the peninsula.[3] He set up headquarters at the silver mines of Santa Ana and stayed at the house of Manuel Ocio, the "wealthy" proprietor. Don José shortly solved the problem of the temporalities by removing the soldier comisionados and restoring control to the missionaries. Reports from the comisionados, obtained with considerable difficulty, so displeased Gálvez that he dismissed several of the least competent soldiers and reassigned some others despite clemency pleas by the missionaries.

Both Gálvez and Portolá were deeply concerned about the extreme poverty of the California missions. Various grandiose plans were considered for improving the situation, but most of these proposals "died in committee." Eventually, missions La Pasión and San Luis Gonzaga were discontinued; their converts were sent to nearby missions where the water supply was better. Because of the great distance between Loreto and the tip of the peninsula, San Luis Gonzaga was established as a ranch and shelter house for travellers. It was put in the charge of the soldier, Felipe Romero. The problem of too great an Indian population for the carrying power of mission agricultural lands was also noted at Guadalupe, Santa Gertrudis, and San Borja. Surplus Indian population at Guadalupe and Santa Gertrudis was moved to San José Comondú and La Purísima Concepción, respectively, without serious trouble. The southern missions, then and now, had a much greater agricultural potential than those to the north.

The last overpopulation problem at mission San Borja was considered by José de Gálvez, who proposed to move the surplus population by boat south to mission San José del Cabo. This would have transplanted a large number of recent converts into a climatically different area with accompanying cultural and linguistic problems. A long series of letters between Fr. Fermín Lasuen and José de Gálvez made it apparent that this

---

[3]José de Gálvez, Visitor-General of New Spain, was born in Macharaviaya, Spain, in 1720. Trained as a lawyer, he held several judicial positions in Spain, eventually serving on the Council of the Indies. He came to the New World in 1761, took an active part in the Jesuit expulsion, and travelled extensively in California and Sonora. He was instrumental in the organization of the Provincias Internas despite recurrent mental breakdowns. In 1785 Gálvez was appointed Marqués de Sonora. He died in Madrid in 1787.

transfer of populations probably would not work.[4] The mass deportations were suspended "for the time being" and were never resumed. Father Lasuén's successful argument here was that the relatively new converts at San Borja would forsake Christianity rather than move some 600 miles from their traditional homeland.

By early 1769, the missions of Baja California except for La Pasión and San Luis Gonzaga were staffed by Franciscans, who had charge of the temporalities except Loreto and who carried on work of the Jesuits almost without change. The only major difference was that the missionaries no longer had "hire and fire" authority over the soldiers, an administrative change which unavoidably caused friction and misunderstanding for the remainder of Spanish rule in the Californias.

During this time various plans were proposed for the establishment of trade schools for converts at selected missions. These were re-proposed every few years for the next half century but were never fully carried out, due in large part to lack of teachers willing to serve on the frontiers of New Spain. Despite a general lack of formal training, some converts became literate, and others acquired agricultural, mechanical or nautical skills, largely as a result of individual tutoring by missionaries, soldiers, or visiting artisans. By about 1800, a few of these Indian converts attained minor administrative or supervisory positions in the Californias, and some others served in the always understaffed military forces or worked as arrieros in the chronically overloaded services of supply.

---

[4]Fermín Francisco Lasuén was born on June 7, 1736, at Victoria, Cantabria, Spain. As a deacon, he left Cádiz for the Indies in 1759. After entering the College of San Fernando in Mexico, he was ordained and served under Serra in the Sierra Gorda until 1767. Then, still under Serra (1768-1769) and Palou (1769-1773) he was missionary at San Borja. Lasuén came to Alta California in 1773, spending two years at mission San Gabriel. After service as chaplain at Monterey Father Lasuén, aided by Father Gregorio Amurrio, began the establishment of mission San Juan Capistrano, an enterprise interrupted by the San Diego revolt of 1775. Ordered to San Diego to pacify the troublesome Indians, Fr. Lasuén remained on duty there until his appointment as president of the Californias missions in the fall of 1785. An able administrator as well as a competent and diligent missionary, he continued in that office until his death at mission San Carlos June 26, 1803, at the age of sixty-seven.

Figure 7. Bahía San Luis Gonzaga and the offshore islands, as seen from the north. Photo by R.L. Ives.

THE NORTHWARD MARCH

rior to 1769 Spanish claims to Alta California were based solely on sea explorations from the Pacific. There was one major conflicting claim — that to the lands of New Albion made by Sir Francis Drake during his occupation of Drake's Bay in 1579. Interest in the Pacific shores of California had been shown by a number of unauthorized visitors — French, Dutch, and English — who were either pirates or privateers, depending upon the current political situation in Europe. Additionally, French and English fur traders and trappers certainly by 1769 were entering the Rocky Mountain region, and Russian explorers had reached the Aleutian Islands. With this information at hand, it became apparent to the Spanish court and to José de Gálvez that an immediate occupation of Alta California was in order.

Plans for the occupation of Alta California were prepared by José de Gálvez, apparently on his own initiative because we find no royal orders specifically covering the matter. Don Gaspar de Portolá, already civil and military governor of California, was named military commander of the expedition. Father Junípero Serra, apparently over the protests of the College of San Fernando, was appointed president of the missions including those eventually to be founded in Alta California. Ships, soldiers, and supplies, originally destined for the Elizondo campaigns against the Seri Indians were "borrowed" from Sonora.

As it finally came about, this was not a single expedition, but consisted of three groups going separately by sea and two by land. Also involved, although in a minor capacity, were several mission launches which carried supplies from Loreto to Bahía San Luis Gonzaga. Thus, if any one group failed to arrive, the occupation of Alta California would still take place. As things worked out, two of the three ships eventually reached San Diego as did both overland parties.

The three vessels were the *San Carlos*, the *San Antonio* (also known as *El Principe*), and the *San José*. The first two ships were built to carry troops to Sonora. The third, the *San José* had been designed for voyages to the north coast. The *San Carlos*, also known as *El Toyson — The Golden Fleece*, came from Sonora and needed extensive repairs on arrival in Baja California, and it eventually sailed for Alta California on January 9, 1769, captained by Vicente Vila. Passengers included Lieutenant Pedro Fages with twenty-five Catalonian volunteers, Doctor Pedro Prat, surgeon, Father Fernando Parrón, O.F.M., the engineer and diarist Miguel Costansó, two blacksmiths, and a baker.[1]

The *San Antonio* likewise arrived in Baja California badly in need of repairs. After extensive and time consuming overhauling, it was loaded with supplies and sailed north on February 15, with Juan Pérez, who had piloted a Manila galleon, in command. Among the passengers were Fathers Juan Vizcaino (Vicaino in some accounts) and Francisco Gómez.

The third ship, the *San José*, had been built at San Blas on the west coast of Mexico at the orders of José de Gálvez. After several local shake down voyages, it took on a cargo of mixed supplies on the Sonoran coast, then sailed to Loreto where it was loaded an additional cargo of church goods ("three tower bells," etc.). Departing for La Paz, the *San José* was buffeted by winds and currents in the Gulf of California for three months, and finally put in at Escondido Bay about sixteen miles south of Loreto with a broken mast and other damages! After some of the cargo was removed and sent north, overland, the vessel was sent back to San Blas for extensive repairs. Eventually, it sailed for Cabo San Lucas, carrying a cargo of provisions — corn, beans, etc. — and sailors to replace those who died on the northern voyages of the other two ships. Loading additional cargo at the Cape, the *San José* finally sailed for San Diego on July 16, 1770, but was never seen again.

Although the two overland parties travelled almost exactly the same route, only a few weeks apart, they were substantally independent commands. The pioneer party, which "broke trail," was led by Captain Fernando Javier de Rivera y Moncada, an experienced and competent

---

[1]Little is known of Doctor Pedro Prat prior to 1769. Assigned as a surgeon, he sailed north on the *San Carlos* and arrived in San Diego suffering from scurvy along with the rest of the ship's company. While a part of the expedition travelled north from San Diego, seeking the port of Monterey, Dr. Prat stayed in San Diego, apparently doing good work. He treated Father Vizcaino's wounded hand after the Indian raid of mid-August in 1769 and somehow restored many of the soldiers and sailors to health, although the cause and treatment of scurvy was poorly understood at the time. On April 14, 1770, he sailed to Monterey on the *San Antonio*. Shortly thereafter, he lost his reason and was sent back to the mainland of Mexico where he apparently died in 1771.

frontier soldier. This group, which assembled at Velicatá, departed north on Good Friday, March 24, 1769; in addition to Captain Rivera it consisted of Father Juan Crespi (diarist), José de Canizares (engineer), a *pilotin*, twenty-five soldados de cuera, three muleteers, and forty-odd Indian auxiliaries.[2]

For several months prior to the departure of the first land party northward from Velicatá, Captain Rivera and his soldiers were busy visiting the missions of Baja California, collecting supplies, livestock, and materials for the expedition. These essentials were originally assembled at Santa María de Los Angeles, the northernmost of the Jesuit missions, which had not been completed by the time of the Jesuit expulsion. Because this barren location did not have enough forage for the several hundred animals assembled there, Captain Rivera moved his camp northwest about forty-five miles to Velicatá, a somewhat better site discovered by Father Linck in March of 1766. The military governor, Don Gaspar de Portolá, was informed of the change and made minor shifts in his scheduled itineraries. Plans were also made at this time to ship supplies by sea from Loreto to Bahía San Luis Gonzaga, and thence overland, via Santa María, to Velicatá.

The second land party which was smaller than the first was led by Gaspar de Portolá and departed north from Velicatá on Monday, May 15, 1769. Accompaning Don Gaspar on this journey were Fray Junípero Serra, Sergeant José Francisco Ortega, nine or ten soldiers, two servants, and probably forty-four Baja California natives, many of whom died or deserted en route.[3] During much of the journey from Loreto to Velicatá Father Serra travelled separately from the main (second) party, accompanied by two servants (one of whom was José María Vergerano) and a military guard. Despite often-repeated folklore, Father Serra did not

---

[2]A *pilotin* was an assistant guide, whose duties included determining and recording the distance travelled each day.

[3]José Francisco Ortega was a Mexican soldier, born in Celaya, Guanajuato, probably in 1734. He came to Baja California with Portolá and was already an experienced soldier at the time. Having enlisted in 1755, he became a corporal in 1756 and was promoted to sergeant in 1757. After service on the march to San Diego, he joined the northern expedition and is credited with the discovery of San Francisco Bay (November 1, 1769). Promoted to Lieutenant in 1773, he held a number of important commands in Alta California, retiring as brevet captain in 1795. José Francisco Ortega died in Santa Barbara in 1798. For him is named the modern mountain highway connecting San Juan Capistrano and Lake Elsinore (California Highway 74).

walk this distance but rode "a broken-down mule," as is clearly shown by several contemporary diaries.

Only a few days, and a few miles, before arriving at Velicatá, on his journey north from Loreto, Father Serra spent several days at Santa María de Los Angeles, supervising the building of an improved trail to the east toward Bahía de San Luis Gonzaga and inspecting the work. Parts of this trail through a rugged granite area are still visible (1977). It is not suited for travel by four-wheeled vehicles, and parts of it are obstructed by thick brush.

Major accomplishment on the northward journey was the establishment of mission San Fernando de Velicatá — the only Franciscan mission founded in Baja California.[4] The site of Velicatá was discovered and described by the Jesuit, Wenceslaus Linck, on March 5, 1766, while he was on a journey of exploration from mission San Borja toward the Colorado delta. According to some of the soldiers who had accompanied him, mass was not celebrated at Velicatá by Father Linck. When the first overland party, headed by Captain Rivera, assembled at Velicatá, prior to its departure north, mass was celebrated in a temporary shelter by Father Fermín Lasuén, March 23, 1769. When the second overland party, headed by Don Gaspar de Portolá, travelled northwest from Santa María in May, 1769, the two leaders, Governor Portolá and Father Serra, were favorably impressed with the site and determined to found a mission at Velicatá.

Actual dedication of the mission took place after a forced march northwest from Santa María, via Agua Dulce which is still a good watering place, so that the two Fathers Serra and Campa, Governor Portolá, one soldier, and two servants might arrive at Velicatá on the eve of Pentecost. The next day (Pentecost, May 14, 1769), the temporary shelter used by Father Lasuén was "cleaned and adorned." Governor Portolá took formal possession of the country in the name of the Spanish king, and mass was celebrated with such ceremony as was possible on the frontier, where candles were lacking, and gunpowder smoke replaced incense. Father Miguel de la Campa, previously of Santa María, was placed in charge with a guard of a corporal and a few soldiers. When the

---

[4]Numerous accounts of the founding of mission San Fernando de Velicatá are available. See Pablo Martínez, *A History of Lower California*, pp. 262-264; Maynard Geiger, *The Life and Times of Junípero Serra*, Vol. I, pp. 218-220; H. E. Bolton, *Historical Memoir of New California*, Vol. I, pp. 214 et seq. II, pp. 30-35.

pack train arrived the next day and candles became available, both fathers celebrated mass again.[5]

Both land parties followed almost exactly the same route from Velicatá to San Diego — a route which was used for a very short time and was soon replaced in the southern part by an easier and more direct route, which with minor changes and improvements is in use today as Mexican Highway 1. For the first few days of the journey, march was along the trail originally used by Father Linck in 1766. From Velicatá the route went northeast over a ridge to San Juan de Dios, a well-watered inhabited oasis on an arroyo of the same name. The modern back country road from San Fernando to San Juan de Dios approximates the route followed by both expeditions.[6] Here Father Serra's leg gave him so much trouble that it was feared that he would not be able to continue to California.

Disregarding Portolá's strong urging that he return to Velicatá for rest and recuperation, Serra consulted with one of the muleteers, Juan Antonio Coronel by name, regarding treatment of his leg. The reported conversation follows in translation:

"Son, do you know how to prepare a remedy for the wound in my foot and leg?"

Don Juan, somewhat surprised, replied "Why, Father, what remedy could I know of? Do you think I am a surgeon? I'm a muleteer; I've healed only the sores of animals."

"Well then, son," replied Serra, "just imagine that I am an animal and that this wound is the sore of an animal, from which developed this

---

[5]Comparison of 1976 and 1977 conditions at San Fernando de Velicatá with those shown in Hendry's 1926 photograph (H. E. Bolton, *Historial Memoir of New California,* Vol. I, opp. p. 216) discloses that the missions ruins proper have disintegrated markedly in the last fifty years. The two houses close to the ruins (at left in Hendry's photograph) are now unoccupied, unroofed, and rapidly disintegrating; and the croplands (middle distance in Hendry's photograph) have been deeply channeled by flood erosion. Much of this erosion, according to local residents, took place during *diluvias* in the early fall of 1976.

[6]From San Fernando de Velicatá to San Diego; and from San Diego to San Francisco Bay, and return to San Diego, the detailed diaries of Father Juan Crespi are our principal source of information. These are published by H. E. Bolton *Fray Juan Crespi, Missionary Explorer*; Diary from Velicatá to San Diego pp. 59-121; Diary of the journey northward in search of Monterey, pp. 122-236; Diary of the return to San Diego, pp. 237-273. This work also contains much collateral data in the form of letters, and many site identifications by Bolton. Contrary to Bolton's note (p. 63), the arroyo San Juan de Dios flows westward, joining the arroyo Rosario and eventually emptying into the Pacific Ocean.

swelling of the leg and the great pains which I experience, which permit me neither rest nor sleep. Make me the same remedy which you would apply to an animal."

More to please Serra than because of expected results, Don Juan replied: "Father, I shall do so in order to please you."

Coronel then crushed some tallow between stones, added some green herbs, heated the mixture, and applied it to Serra's foot and leg as a hot poultice. This primitive medication worked. Father Serra slept that night, arose the next morning "much improved," and celebrated Mass. From San Juan de Dios to San Diego Father Serra had no further serious trouble with his inflamed leg and foot. The account of this effective first aid constitutes Juan Antonio Coronel's only known appearance in the pages of history.[7]

From San Juan de Dios, the trail of the land expeditions tended slightly west of north, almost perpendicular to the trends of the ridges and valleys of that part of the peninsula, so that travel was a seemingly endless series of ascents and descents. For the first forty miles or so beyond San Juan de Dios, this trail was almost exactly that used by Father Linck in 1766. At La Cieneguilla (somewhere near modern Rosarito), reached by the first land party on April 1, 1769, the trails diverged. Here, according to the soldiers who accompanied him, Father Linck turned eastward, crossed the Sierra San Pedro Mártir, and eventually reached the Arroyo de Agua Caliente which drains into the Valle de San Felipe on the east side of the Sierra.[8] The expedition bound for San Diego continued north-northwest through totally unexplored and unknown lands, aiming for a point on the Pacific coast, at a supposed latitude of 34° north.[9] Leaving La Cieneguilla, the expeditions continued roughly northwest, travelling slowly because of rough terrain and scanty

---

[7]Condensed from Maynard Geiger, *The Life and Times of Junípero Serra*, pp. 220-221.

[8]Although identified with confidence by the soldiers, Father Linck, in his surviving diaries nowhere mentions La Cieneguilla. See E. J. Burrus, *Linck's Diary*. Father Serra had another version of Linck's diary with him on the second land expedition. This, if still extant, has not been found.

[9]This latitude, which is more than a degree too high, is found in J. G. Cabrera Bueno, *Navegación Especulativa y Practica*, (many reprintings, piracies, plagarisms and translations) p. 305. Part IV of this work contains descriptions of the California coasts as seen from the Pacific. Modern "official" latitude of San Diego is 32°42'53" N. The latitude error here is due to the use of the meridian altitude method of determination, the meridian being found by magnetic compass, not corrected for local declination. As

provisions. Little trail information could be obtained from local Indians because of linguistic problems. The ranks of the Indian aids, brought from southern Baja California, thinned rapidly because of desertions, illness, and death.

Nine days after the first land expedition left La Cieneguilla, the interpreter, Manuel Valladares, died. Father Juan Crespi in his diary of the expedition (April 10, 1769), states: "Before leaving this place I buried an Indian named Manuel Valladares of the mission of San Ignacio to whom I administered the holy sacraments of penance and extreme unction. I felt his death very keenly because he had served me as interpreter. A cross was planted over his grave. *Anima ejus requiescat in pace.*"[10] When the second land party came to the site, the grave had been disturbed. Father Serra and his party collected the scattered bones and reburied them with the pious wish "May his soul rest in heaven," added in Serra's diary.

Additional laborious, northwest travel, diagonally across the western foothills of the Sierra San Pedro Mártir, brought the land parties to the coastal plain of northern Baja California at a point near the Pacific, somewhere between San Telmo and Colonet. From this point to San Diego the trail was smoother although there were a few ridges directly across the line of march. General route is approximately but not exactly that now followed by Mexican Highway 1 and U.S. Interstate 5.

---

the land parties used the same method of measuring latitudes, their determined positions were likewise "high," and the very real errors (here slightly more than eighty-eight statute miles) cancelled out. About 1770, shortly after and perhaps in part because of, the international astronomical expedition from France to San José del Cabo led by the Abbé Jean-Baptiste Chappe d'Auteroche, the errors in Spanish-measured latitudes decreased from almost a degree "high" to a few minutes "plus or minus." Further applications of the observations of the transit of Venus, June 3, 1769, showed that the traditional longitudes in New Spain, then measured from Hierro in the Canary Islands, were in error by almost five degrees (almost 330 statute miles at 20° N.). The first major map to show this improvement in position accuracy was probably Miguel Costansó's *Carta Reducida del Oceano Asiático o Mar del Sur*, printed in Madrid (Hipolito Ricarte) in 1771. See: J. B. Chappe d'Auteroche, *Voyage en California pour l'observation du Passage de Venus sue le disque du soleil, le 3 Juin 1769*, 1772; I. W. Engstrand, *Royal Officer in Baja California 1768-1770: Joaquín Velázquez de León*. This latter work contains an excellent print of Costansó's 1771 map.

[10]H. E. Bolton, *Fray Juan Crespi*, p. 82. Near the gravesite is the modern small town of Valladares which subsists by cattle-raising and sporadic mining. Valladares can be reached by a back-country road from San Telmo.

As might be expected, the various parts of the northern expedition did not arrive in San Diego together, or in equal condition. First arrival was the *San Antonio* on April 11, (or April 14 according to other accounts).[11] This vessel, commanded by Juan Pérez, brought Fathers Juan Vizcaino and Francisco Gómez, some carpenters and blacksmiths, a crew, and miscellaneous supplies. There were no soldiers aboard. According to somewhat confused reports, eight of the *San Antonio's* crew died of scurvy. Next arrival at San Diego was the *San Carlos* commanded by Vicente Vila, which cast anchor in the bay on April 30. Ship's company initially consisted of Captain Vila, an unnamed mate, Alférez Miguel Costansó (cosmographer), twenty-three sailors and two boys. Passengers included Lieutenant Pedro Fages, twenty-five Catalonian volunteers under his command, Father Hernando Parrón, Dr. Pedro Prat, four cooks and two blacksmiths. Unfortunately, not all of these survived the voyage which lasted about 110 days, and more died later ashore at San Diego as a result of dietary deficiencies. Starting from La Paz with 3800 gallons of water (for sixty-two people and six cattle), trouble was early experienced with leaky casks. Replacement water, obtainable at Cedros Island, was of bad quality. This aggravated the scurvy always present on long voyages at that time, probably by adding dehydration to the avitaminosis already present. When the *San Carlos* dropped anchor in San Diego Bay, but did not lower a boat, the crew of the *San Antonio* investigated and found all hands incapacitated with scurvy. The sick were taken ashore, sheltered under canvas, and given

---

[11]Indian tales, recounting the coincidence of an earthquake and an eclipse of the sun with the arrival of the *San Antonio*, are condensed in H. H. Bancroft, *Early California Annals*, p. 127, n. 3, from Serra's correspondence. These give some hope of determining this date exactly, even though, as Serra stated, the Spaniards noted neither an earthquake nor an eclipse. Reference to T. R. von Oppolzer, *Canon der Finsternisse*, p. 284, chart 142, indicates that there were three solar eclipses in 1769. Of these, No. 7085, occurring on January 8, was partial and not visible in San Diego. No. 7086, occurring on June 4, was total, but the path of totality extended from Labrador over the North Pole to Kamchatka, so the eclipse was not visible in San Diego. No. 7087, occurring on November 8, was a non-central annular eclipse, also not visible in San Diego. As a cross-check the state of the moon in mid-April of 1769 was determined from astronomical tables. At this time, the moon was about a week old (first quarter), so that a solar eclipse, which can occur only at new moon, could not have occurred. Hence, as there was no possibility of a solar eclipse in mid-April of 1769, the Indian tales give us no help in determining the exact date.

Figure 8a. Ruins of mission San Fernando de Velicatá, October, 1977. Photo by R.L. Ives.

Figure 8b. Modern small settlement at San Fernando de Velicatá, October, 1977. Photo by R.L. Ives.

such care as Dr. Prat, who was himself not in the best of health, and the three friars could furnish. Unfortunately, the survivors at San Diego subsisted on supplies brought by the two ships — the same supplies that caused the scurvy in the first place — and the "contagion" spread to the crew of the *San Antonio*. Eventually, despite valiant but futile efforts by Dr. Prat, many more than half of the ninety or so persons ashore at San Diego died of scurvy, and those who survived recovered most slowly.[12]

When the first land party, headed by Captain Fernando Javier de Rivera y Moncada, arrived at San Diego, they found the beach camp a combination infirmary and morgue with the few well and slightly ill persons caring exhaustedly for the many who were seriously ill. The first land party, which consisted in addition to the leader, of twenty-five soldiers, Father Juan Crespi, pilotin José de Canizares, three muleteers, and a few Indians — remnants of the forty-odd who started from Velicatá, arrived tired and probably hungry. Although supplies were limited on the northern journey, they managed to stay in general good health. This group gave aid to those already at San Diego and began construction of the presidio, whose ruins are still visible on Presidio Hill in "Old Town."

Imminent arrival of the second land expedition was announced in late June by Sergeant Ortega who had ridden ahead of the main party. With a patrol of ten soldiers from San Diego, he then rode south, rejoined the expedition, and brought them all into San Diego by July 1. This party, on arrival, consisted of Governor Portolá, Father Serra, Sergeant Ortega, six or seven soldiers (a corporal and several soldiers had been left at Velicatá), four muleteers, two servants, and about a dozen Indians out of the forty-four who had started from Velicatá. The sailors and supplies scheduled to be delivered by the *San José* never arrived in San Diego because that vessel was lost at sea. Diaries of the journeys from Loreto to San Diego, and on to San Francisco are numerous, circumstantial, and in close agreement. Furthermore, as all of the diarists were

---

[12]Records for this period, as might be expected, are not as complete as we would like. Study of the manifest of the *San Carlos* (Provincial State Papers, MS., i. 13-21, Bancroft Library) shows that the supplies were almost totally lacking in antiscorbutics such as oranges, potatos, and sauerkraut. As the causes and cure of scurvy at that time were only vaguely understood, this unfortunate dietary omission was due to ignorance, rather than to stupidity.

experienced in the field and most had skill in navigation, the accounts contain clear geographic references which in conjunction with surviving sectors of the Camino Real permit much of the route to be recovered even today.[13]

The personnel tallies in the various accounts and diaries enable us to determine with some confidence how Corporal Velásquez reached Alta California, even though he was not mentioned directly by name in any diary seen. From his service record and numerous other documents we know that the corporal was physically present at Monterey on June 3, 1770, and that he was a member of the second expedition to travel north from San Diego. His service record is ambiguous regarding the first expedition and tells us nothing of his journey north from Loreto to San Diego. As no new soldiers went to Alta California after the overland journey of 1769 until some time shortly after June 14, 1770, it seems certain that Corporal Velásquez came to California with the 1769 expedition. He did not come on the *San José* which was lost at sea. Likewise, he did not travel on the *San Antonio*, because it carried no soldiers. He also was not aboard the *San Carlos*, because all of the soldiers on board were Catalonian volunteers under the command of Lieutenant Pedro Fages. Corporal Velásquez was attached to the presidio of Loreto, commanded by Captain Fernando Javier de Rivera y Moncada.

The land expedition commanded by Gaspar de Portolá had a military escort of about a dozen men, including a sergeant, José Francisco Ortega, and a corporal, not named. At Velicatá, the corporal and several soldiers were detached to serve as mission guard. There is no mention of a second corporal in any of the documents, and no military requirement

---

[13]For most historical purposes, the diaries of Father Juan Crespi will be found adequate and dependable. A very complete listing of the expedition diaries, their translations, and a rather complete pertinent bibliography, is found in Ray Brandes, *The Costansó Narrative of the Portolá Expedition*, pp. 102-110. This same work also contains a laudatory description (p. 96) of the presidial soldiers of Baja California by Gaspar de Portolá, which is considerably at variance with Father Baegert's diatribe. Discussion of the trails followed by the northward expedition is found in R. F. Pourade, *The Call to California*, pp. 1-87; Harry Crosby, *The King's Highway in Baja California*; R. L. Ives, "Problems of the Serra Route," *Journal San Diego History*, Vol. XXI, No. 4, Fall, 1975, pp. 21-37. Although these three works are in substantial agreement on most points, none of them completely resolve the problem of Serra's route from Santa Gertrudis to San Borja.

for a second corporal in such a small group. Several vague documentary references to "Sergeant Ortega's company" hint that his soldiers came from Sonora, as did he. There is no evidence or suggestion that Corporal Velásquez was in this group. By elimination, this places him in the first land expedition, commanded by Captain Rivera y Moncada, militarily staffed by twenty-five soldados de cuera "selected from the company of California." Although a reasonable table of organization would call for one sergeant and two corporals in a group of this size, no mention of the non-commissioned officers in the first land expedition is made in the diaries.[14]

---

[14]The only soldier mentioned in Crespi's diary is one Guillermo, who was seriously ill on the journey north. This was almost certainly Guillermo Carrillo, who recovered from his illness, and later became corporal and then sergeant at San Diego where he died in 1782. His service record is ambiguous regarding the first expedition and tells nothing of his journey north from Loreto to San Diego. As no new soldiers went to Alta California after the overland journey of 1769 until some time shortly after June 14, 1770, it seems certain that Corporal Velásquez came to California with the 1769 expedition. He did not come on the San José because it was lost at sea. Likewise, he did not travel on the San Antonio because it carried no soldiers. He also was not aboard the San Carlos because all of the soldiers on that ship were Catalonian volunteers under the command of Lieutenant Pedro Fages and Corporal Velásquez was attached to the presidio of Loreto commanded by Captain Fernando Javier de Rivera y Moncada.

THE SEARCH FOR MONTEREY

eunion of the four surviving contingents of the northern expedition at San Diego raised a family of new problems for the commander, Gaspar de Portolá. Although he had two vessels in port and the *San José* expected, those at San Diego could not be used for further exploration because their crews were either dead or disabled by scurvy. Also, more than half of the Catalonian Volunteers were either dead or disabled from the same disease. Most of the Indian aides who started with the land expeditions had either died or deserted en route. Establishment of a mission and presidio at San Diego was delayed by widespread sickness, and the ordered march northward to find, claim, and settle Monterey was not only delayed, but the planned marine reinforcements were unavailable. As the victims of scurvy either died or recovered, new plans were made by Governor Portolá.

When a minimum crew was well enough to function, after a fashion, the *San Antonio* was sent to San Blas for supplies and for replacement crews, not only for the *San Antonio* but also for the *San Carlos* which was anchored, crewless, in San Diego. Captain Pérez sailed on the ninth of July for San Blas and arrived there twenty days later, less nine sailors who had died of scurvy en route. Just how Captain Pérez brought his ship into San Blas with his remaining crew (probably eight) is not told by surviving records. While supplies were being collected and loaded and replacement crews gathered, preliminary reports of the California expedition went inland from San Blas to the viceroy in Mexico City.

At San Diego, Governor Gaspar de Portolá determined to carry out his orders to occupy Monterey despite lack of sea support, the non-arrival of the *San José*, shortage of personnel, and the poor physical condition of many of those present. The forces were divided. One group — consisting of Captain Vicente Vila, pilot José de Canizares, Dr. Pedro Prat, Fathers Junípero Serra, Fernando Parrón, and Juan Vizcaino, eight sickly soldiers, a blacksmith, a carpenter, several servants, eight Lower California Indians, and an indefinite but small number of sick sailors — was designated to stay in San Diego. One of the soldiers "held the rank of corporal." He was Juan Puig, a Catalonian Volunteer who later became sergeant. Hopefully, after recovering from scurvy, this group would build a presidio and mission, making San Diego a permanent settlement. A second group — consisting of Governor Gaspar de Portolá, Captain Rivera y Moncada, Lieutenant Pedro Fages, Miguel Costansó, Fathers Juan Crespi and Francisco Gómez, six or seven Catalonian Volunteers (all that were still able to travel of the original twenty-five), twenty-seven soldados de cuera from Baja California, seven muleteers, fifteen Indian aides, and two servants — about sixty-four persons in all — departed north from San Diego on July 14, 1769, in search of the port of Monterey. Because he did not sail on the *San Antonio* and was not among those assigned to San Diego, Corporal José Velásquez was a member of the first expedition to search for Monterey. His service record did not state this unambiguously.

Itineraries of the two successive expeditions that searched for Monterey are given with laudably accurate detail in pertinent diaries. These have been subsequently studied and the original routes have been "tied in" to modern geography. Quite interestingly, many of the original placenames are still in use; the route over much of its course, with minor improvements, became the historic "Camino Real," and later modern Highway 101 from San Diego to Monterey. The "Camino Real" from Monterey to San Francisco was explored a few years later to replace the original difficult trail through the redwoods in the Santa Cruz Mountains.[1]

Northward from San Diego the trail parallelled the beach for some miles, passing a short distance inland (east) of modern Highway 1, and making detours far inland, where necessary, to pass around various inlets, lagoons, and swampy places. Along this route a few years later,

[1]Important diaries here include H. E. Bolton, *Fray Juan Crespi*, pp. 122-274; Ray Brandes, *The Costansó Narrative of the Portolá Expedition*. Crespi's diary is substantially duplicated in H. E. Bolton, *Historical Memoirs of New California*, Vol. II, pp. 109-260. An excellent nearly contemporary description of the route northward from San Diego to San Francisco is given in H. I. Priestley, *A Historical, Political and Natural Description of California by Pedro Fages*. Pedro Fages, in addition to his competence as a military commander, was a keen observer and a prolific writer of clear and accurate reports. Among the later studies of the route are H. H. Bancroft, *Early California Annals*, pp. 140-172; Maynard Geiger, *The Life and Times of Junípero Serra*, Vol. II, pp. 202-208; R. F. Pourade, *The Call to California*. The term "Sacred Expedition" used in this work is a twentieth-century addition not found in the original documents.

mission San Luis Rey was founded. Near the site of modern San Clemente the trail turned almost due north, went inland, and parallelled modern Interstate 5 to the east, to and beyond the place where the first mission San Juan Capistrano was later founded. Modern mission San Juan Capistrano, a few miles to the west, has become famous for its commuting swallows. North and west, the trail continued inland, passing the places where El Toro Marine Base, Tustin, and Anaheim were later founded. In late July the expedition experienced "a terrible earthquake, which was repeated four times during the day." As a result, the river which they crossed was named the Río de los Temblores. It is modern Santa Ana.

Extensive travel and exploration in the area northeast of Cabrillo's "Bahía de Humos" led to the discovery and naming of the San Gabriel River and of the Río de Porciúncula, now known as the Los Angeles River. A large dry wash, later named the Arroyo Seco, was encountered. Many earthquakes were felt and noted. A scouting party under "the Captain" found some "forty springs of tar, or pitch, boiling up out of the ground, molten enough to caulk many ships."[2] Governor Portolá noted that this area — the Los Angeles Basin — was a suitable place for a mission. Not long after, mission San Gabriel was founded there. Egress from the Los Angeles Basin was found difficult because the Santa Monica Mountains loomed across the logical northern route, ending in steep cliffs at the ocean's edge. Eventually, the expedition crossed the eastern part of the mountains by a path that was "rough and difficult" and entered the San Fernando Valley. Here, they were visited by many surprisingly well-informed Indians, who told among other things of a visit to their country by bearded and armed men who had come from the east. This vague legend, which occurs in many accounts, refers to no known expedition, and seems to be a "hardy perennial," first being recorded before 1700. Leaving the valley, which later became the site of mission San Fernando, the expedition struggled over San Fernando pass and thence travelled down the Santa Clara valley to the sea. At the mouth of this river mission San Buenaventura was later founded and surrounding it the modern town of Ventura developed.

---

[2]This was Captain Rivera y Moncada, no other person of that rank being a member of the expedition. Names of the soldiers who accompanied him on this exploration are not given.

Here began the country of the Chumash Indians who had a considerably more advanced material culture than did the natives to the
south. Proceeding west-northwest close to the beach, the diarists of the
expedition noted the excellent canoes built by the Chumash people. At
one Indian town which they named Carpinteria (still there), they saw a
canoe nearing completion and noted some tar springs ''set hard and
steaming slightly'' nearby. Three leagues farther along the shore, the
party camped at a large fresh-water lagoon and was entertained by Indian
dancers who also supplied plentiful food. This was in the area where
Santa Barbara — mission and presidio — was founded a few years later.
About eleven leagues (about twenty-eight miles) west of Santa Barbara,
the modern road (Highway 101) turns sharply to the north, goes through
a narrow defile (Gaviota Pass), and runs inland for some miles, returning
to the shore near Pismo Beach. This pass was not used by the Portolá
expedition which continued with some difficulty along the shore, passing
points Concepción and Arguello (both named in honor of Concepción
Arguello, whose futile wait for the return of her betrothed, Count
Rezanov, has been detailed elsewhere). They continued to a point some
distance north of the Santa Inez River. Route of the expedition from the
Pacific end of Gaviota Pass to the site of modern San Luis Obispo has
been followed very closely by the right-of-way of the Southern Pacific
Railroad. This route turns inland about midway between the Santa Inez
and Santa María rivers, passes through Schuman Canyon, skirts the
eastern edge of the Santa María dune field, and then angles seaward
(west), reaching the shore again near modern Pismo Beach. Bears and
bear tracks were noted along this line of march, and one bear was killed.
They ''ate of the flesh and found it savory and good.'' North of this
route, and inland, at a much later date, missions Santa Inez and La
Purísima were founded. Close to the route, mission San Luis Obispo de
Tolosa was later constructed, and gives its name to the nearby city.

Had they known it, the explorers could have gone northward
through the site of modern San Luis Obispo, climbed for two leagues
(about five miles) over Cuesta Pass (1520 feet), and entered the headwaters of the Salinas River which furnished a relatively smooth and easy
route to Monterey Bay. This easier route which is not visible from the
sea, and is certainly not obvious to an observer on land near Pismo
Beach, was discovered and put into use soon after the end of the search
for Monterey. Some years later, mission San Miguel Arcangel was
founded in the upper part of the easier route, which is part of the historic

Camino Real close to Highway 101. Lacking this geographical knowledge, the Portolá party struggled through coastal hills, hunted plentiful
bears en route, and came again to the sea at a clearly identifiable point.
Costansó writes:

> An estuary of immense size, which to us seemed a harbor, enters this
> canyon (the Cañada de los Osos - the name dates from Portolá's
> time) on the south side. But its mouth, opening up to the southwest,
> is covered with reefs that cause a furious surf. At a short distance to
> the north of the mouth, and in front of our camp, there is a very large
> rock (Morro Rock) shaped like a round head. At high tide it becomes
> an island and is then separated — a little less than a gunshot — from
> the shore.

This area today is much the same except for minor, and mostly
man-made changes. Because of its scenic and historic interest, much of
the area has been incorporated into Morro Bay State Park. The mouths of
Los Osos and Chorro Creeks, which empty into Morro Bay, have silted
up considerably since 1769. The great bay-mouth bar which separates
Morro Bay from Estero Bay has grown somewhat in recent years due
partly to efforts to stabilize the sand dunes upon it. Morro Rock is now
tied to the mainland by an extensive fill, and breakwaters have been built
out into Estero Bay from Morro Rock and the bay-mouth bar. A channel,
suitable only for shallow-draft vessels, has been dredged into Morro
Bay.[3]
From this clearly described and accurately located site, the expedition continued northwest, close to shore, along a route much like that of
Highway 1. The next stop which they named El Estero was on the shore
of what is now called Estero Bay. Here, Costansó measured the latitude,
and found it to be 35°27' North. His navigation, as usual, was good, for
that parallel does pass through Estero Bay. Still continuing northwest
along a narrow coastal shelf between the sea and the mountains, the party
passed the site of modern Cayucos, and then travelling almost due west,
they came to the mouth of Villa Creek where the coastal shelf ceases and
is replaced by hills. As nearly as can be determined, they went up
Ellysley's Canyon (as does modern Highway 1), emerging out beyond
the coastal hills on Santa Rosa Creek near modern Cambria. Continuing,
they came to a ''very high mountain range falling to the sea that shuts off

---

[3]This area is excellently mapped on the U.S. Geological Survey 7.5' Quadrangle,
''Morro Bay South, California,'' 1965.

our way by the shore.'' Camp was made here, somewhere near San Carpóforo Creek, and eight scouts led by Captain Rivera y Moncada sought, found, and improved a workable route into the range (Santa Lucía Mountains).

Although only casually and briefly mentioned in the various diaries, the role of the Rivera's Lower California soldiers as trail finders and builders for the expedition was quite important. Whenever the advance trail was uncertain or needed impovement, Captain Rivera and his scouts were delegated to find a trail and to improve it if necessary. This work probably prompted Costansó, in his diary, to comment that ''we do not hesitate to say that they (the soldiers of the presidio of Loreto in California) are the best troopers in the world.''[4] This statement is in marked contrast to numerous missionary opinions.

The ascent and crossing of the Sierra de Santa Lucía began at San Carpóforo Canyon and continued roughly northeastward. Extremely difficult, their forward progress was little more than a league (two and a half miles or four kilometers) a day. Not only was the terrain rough and steep, but the area was on the windward side of the sierra and hence received heavy orographic rainfalls compounded by fog. Consequently, heavy matted brush and unstable soils added to the problems of gradient. While the scouts worked on the trail, resting frequently, they eventually crossed the summit (perhaps 2500 feet above sea level), entered the lower and more open country around the headwaters of the Nacimiento and San Antonio Rivers, and came to the general area of Jolón where mission San Antonio was later established.[5]

Terrain was not the only problem encountered by Portolá's expedition. Shortly before they reached Morro Bay, Sergeant José Ortega became ill with scurvy and the sickness spread until eventually seventeen soldiers were unfit for duty. An unknown number of others had pains in their legs apparently from the same cause. This problem is understandable

---

[4]Ray Brandes, *Costansó Narrative*, p. 90. As this was an official diary of the expedition, we cannot be sure whether the opinions expressed are those of Costansó, of his commander Portolá, or were jointly held by both of them.

[5]The history of mission San Antonio is succinctly told in Regis Rohder, *Mission San Antonio*, (Jolón: Franciscan Padres, undated). Parts of this area are now occupied by the Nacimiento and San Antonio Reservoirs and by the Hunter-Liggett Military Reservation. Southeast of the reconstructed line of march is the large Camp Roberts military establishment and angling northwest from Paso Robles is the route of the "historic" Camino Real, established shortly after Portolá's march.

when it is remembered that their supplies had been brought from San Blas by ship and were markedly lacking in vitamins, particularly in Vitamin C, the specific for scurvy. Apparently Lind's famous treatise had not yet become known in western North America.[6] Sketchy Spanish knowledge of antiscorbutics in 1769 seems to have been limited to pitahayas which did not grow in western Alta California, and to tunas which were not in season at the time of Portolá's expedition.

Scouts exploring north from the Jolón area soon found a workable trail which led to the valley of a river assumed by them to be the Carmel. Actually, it was the Salinas. The main expedition followed, coming to the river near the site of modern King City. About midway in the journey down the Salinas Valley to the sea they passed the rather barren site where Soledad mission was later founded. On September 30, the expedition camped near the mouth of the Salinas and began looking for Monterey Bay which from the marshy flatlands of the lower valley looks more like an open roadstead than an important harbor. Certainly, nothing that they saw very closely resembled the descriptions given by Vizcaino and Cabrera Bueno. Besides, the latitude was wrong. Cabrera Bueno placed Monterey at 37°, but Costansó's careful observation showed that they were at about 36°44'. To add to their woes, the hoped-for supply ship the *San José* did not appear and provisions were running low.

Careful and thorough exploration of the area suggested that they were actually at Monterey Bay, but no evidence gave conclusive proof. A rocky point, which resembled (and was) Vizcaino's "Point of Pines" was found, but it was southwest of the river mouth, not north, as they believed it should be. Much of this confusion arose because most of the expedition members had mistaken the Salinas River for the Carmel. Captain Rivera y Moncada and his scouts explored south of Point of Pines, finding a small bay fed by a feeble stream. This was almost certainly Carmel Bay and River, but at the end of the fall dry season they bore no resemblance to the older descriptions which were written during the winter rainy season.[7] Father Crespi, noting the great sand dunes northwest of modern Fort Ord, suggested that the bay had been filled with sand between 1603 and 1769.

Local explorations, mostly west and southwest of the mouth of the Salinas, failed to convince the leaders that the expedition was actually at

---

[6]James Lind, *A Treatise on Scurvy*, reprinted with an evaluative introduction.

[7]Vizcaino spent the period December 17, 1602, through January 3, 1603, at Monterey Bay.

Monterey Bay. A meeting of officers was held and plans were made to continue northward after a short rest, despite sickness of many of the soldiers and rapidly diminishing supplies. March was resumed October 7, the course being near shore and roughly northward. Scouts found a river north of the Salinas and named it the Río de Pájaro because of a large stuffed bird left along its course by Indians. The name is still in use. Continued travel brought them near the sites where Branciforte and Santa Cruz were later founded. Still bearing north, they came to the rainy and foggy windward slopes of the Santa Cruz Mountains with their dense growths of giant *savin* trees (redwoods). Thence, they labored north to within a few miles of modern San Francisco. There are probably worse routes from Santa Cruz to San Francisco, but not much worse. No promising sites for missions were found along this line of march and none were subsequently established in the immediate area. All of the missions later built north of Monterey Bay — San Juan Bautista, Santa Clara, San José de Guadalupe and San Francisco de Asís — were east of the Santa Cruz Mountains on more level land, accessible from the improved course of the Camino Real, established shortly after Portolá's expedition.

Near the northern limit of their march, the members of the expedition noted seven rocky islands to the west and a rocky headland, enclosing a bay, to the north. These islands were the Farralones, and the headland was Point Reyes, north of what we now call Drake's Bay. Study of the sailing directions of Cabrera Bueno convinced all that they were seeing the (old) Port of San Francisco and that Monterey Bay was behind them. Exploration northward by Sergeant José Francisco Ortega (November 1-3) disclosed a vast bay, hitherto unreported; a party of soldiers on a hunting expedition returned with an almost identical report. Subsequent exploration (November 7) by Sergeant Ortega gave an indication of the size of the bay and showed that it would take many days of travel to reach old San Francisco Bay, now known as Drake's Bay. As a result of these explorations, San Francisco Bay, as we now know it, was shown in recognizable form on Costansó's map, published in 1771. Later exploration by land and sea augmented Spanish geographical knowledge of the area.[8] The expedition began its return journey on November 11.

---

[8]H. E. Bolton, *Crespi*, pp. 275-305. This is Crespi's account of the Fages expedition of 1772. John Galvin (ed.), *First Spanish Entry into San Francisco Bay, 1775*. This is the account of Captain Juan Manuel de Ayala's voyage into San Francisco Bay aboard the *San Carlos* in 1775.

The supply situation, which had become worrisome for the expedition as they travelled north of the mouth of the Salinas, became acute as they entered the Santa Cruz Mountains. As the supplies brought from San Blas were exhausted, the party subsisted on game, such as ducks, pinole and seeds obtained from the natives, and acorns which produced indigestion and fever. During this change of diet, some of the soldiers suffered not only from scurvy, but also from diarrhea. Very thorough soakings from the winter rains caused much worry among the leaders but seemed to do no harm. Later, the expedition members were forced to eat the meat of exhausted mules, which they apparently did not enjoy. This exhaustion of imported supplies was perhaps a blessing in disguise because the foods brought from San Blas were sadly deficient in vitamins and produced scurvy among most who ate them. Improvement of the sick, following the change of diet, is clearly described by Costansó, who wrote: "The swellings, and the contractions of the limbs . . . disappeared little by little. At the same time their pains left them, and all symptoms of scurvy disappeared. Their mouths became clean, their gums solid, and their teeth firmly fixed." As far as we can determine, Miguel Costansó was not trained in medicine, but his observations concerning the onset of and recovery from scurvy are laudably accurate and revealing.

Return route to the mouth of the Salinas was much like the outgoing route, but progress was a bit faster because they did not need to explore the route as they went. The pack train was lighter, and they were less retarded by the sick who were recovering. The expedition arrived at Point of Pines on November 28 and remained in the area until December 10, making additional local explorations but discovering little of immediate value. A large cross was erected near the beach, and a brief account of the expedition was buried at its foot. After a lengthy council, it was decided to return to San Diego. The outgoing route with minor improvements was followed south to the Ventura area. South of San Luis Obispo, the natives generously supplied food so that there was no more suffering from hunger. From Ventura across the area now occupied by Los Angeles a new route was chosen, roughly midway between the Santa Clara River and the course of the modern Ventura freeway. Although difficult in some places, this shortened the march considerably. Travel from the future site of Los Angeles back to San Diego was via the outgoing route (with very minor changes). Progress was rapid, and there were no serious problems. The expedition, "smelling strongly of mules," arrived in San Diego on January 24 after more than six months on the trail. With modern roads and transportation, it is no great feat of endurance to drive from San Diego to San Francisco in one day, and to return the next.

Conferences at San Diego between Portolá and his officers, and Father Serra and Captain Vila, who had remained in San Diego, made it apparent that the Portolá expedition had reached Monterey Bay, but, not recognizing the site, it had proceeded onward to the San Francisco area. Father Serra, perhaps in disgust, remarked, "You have come from Rome without having seen the Pope." Reasons for the non-recognition of Monterey Bay were many and varied. Most important, perhaps, was the mis-identification of the Salinas River as the Carmel. Because of this error, the landmarks described in Cabrera Bueno's sailing instructions seemed to be in the wrong places. Not previously considered, so far as can be determined, was the mental condition of the explorers, who suffered from fatigue, under-nutrition and scurvy. These physiological stresses usually produce mental impairments, largely confusion and disorientation, of a highly selective nature, so that some mental functions are markedly impaired and others are not. Although analysis after more than two centuries may be a bit uncertain, this seems to have been the case with the Portolá expedition because Costansó's latitude determinations continued very good indeed throughout the more than six months that he was on the trail; and the diaries of Costansó, Crespi, and Portolá were reasonably clear at all times. Ability of the leaders to recognize landmarks from descriptions and to pick the optimum trail seems to have been impaired. Despite the seriousness of their illnesses, particularly scurvy, the expedition members recovered rather promptly on receiving an adequate diet; many of them continued in military service for years or decades after 1770 with no evidence of lasting physical or mental impairment. The residual effects of scurvy, however, many have been a major contributing factor in the mental breakdown and eventual death of Dr. Pedro Prat.[9] They should also be considered among the many factors leading to the premature ageing and occasional irrational behavior of Captain Fernando Javier de Rivera y Moncada.

During the absence of Governor Portolá on his initially unsuccessful search for Monterey, things did not go well at the little outpost of San Diego. Most of the personnel were sick with scurvy, and the best efforts

[9]Clifford Graves, "Don Pedro Prat," *Journal of San Diego History*, Vol. 22, No. 2, Spring, 1976, pp. 1-8.

of Dr. Prat, who had neither the knowledge nor the supplies to treat it, were of no avail. What he most needed were antiscorbutics — a barrel of sauerkraut, a sack of potatos, or a carton of oranges — and these he did not have. Eventually, eight soldiers and some others died, and the rest recovered slowly. Construction of the first mission-presidio went very slowly. Attempts to convert the local Indians were unsuccessful. An Indian raid in mid-August (1769) resulted in the death of José María Vergerano from an arrow wound and the injury of Father Vizcaino, a blacksmith, a soldier, and a Lower California Indian. After this raid the Indians, who lost three killed and others wounded, developed a considerable respect for firearms and became a bit more tractable for a time, even seeking and receiving medical attention for their wounded.

The return of the Portolá expedition from the north brought about a supply crisis at San Diego, for the number of mouths to be fed increased from twenty-odd to eighty-odd. The *San Antonio* had been sent to San Blas some time previously for supplies but had not yet returned. The long-hoped-for *San José* with its cargo of supplies and a replacement crew for the *San Carlos* still had not appeared at San Diego. Unknown to Portolá, the vessel had been sent to San Blas for extensive repairs, and did not actually sail from San José del Cabo until May, 1770. Then, captained by Don Domingo Callegán, it put to sea and vanished. Recently, a bell, believed to be part of the cargo, was found by divers in Baja California waters. To alleviate the supply situation at San Diego, Governor Portolá sent Captain Rivera y Moncada, twenty or so soldiers, and some aides south to Velicatá with horses and mules to bring up the cattle that had been left there and to collect such supplies as could be obtained. Father Vizcaino, who was still recovering from an arrow wound in his hand, accompanied the party which left San Diego on February 11 and arrived at Velicatá on the 25th of the same month.

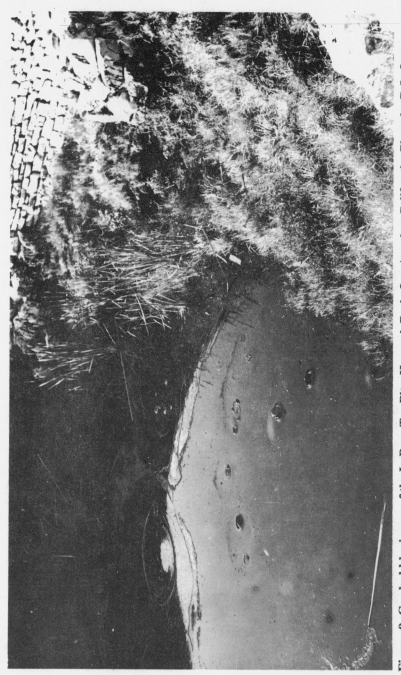

Figure 9. Gas bubbles in one of the LaBrea Tar Pits, Hancock Park, Los Angeles, California. Photo by R.L. Ives.

THE FIRST MAIL FROM MONTEREY

ritten word of the successful occupation of Monterey was carried south by two volunteer couriers, Corporal José Velásquez and an unnamed sailor who left Monterey with the documents on June 14, 1770. They travelled by now-familiar trails, passed through San Diego, and met Captain Rivera y Moncada and party about fifteen leagues south of San Diego.[1] Captain Rivera was returning from Velicatá with cattle and supplies. Because of Indian hostility farther south, he detached five soldiers from his company and sent them, as guards, with the two couriers. The messengers, now numbering seven, travelled south over what is now known as the Camino Real, passing through Loreto, and eventually delivering the documents to Governor Matías Armona, who had recently been appointed to succeed Portolá, and to Father Francisco Palou at the mission of Todos Santos where they arrived on August 2. Text of one version of Gaspar de Portolá's "Act of Formal Possession of the Port of Monterey," has survived complete with endorsements by Miguel del Pino, Juan Pérez, and Pedro Fages, as witnesses. *(Cf. Appendix E)*

Father Palou celebrated a solemn mass of thanksgiving at Todos Santos on August 3; other celebrations took place at Loreto and Santa Ana. Governor Armona immediately dispatched a vessel to carry the good news to the mainland. Meanwhile, the *San Antonio* made a rapid voyage from Monterey to San Blas, and Governor Portolá, who arrived at the west coast port on August 1, reached Mexico City with his version of the founding of Monterey on August 10. There were numerous official celebrations, and great plans were made for the new domains, including those for five new missions for which friars were available. Most of these plans were eventually carried out.

Corporal José Velásquez' courier journey from Monterey to Todos Santos was a most respectable equestrian feat. The trail distance of about

---

[1]This encounter was somewhere near modern Rosarito about seventeen miles south of Tijuana.

1440 miles was covered in forty-nine days, giving an average rate of travel of about thirty miles per day. This, it must be remembered, was during the hottest season, when water supply and forage were at a minimum and daytime temperatures commonly exceed 100° F. Although changes of mounts (mules) were available at various missions en route, the riders journeyed "straight through." At this time, Corporal José Velásquez was in his fifty-fourth year of life, and well into his twentieth year in military service. During the previous fifteen months or so, he had travelled on horseback or muleback considerably more than 3,000 miles. The excess here is hard to determine, as his duties included scouting out the trails in advance of the main party, and, where necessary, improving those trails.

Corporal Velásquez wrote a report on his courier journey, or a large part of it, but the account has not been found. However, a summary of the data contained therein was prepared by Governor Armona; it provides useful information and is presented below in translation.

GOVERNOR ARMONA'S SUMMARY OF JOSÉ VELÁSQUEZ' ACCOUNT OF THE JOURNEY SOUTHWARD FROM MONTEREY

From Monterey to San Diego it is 159 leagues, which the said courier (José Velásquez) covered in ten days.

As far as the channel of Santa Barbara he passed thirty-five rancherías whose heathen Indians number more than 2500 souls.

In the course of the channel there are found sixteen villages with more numerous inhabitants than those passed.

From the channel to San Diego, seventeen villages. Their inhabitants number some 1500 souls.

Along this distance he forded nine arroyos of running water. They almost resemble rivers due to their abundance of water, spacious channels and thickly-wooded banks. They have much land fit for sowing, since water is easily diverted from them.

There are found wild animals such as bears, deer, antelopes, jackrabbits, cottontail rabbits, and many birds of all kinds.

Along the way between rivers, there were many other arroyos, intricate lagoons, extensive marshes, and broad valleys, all with plenty of water.

He passed over several mountain ranges, counting six of them; along the seacoast they are very craggy, but offer passage through their midst for they are easily climbed. The most rugged of these are those of the Santa Lucía and along the channel (particularly) that of the Conversion, which terminates in the sea.[2]

In addition to these sierras and the rivers which flow into the sea, the rest of the terrain is made up of mesas and most extensive valleys. All of them are well-wooded and covered with good pasture of every description, down to the very seashore.

The kinds of timber to be found in abundance are cottonwood, willow, sycamore, live oak, deciduous oak, pine, juniper, and another species which he could not identify. The latter are all very large and towering trees.[3]

There are several salt deposits near the sea.

From Monterey to the channel there are seen two flows of bitumen; from the channel on the second day's journey to San Diego the same is seen.[4]

From Monterey to the channel there are many outcroppings of building stone of every description and color.

The said courier having explored as far as San Diego, the diary follows as far as the first mission of (Baja) California, which is that of Velicatá. From San Diego to this mission there are 111 leagues, which the said courier travelled in seven and a half days.

From San Diego to Velicatá there are nineteen villages, which contain some 2,000 souls, more or less.

Thirty-five leagues along the way there is a running arroyo, which has some land for sowing, and is a likely site for a small mission.[5]

Forty leagues farther on there is an excellent arroyo, fed by a spring which gushes by the roadside. Here, another small mission could be founded.[6]

---

[2]La Punta de la Conversión at Point Mugú, Lat. 34°7' N., is mentioned by Fr. Antonio de la Asención on the voyage of Sebastián Vizcaino, January 25, 1603. This is the seaward (west) end of the Santa Monica Mountains. See H. R. Wagner, *The Cartography of the Northwest Coast of America to the Year 1800*, Vol. II, p. 444.

[3]Velásquez was almost certainly describing the California redwood, Sequoia sempervirens, which grows in a few isolated groves in the foggier parts of the Santa Lucía Mountains south of Carmel, and in larger numbers in the Santa Cruz Mountains north of Monterey. This tree, which is not found in Europe or Mexico, posed an identification problem for the chroniclers of the Portolá expedition.

[4]These flows are discussed in some detail in Appendix F.

[5]Mission Santo Tomás de Aquino was founded near this site on April 24, 1791, by the Dominicans.

[6]Mission Santo Domingo was founded near this site on November 26, 1775, by the Dominicans.

In the vicinity of Velicatá there is an arroyo of running water where a good-sized mission could be founded, since it has adequate fields for sowing and good pasture for both cattle and sheep.[7]

Along the rest of the way, the terrain has nothing to produce since it consists of stretches of interminable hills, very bare of trees. Its arroyos are dry and very rocky. Its pasture land is very scarce and of the poorest kind, and is found only in certain designated places. There are great thickets of thorn bushes. Few animals are to be seen. Finally, this stretch from San Diego to Velicatá resembles the rest of (Baja) California in its sterility.

LIST OF THE SPANIARDS PRESENTLY EMPLOYED IN THE EXPEDITIONS OF THE CALIFORNIAS

At San Fernando de Velicatá, 224 leagues from Loreto, are Fr. Miguel de la Campa, a corporal, and twenty-two men who are soldiers or recruits from the royal presidio of Loreto. Included (in this figure) are four men on detached service at Santa María on the inlet of the Bay of San Luis Gonzaga, eighteen leagues from Velicatá.

At San Diego, 111 leagues beyond (north of) Velicatá, are Fr. Fernando Parrón, Fr. Francisco Gómez, Captain Don Fernando Rivera y Moncada, and twenty soldiers from the royal presidio of Loreto.

At Monterey, 159 leagues north of San Diego, are Fr. Junípero Serra, Fr. Juan Crespi, and the Lieutenant of Catalan Volunteers, Don Pedro Fages, with twelve soldiers from his company and seven from the royal presidio of Loreto.

Mathieuw de Armona (Rubric)[8]

Comparison of José Velásquez' trip report, as summarized by Governor Armona, with the various reports of the Portolá expedition, disclose many substantial agreements and a few minor discrepancies.

---

[7]This may be an early reference to the lower part of the Arroyo del Rosário, later explored by José Velásquez and others. Here, in July, 1774, mission Nuestra Señora del Rosário was founded by the Dominicans.

[8]Although this name is commonly rendered as Matías de Armona, this is the way he signed the document which is in the Archivo General de la Nación (Mexico City), Tomo 76, f. 233, item 15, dated June 14, 1770, by an unknown hand. This is the date of the beginning of the courier journey, not that of the writing of either the report or of the above abstract.

largely confined to the number of native rancherías passed on the journey. Whether these discrepancies are due to a miscount or to the abandonment of the rancherías (some of which were definitely temporary, "overnight" camps) between Portolá's visits and that of Velásquez, remains an open question. Velásquez' description of his journey from San Diego to Velicatá, as summarized, suggests quite strongly that the trail had been moved coastward north of Velicatá, eliminating the difficult and unnecessarily lengthy detour through San Juan de Dios and Valladares. No mention is made in the abstract of Corporal Velásquez' meeting with Captain Rivera y Moncada, south of San Diego, at which time Captain Rivera opened and read the south-going mail — a most definite faux pas.[9]

The remainder of the courier journey from Todos Santos to the City of Mexico is practically undocumented except for a specific mention of it in Corporal Velásquez' military service record (Cf. Appendix A). From the small amount of evidence remaining and from collateral data, we can determine what probably happened. After his arrival at Todos Santos on August 2, 1770, Velásquez prepared a trip report covering his journey from Monterey to Velicatá. This report has not been found. The remainder of the trip from Velicatá to Todos Santos, being over familiar trails through known country, was of little interest to either the governor or the viceroy. Governor Armona prepared a summary of this report (as translated above). The governor also dispatched a vessel to carry the news of Portolá's successful journey to San Blas, en route to Mexico City. As Todos Santos is not a seaport, the vessel was elsewhere, probably at either Cabo San Lucas or San José del Cabo. Because a sailing vessel cannot usually be dispatched as promptly as a modern prowl car, there was a delay of several to many days while supplies were loaded, water casks filled, and a crew rounded up and readied for duty. This latter task was often time-consuming because the sailors of that time and others "tended to be disorderly ashore;" many of them, following the tradition of Noah, were not models of sobriety.

While the vessel was being readied for the voyage across the Gulf, the courier, Corporal José Velásquez, rode to the port of embarkation

---

[9]This is reported in a letter to Antonio Bucareli y Ursua by Felipe Barri, dated Loreto, August 24, 1770. See Amado Aguierre, *Documentos Para la Historia de Baja California*, Document 18, p. 17.

(not specified) and thence sailed for San Blas. In addition to the Portolá reports, which he had brought from Monterey, and local mail, he almost certainly carried Governor Armona's abstract of his trip report, because that document found its way into the Archivo General de la Nación, whereas the original report apparently did not. From San Blas Velásquez rode over the well-worn trail to Mexico City and delivered the packets of mail to the office of the viceroy. In view of travel times by land and sea in 1770, the mail from Todos Santos probably did not arrive at its destination before the latter part of September, 1770. The courier could hardly have returned to Baja California before the end of October. As the late summer and early fall are the hurricane season in the waters off southern Baja California, travel times may well have been very much longer. Sea travel time from San Blas to peninsular California varied from less than a week to more than nine months, depending upon wind, weather, and the competence of the navigators. Some of the journeys of San Blas ships resembled the legendary voyages of Philip Vanderdecken.

TROUBLE ON THE PENINSULA

n completion of his courier journey to Mexico City, Corporal Velásquez returned to Baja California to resume his military duties at Loreto. He probably arrived there late in 1770 or very early in 1771. Shortly thereafter, he was promoted to sergeant, the date of the promotion being April 20, 1771. In his new rank, Sergeant Velásquez served at Loreto for almost two years, eventually becoming "the soldier most in the governor's confidence." During the major part of his first tour of duty at Loreto (1751-1768), the military and missionary establishments were closely integrated; many facilities were shared by the soldiers and the missionaries. The military commander, Don Fernando Javier de Rivera y Moncada, was sympathetic with the missionaries and got along well with them. The common warehouse at Loreto was managed by Brother Juan Bautista Mugazabal, S.J., who had an excellent record as a soldier, advancing to the rank of alférez before he became a Jesuit brother. He served at Loreto from 1720 until his death in 1761.

The sudden expulsion of the Jesuits in 1767 completely disrupted this smooth-working symbiosis, replacing it with a divided command, under which the soldiers received their orders from the viceroy via the governor, and the missionaries theirs from the College of San Fernando. Both commands were overcentralized; liaison between them was poor and communication with the peninsula was slow. In consequence, small problems that should have been resolved in a few hours dragged on unsolved for months, or sometimes for years. The unhappy situation was further complicated by frequent changes of governors — there were six in Baja California during the period 1767-1772. The first governor, Don Gaspar de Portolá, was sent to the peninsula in 1767 to superintend the expulsion of the Jesuits. That difficult and unpleasant task completed, he remained in Baja California working with the Inspector General, Don José de Gálvez, to reactivate the missions. Then he was ordered north as commander of the expedition that founded San Diego; he discovered San Francisco Bay and established the mission and presidio at Monterey. On his departure from Loreto March 9 (or 14th according to other accounts), Juan Gutierrez was appointed as temporary governor, serving until October 23, 1769, and "leaving no footprints." During this time on June 12, the newly-appointed governor of the peninsula, Don Matías de Armona, visited Loreto; he did not like what he saw and returned to Sonora to confer with the inspector general at Arizpe. He was unwilling to accept the governorship until a number of serious problems, specifically including absence of funds to pay the soldiers, were resolved.

On October 23, Antonio López de Toledo became temporary governor in addition to his regular duties as commissary of the warehouse at Loreto. Apparently his only major official act was to tangle with Father Francisco Palou, who was acting president of the Lower California missions. López came out a very definite second-best. His problem had been inherited from Gálvez who ordered that the salt mines of Isla Carmen (about twenty miles east-southeast of Loreto) be worked by Indians levied from the missions, particularly Loreto. These workers were to be given subsistence while working, but no other wages. When Don Antonio asked Father Palou for a levy of Indians under these conditions, he received a firm refusal on the grounds that there were no Indians to spare. No provision had been made to clothe the workers, to care for them if they were sick, or to support their families. After further arguments with Father Palou, the levy request was suspended for the time being, and the matter eventually became the subject of a memorial submitted to Inspector-General José de Gálvez by Father Dionísio Basterra, O. F. M., procurator of the Baja California missions (July 10, 1770).[1]

Having arrived at Cerralvo June 13, 1770, Matías de Armona left immediately for Baja California apparently in response to a direct order to assume the office of governor.[2] During his relatively short tenure, he

---

[1]Father Basterra's memorial and a full statement of the grievances of the Franciscans is given in Zephyrin Engelhardt, *The Missions and Missionaries of California*, Vol. 1, pp. 415-426.

[2]Matías de Armona, a professional soldier, had been Sergeant-Major of the La Corona Regiment, and later a secretary to José de Gálvez, the inspector-general. He was appointed governor of Baja California early in 1769, apparently against his will, and did not actually assume the office until after June 13, 1770. Later in the same year, he was permitted to resign, leaving the peninsula on Nov. 9, 1770. At this time, José de Gálvez was mentally disturbed (he may have had cerebral malaria) so that old problems were not solved, and new troubles proliferated. See C. E. Chapman, *A History of California*, pp. 234-238.

expedited the forwarding of mail from Monterey to Mexico City, had difficulties with the fractious Indians at Todos Santos, and found immediate solutions to few problems. Armona eventually received permission to resign and left the peninsula November 9, 1770, taking with him a list of problems, requests, and suggested solutions (prepared in conjunction with Father Palou) for later consideration by the viceroy. Eventual action on these requests lessened the problems of the missionaries only slightly. Governor Armona's extensive correspondence about the ill-fated French scientific expedition, which observed the transit of Venus from San José del Cabo on June 3, 1769, has been detailed elsewhere.[3] After Governor Armona's "escape" from his apparently unwanted position, Bernardo Moreno became acting governor. He served until April 19, 1771, accomplishing little of note.

The next governor of Baja California was Felipe Barri who was appointed by the viceroy some time before March of 1771.[4] He arrived at Cerralvo on March 22, and at Loreto on April 19 of that year. Almost immediately, friction developed between the Franciscan missionaries and the governor, much of it resulting from inherited problems over which neither the missionaries nor the governor had any immediate control. Although solutions to some of these problems were outlined to the viceroy by former Governor Armona and were already being considered, the ill-conceived and largely unworkable "reforms" imposed by José de Gálvez still prevailed since they could not be evaded. To complicate matters still further, the Indians who had been moved from declining mission areas to Todos Santos did not like their new location and kept the administration busy with spurious complaints of ill-treatment. A series of plagues killed off many Spaniards and Indians alike. These epidemics included measles, smallpox, syphilis *(mal*

---

[3] I. W. Engstrand, *Royal Officer in California.*

[4] Felipe Barri, whose name is spelled Barry in some documents, was an experienced career soldier. He was appointed to the governorship of California by the viceroy, probably early in 1771. While in that office he had trouble with the missionaries, as did his predecessors and successors. Leaving that troubled realm in 1774, he was active in campaigns against various rebellious Indian groups, particularly the Mescalero and Lipan Apaches, who kept the Bolsón de Mapimí in a turmoil in the 1770s. He was appointed Governor of Nueva Viscaya by Viceroy Bucareli some time before 1778, and died, while on campaign, on February 2, 1784. Among his writings is a census of Indian depredations in 1776-1777 (Archivo General de Indias 103-4-16). Details of his service on the mainland of Mexico are given in Luis Navarro García, *José de Gálvez y la Comandancia General de las Provincias Internas,* pp. 282-284, 338, 508.

Gallico), and perhaps typhus or typhoid. Malarial fevers, then endemic in parts of the peninsula, complicated other ills.

In this troubled area, Governor Barri attempted to carry out the sometimes incompatible orders of the viceroy and of the inspector-general. He maintained a semblance of order to insure adequate supplies for the missions in the province (Baja California) and to care for the growing supply needs of the new settlements in Alta California. He kept the Franciscan missionaries happy. Sergeant Velásquez, then stationed at Loreto, was kept busy with problems of supply, transportation and property accountability, including investigations of apparently baseless reports of misappropriation of mission equipment by the Franciscans. At this time, it became apparent that the Franciscans were overextended and did not have the manpower to staff both the existing missions of Baja California and those founded and planned in Alta California. After extended negotiations, the California mission field was divided between the Franciscans and the Order of Preachers (Dominicans). The new missions of Alta California were placed under the Friars Minor while the older missions in Baja California were ceded to the sons of Dominic. This division of mission territories was formalized by a concordat, signed April 7, 1772. A new deployment of missionaries took place all over the peninsula as the Franciscans moved north and the Dominicans took new places in Baja California.

During this restaffing of the missions, the second in about four years, word came through the governor's office (and was attributed to the governor) that the Franciscans were robbing the peninsular missions of "vestments and sacred vessels for the mission of Monterey."[5]

Sergeant Velásquez was ordered to check the Franciscan packs in Loreto. He did so, found nothing wrong, and so reported. Later, his inspection was repeated and confirmed by a committee of Dominican friars. One of his related investigations is reported by Father Palou:

> I have no doubt the soldier gave this report to the governor who had sent him on the errand. But, not content with it, he made use of a new scheme to bear out the false accusations that he had raised against us with the Dominican fathers. This was the soldier most in his confidence in Loreto, named José Velásquez. He called some Indian muleteers to his house from the mission of San José de Comondu; they had brought the things belonging to the first friars who left California shortly after the arrival of the first Dominicans. After assuring them that they need fear nothing and that if they told the

[5]Zephyrin Engelhardt, *Missions and Missionaries.* Vol. 1, p. 519.

truth they would be heeded by the governor, but if not, they would be severely punished, he asked them what vestments the father at San José had taken out and carried to Mexico.

"Now, tell the truth," he said, "or everything is known because two Indians from San Xavier have told about it . . . ."

They replied that they knew no such thing; that what they had brought when the fathers came consisted of some little articles and a bed for him as for the others who had gone down to San José from the other missions, and food for the voyage on the bark. He threatened them with punishment for hiding the truth, as a partisan of the fathers, to which they replied that no matter what might be done to them, they could tell no more than what they said. "If they took vestments or anything you say, you can find it out by looking to see if anything is missing."

To this Velásquez replied: "Yes, it will be investigated, and you will be punished for not having told it." With this he sent them away.

As soon as these muleteers arrived at their mission of San José they informed the missionary father in his presence and that of the Dominican friars who had been at the mission since they landed. They told me about what had happened to them and about the soldier, Velásquez; they informed me without delay. All of these occurrences took place between the middle of October, 1772, when the first ten Dominican fathers landed at Loreto, and the latter part of November.[6]

Although Father Palou's report consists largely of unsupported accusations and hearsay, it marked the approximate beginning of a long period of ill-will, friction, and suspicion between the governor and the missionaries; it does show that Sergeant Velásquez followed his orders diligently, used a fairly standard method of police interrogation, and found that the Franciscans were not "robbing the peninsular missions."

During this time the missionaries in Alta California made slow and steady progress, hampered as always by supply shortages, fractious Indians, and continuing manpower scarcities. When Corporal José Velásquez left Monterey with the mail on June 14, 1770, there were just two missions in Alta California — San Diego, founded July 16, 1769, and Monterey, founded June 3, 1770. Despite numerous obstacles,

---

[6]H. E. Bolton, *New California*, Vol. III, pp. 326-327. This work, a fundamental source on early California, is a translation and annotation of Fray Francisco Palou's major writings. Strongly pro-Franciscan and anti-government bias is evident as several places in the work.

Father Serra and his co-workers immediately planned expansion of the mission system. During the next two years mission San Antonio de Padua was founded near modern Jolón July 14, 1771. Mission San Gabriel (old site) was founded from San Diego on September 8, 1771, and mission San Carlos Borromeo was moved from Monterey to Carmel, the work being substantially completed in December, 1771.

In the spring of 1772 in obedience to various orders and requests, Captain Pedro Fages led an extensive and careful exploration of the San Francisco Bay area, travelling along the south shore to Carquínez Strait and the mouth of San Joaquín River, near modern Antioch. This extensive journey was ably described by Father Juan Crespi.[7] While Fages was away on this expedition, the supply situation at Monterey grew serious due to late arrival of the supply ships which had been fighting adverse winds and the crews suffering from scurvy. Shortly after his return to Monterey, Fages organized a hunting party which went to the Cañada de los Osos (May, 1772) between Morro Bay and San Luis Obispo. They supplied the northern missions with bear meat until supplies could be forwarded north from San Diego and Velicatá. Most unfortunately, this hunt apparently exterminated the California grizzly bear in that area. Shortly after this hunt mission San Luis Obispo was founded (September 1, 1772).

The southern missions, San Diego and San Gabriel, continued to be plagued with deserting soldiers who were not happy with conditions of service in Alta California. Most of these eventually returned to duty under various amnesties. Relations between the Indians at these missions and the soldiers likewise were strained because the soldiers had taken no vows of chastity, and the only women available were Indian. These problems continued throughout Spanish and Mexican rule in Alta California. The chronically low soldier morale was exacerbated as a result of pay cuts imposed by José de Gálvez. Moreover payment was only in merchandise and at very high prices. Extended tours of duty were common in the Californias, which most soldiers regarded as anus mundi. Early in 1772, Captain Don Fernando Javier de Rivera y Moncada journeyed south from San Diego, leaving Loreto in mid-January en route to what he hoped would be retirement on the mainland of Mexico.

On February 2, 1773, Sergeant José Velásquez was promoted to the rank of alférez. This rank, normally translated as ensign, is the military rank between sergeant and lieutenant.

---

[7]See H. E. Bolton, *Fray Juan Crespi*, pp. 275-304.

COMMANDER AT VELICATÁ

hortly after his promotion to the rank of alférez, José Velásquez was transferred to San Fernando de Velicatá, to serve as commander of the military detachment there. San Fernando de Velicatá, at this time, was the northernmost mission in Baja California, the site having been discovered by Father Wenceslaus Linck, S.J., in March, 1766. The mission was founded on May 14, 1769, by Father Junípero Serra, O.F.M., this being the only mission founded by the Franciscans in Baja California. At the time of our immediate interest (1773) the Franciscans were relinquishing control of the mission to the Dominicans. Unlike the missions farther south, Indian troubles were few and minor at San Fernando because of the excellent work by Father Wenceslaus Linck, whose work was carried on and augmented by Father Fermín Lasuén, O.F.M., both of whom, based at San Borja, developed friendly relations with the native population over a large area north and west of their base.

In addition to being a mission settlement, San Fernando de Velicatá was also a supply depot and transshipment point, being the nearest habitable place to an important three-way trail junction. Here terminated the "Jesuit" Camino Real, whose several branches wound through the mountains in the central part of the peninsula from their origin at Loreto. Here also terminated the trail from Bahía San Luis Gonzaga where supplies were brought by mission lighters from Loreto.[1] Northward, the trail ran for about 112 leagues (280 miles) to San Diego in Alta California. Much of the traffic through Velicatá were mule-trains laden with supplies for Alta California. San Fernando de Velicatá soon became a base for explorations, as the Dominicans extended the mission chain north toward San Diego, in obedience to orders from the viceroy. These orders were originally given to the Franciscans who could not carry them out. The

---

[1]The actual junction of these two trails was in the Arroyo Santa María about seven miles southeast of mission Santa María de los Angeles. As the mission had water, but no forage and no arable land, the trail terminal was placed by Velicatá by the Portolá expedition. Sections of the old trail can still be seen east of Santa María.

mandate was inherited by the Dominicans, who eventually built all the missions, substantially as ordered.

Because relatively little has been written about the Dominican work in peninsular California and few Dominican documents are known, the belief has become widespread, even among some professional historians, that the Dominicans did very little there. Actually, they apparently did all that was humanly possible under the conditions, and their accomplishments, although somewhat sparsely documented, were very real.[2] For several years, while military commander at Velicatá, Alférez José Velásquez worked closely with the Dominicans, particularly in exploring for and evaluating mission sites.

Choosing a mission site and the founding it in the 1770s entailed some very careful and extensive exploration, plus a large amount of administrative paper work. The same effort today would probably be called a feasibility study. Father Luis Sales, in his "Observations on California" tells how this was done:

> When the missionary is assured of having a site with water, firewood, stone, and other needs for the founding, he advises the viceroy. The consent of His Excellency having been obtained, he notifies all the missionaries in order that they may give alms and assist in the founding of the village. Some send sheep, others cows, mules, horses, and converted families to begin the work. Then he takes an escort of soldiers, since, although they are detrimental, it would be imprudent of the missionary to expose himself without them. With all this train he sets out for the selected location, begins to sow seed, to make corrals and a stockade of posts for defense. All this done, he goes out through barrancas, caves and forests to look for heathen, and this is the climax of his difficulties, for the Indians are wont to hide themselves, to attack the troops and the missionary and to do them harm, as has happened to me. When he has the luck

---

[2]Major sources for Dominican activity in Baja California include: C.N. Rudkin, *Observations on California, 1772-1790*; these are the writings of Fr. Luis Sales. H. E. Bolton, *Historical Memoirs of New California*, 4 Vols. This work, Father Francisco Palou's magnum opus, contains several hundred references to Dominican efforts. Zephyrin Engelhardt, *Missions and Missionaries of California*, pp. 555-713. This extensive work, although a mine of information, is sadly tainted by pro-Franciscan, anti-government bias with diatribes against the Masons and the "French Encyclopedists" with their "infidel notions," thrown in for good measure. Peveril Meigs, *The Dominican Mission Frontier in Lower California*, and Homer Aschmann, *The Central Desert of Baja California*.

to find some Indians he talks to them of their unhappy state, their
nakedness, poverty and other miseries from which they suffer, and
entices them with small gifts. . . . It is to be noted that the heathen
Indians, once instructed and baptized, remain inhabitants of the
newly founded settlement although they may have lived forty leagues
away. These expeditions the missionary repeats whenever he finds it
convenient and thus the number of Christians goes on increasing. The
settlement once established, the king assigns one thousand duros
against which the missionary draws for tools, cooking utensils,
pots, etc."[3]

In obedience to inherited viceregal orders, which called for the
establishment of five new missions between San Fernando de Velicatá
and San Diego, the Dominicans planned a northward journey of exploration to investigate workable mission sites. The expedition finally left
Loreto in November, 1773, with Father Vicente Mora, President of the
Dominicans in Baja California, leading. Accompanying him were Fathers
Miguel Hidalgo and Francisco Galisteo. The three fathers reached San
Fernando de Velicatá on December 4. Shortly thereafter, on December
20, the three Dominican fathers, escorted by Alférez José Velásquez and
several soldiers, set out northwestward to the southern-most possible
mission site, known as Miñaraco.[4] After a journey of twelve leagues
(thirty miles or forty-eight kilometers) over relatively easy trails, they
reached the site and made a thorough reconnaisance on December 22.
Returning immediately to Velicatá, Alférez Velásquez wasted no time in
preparing his trip report, which follows in translation:

REPORT ON THE FAMOUS SITE OF MIÑARACO[5]

This is an arroyo spread out like a valley, which lies from
east-northeast to west-southwest. It was seen to have a length of
three leagues, and and its narrowest is six hundred and forty varas
wide, as measured by me and the soldier Morillo, without losing our

---

[3]Luis Sales, O.P, *Observations on California*, pp. 163-165.

[4]This place name of Indian origin, is rendered as Viñaraco by Palou; as Viñadaco,
by Mora; as Miñaraco, by Velásquez; and as Viñatacot by Sales. The site was apparently
first mentioned by Velásquez in his report of his journey in midsummer of 1770, from
Monterey southward. It became known to the Franciscans in late 1771 or early 1772 and
was favored by them as a possible mission site.

[5]Original Spanish text in Archivo General de la Nación, Provincias Internas, Vol.
166, Item 4, pp. 192-193.

line of sight.[6] Here one may dry farm for many years before irrigation becomes necessary. Water is plentiful in the valley; there is a lagoon on the south side, so deep that we could not see its bottom. It is 1,000 *varas* long and just as wide. At the end there is a draw which carries a *buey* and a half of water.[7] On the north side, at the foot of a high hill, there is a marsh at whose source in the bramble thickets one can see a spring which could have about two *bueyes*.

At the source of the marsh, at its highest part near the foot of the hill, the Reverend Father President Fray Vicente de Mora in company with the Reverend Fathers Hidalgo and Galisteo ordered a well to be dug. Within two and a half varas, amidst the best of gravelly soil, a strong spring of water was found, that showed no decrease in flow. This is in addition to the arroyo, for in the same stream bed there are also several deep pools of water. I say this because the site is not only marked but identifiable by an abundance of willows, innumerable tules, swamp plants, and rushes, the latter of three different varieties. And thus I repeat that even though this land be worked hard for years, neither would the natural moisture leave it nor would the soil become sterile. And it would be an exhausting job to farm all the land described here.

This valley ends in an estuary which reaches half a league to the sea, and is fifty varas wide, more or less. Near the ocean we went along testing the water of the estuary, and the water tended to be fresh rather than saline. It can be guessed that the water pressure from this valley is considerable.

The lands mentioned have no alkali, though much *tequesquite*, which is in no way injurious to any planted seed.[8]

In addition to everything I have already mentioned, there exists beyond the arroyo a beautiful plain of open country. The Indians say that there is a plentiful supply of water. The only certain thing is that, given a good start, Miñaraco will be able to maintain new missions and their guards.

---

[6] A vara is a linear measure, usually 33 inches.

[7] This is an archaic irrigation measure, representing a flow of water having a cross section about equal to that of an ox.

[8] *Tequesquite* is a white mineral deposit, usually powdery, found on soil surfaces. It is usually composed of mixed sodium and calcium salts — carbonates, calorides, and sulfates — with no fixed formula.

Commander at Velicatá   † 111 †

It is to be noted that I will vouch for all the aforementioned descriptions and, discharging my conscience in full, I say that I have understated this report on the famous site of Miñaraco.

San Fernando de Velicatá, December 24, 1773

Joséf Velásquez
(rubric)

Appended to this document in a similar hand, but containing information not derived from the reported explorations, is a brief tally of the five proposed mission sites north of Velicatá and the distances between them:

PLACES THAT WERE EXPLORED
TO FOUND THE FIVE NEW MISSIONS
BETWEEN VELICATA AND SAN DIEGO:

From Velicatá to Miñaraco . . . . 12 leagues
From Miñaraco to San Simon . . . . 10 leagues
From San Simon de San Telmo . . . . 18 leagues
From San Telmo to San Solano . . . . 16 leagues
From San Solano to El Encino . . . . 19 leagues
    This last (place) is approximately twenty leagues this side of San Diego.

Alférez Velásquez' exploration report was sent to Governor Barri at Loreto and was probably carried by one of the soldiers who accompanied Father President Vicente Mora and his two missionary companions on their return journey. The provenience of the mission-site tally is not clear, but it almost certainly dates from the 1770s.

Checking Velásquez' descriptions against the terrain of Miñaraco indicates that very little has changed in the area, physiographically, since 1773. As nearly as can be determined because there are so few records, average area rainfall has decreased somewhat since the 1770s, and the valley floor has aggraded considerably, perhaps by as much as two feet since that time. In consequence, the fresh-water lagoon on the south side of the valley has disappeared. There has been some slight filling of the drowned mouth of the Arroyo Rosario which, separated from the sea by a sand bar, contains a long narrow lagoon of nearly-fresh water. This is now known as the Bocana del Rosario. The area now supports the adjacent communities of Rosario de Arriba and Rosario de Abajo with a combined population of perhaps 1500. Local crops include beans, chile peppers, corn and alfalfa. Cattle are raised in the surrounding hilly lands.

Government services, tourism, and sporadic work in the local mines add to local income.[9]

Even in the relatively uncomplicated 1770s, the establishment of a mission required much more than selecting a site and a nod from the governor. Viceregal approval was also necessary and the financing had to be arranged from Mexico City. New Spain, at this time, was territorily overextended on the northern frontier and suffered from a chronic and worsening shortage of missionaries, military leaders, competent administrators and funds. The official conferences, prior to approving a new mission foundation, were somewhat long drawn out. Much consideration was devoted to careful allocation of scarce resources.

As the first step in this lengthy process, Governor Barri sent Velásquez' report along with a covering letter of his own, dated March 1, 1774, to Viceroy Don Antonio Bucareli y Ursua. A translation of Governor Barri's letter follows:

Most Excellent Lordship:
My Dear Sir:
The alférez of the leather jacket company of this peninsula, Don José Velásquez, who was employed in guarding the heathen frontier at San Fernando de Velicatá, has sent me the enclosed letter, which is passed in its original form into the hands of Your Excellency. It describes a reconnaissance of a place called Miñaraco (suggested) for the founding of a new mission on the road from this frontier to the presidio of San Diego. On the occasion of the reported exploration it is known that there came to the mission site for Holy Baptism one hundred and fifteen heathen Indians, both adults and children, who submitted to the Reverend Dominican Fathers.

May Our Lord protect the most excellent personage of Your Excellency for many years.
Royal Presidio of Loreto, March 1, 1774.

Most Excellent Lordship:
Your Excellency's hand is kissed by your most humble servant,
Don Felipe Barri
(Rubric)[10]

---

[9]This area is excellently mapped on the DETENAL sheet "El Rosario." H 11 B 74, 1/50,000, 1974. Ruins of the earliest mission are in the community of Rosario de Arriba.

[10]This letter and the following ones relative to the founding of mission El Rosario are contained in Archivo General de la Nación, Californias, Vol. 36 exp. 4, pp. 19-29.

Almost immediately, Father President Vicente de Mora sent a report to the viceroy, describing the mission site of Miñaraco and the prospects of making many converts. This letter follows:

Most Excellent Lordship:
Sir:

On the fourth of November last year I went out from the mission of Loreto to visit the missions of the north. Upon the conclusion of my visit at the frontier of Velicatá I went to survey the place called Viñadaco, sixteen leagues to the west of the frontier, to see if I could begin the founding of the missions with which we are charged.[11]

I have found that the said site is a pleasing and wide valley with willows with many marshy places or lagoons. It runs from east-northeast to west-southwest. The valley must be six or eight leagues long and nearly one wide. The dense willow grove is about three leagues long. We could not walk through it, though we tried hard, except for two places near the bed of the arroyo which has running water. In these explorations I observed that the ground is pebbly, without any saltpeter. Before the end of the willow grove there is a large lagoon of very good-tasting water, and rather fine.

From here runs a beautiful stream of water, which empties into an estuary of the sea half a league long. This joins the South Sea only during high tide; when the tide is low, one can walk easily between the sea and the estuary (along the barrier bar which separates them).

We tested various parts of the estuary and at the beginning it was normal, almost half way along an unpleasant aftertaste was noticed, although hardly salty. It is possible that the taste was due to the sea breeze blowing then.

This survey finished, we went back to the camp that had been made where the willows began, where we were expecting three heathen chiefs with other people from their same rancherías who came with them. They numbered twenty-six, all with bows and arrows. Without wasting time, I began preaching to them the faith of Jesus Christ, to which they were very attentive. I questioned them as to what they might answer, they all unanimously said that they would embrace the faith without any reluctance as long as they were assured that they would not have to leave their lands. I told them that I would send them priests who would live with them and that they

---

[11]Velásquez gives this distance as twelve leagues. Scaling this distance over the probable course followed and using the best modern map gives a distance of about 13.5 leagues of 2.5 miles (4 km.) each.

would be free from the plundering they suffered at the hands of other heathens. They responded in very happy and positive terms that if they knew when the priests were to come, they would bring their women and children there. I promised them that the priests would come very soon, but that they (the Indians) could not remain here for the time being, as I did not have anything for them to eat, but that I would go get a supply of provisions and the priests then could live with them.

I asked them whether there were many related Indians at this site, and they gave me to understand that there were unbelievers on all sides, and indeed the signs show it because there are main trails which they use to go to the sea to do their fishing, at which they are skillful enough.

They were with me two days and, saying farewell, they told me they were going for their women and children (to be ready) when the priests would come.

Being made aware of the agreeableness of the place and the docility of those unhappy ones and with such a multitude of souls to occupy those lands, I saw myself obliged to undertake the most efficacious measures with the purpose of collecting some supplies on the frontier with the goal in mind of attracting (the Indians) to the knowledge of the true God, those poor sheep gone astray from the flock of Jesus Christ.

I have not been able to gather any more supplies than sixty fanegas of wheat and corn, either because the missions did not have enough for their own children, or because they deny it to me from the warehouse.[12]

With this information at hand, Your Excellency will determine what would be your highest pleasure.

I wish for Your Excellency perfect health, and I ask God to preserve you for many years.

Royal presidio and mission of Our Lady of Loreto, March 11, 1774.

Most Excellent Lord: Your Excellency's hand is kissed by your most humble chaplain, who venerates you,

Fray Vicente de Mora
(rubric)

---

[12]A fanega is a dry measure similar to an English bushel.

These three letters by Alférez Velásquez, Governor Barri, and Father Mora, respectively, gave the viceroy adequate and apparently satisfactory information on the site of the proposed mission and its environs. Remaining to be worked out by the viceroy and his advisors was the problem of financing the new mission. Many months, conferences, and letters later, funds were made available for the founding of the proposed mission at Miñaraco. These deliberations involved, among others, Antonio Bucareli y Ursua, the viceroy; José Antonio de Areche, fiscal of the royal audiencia; Fray Francisco Estabillo, procurador general of the missions of California; and Fernando José Mangino, auditor-general and director of the Pious Fund.

Initially, the Dominicans requested 5,000 pesos — 1,000 pesos for each of the proposed new missions north of Velicatá — plus 1,000 pesos for Velicatá and a settlement of the more than 800 pesos owed for the equipment acquired by the Dominicans from the Franciscans at the time of the Dominican takeover of the missions of Baja California. Final arrangement called for an immediate payment of 1,000 pesos to the Dominicans to assist in the costs of founding the new mission at Miñaraco. Additional fiscal considerations were asked for other Dominican missions when founded. No payment had been made to cover San Fernando de Velicatá which was regarded as already founded — and a Franciscan problem. No provision had been made to settle the Dominican debt to the Franciscans (800 pesos) from the Royal treasury. This is all clearly stated in fiscal José Antonio de Areche's letter to the viceroy, which follows:

Most Excellent Lordship:
    The considerations which have motivated the Director of the Pious fund of the Missions of California to inform Your Excellency that, for now, one thousand pesos should be given to the Father Solicitor Fray Francisco Estabillo in order that a single mission be built in the place called Miñaraco, or Viñadaco, are worthy of being kept in mind. These funds must not be subjected to speculative risks, as this was not the intention of the founders.
    Once this establishment is verified, the others will follow, provided the proper prerequisites have been met, and according to the qualities which are observed in each one of them. Therefore, under such criteria, Your Excellency should order payment to Father Solicitor only in the amount of one thousand pesos, making it clear to him that in the future, as further discoveries are made, and

according to the feasibility of new foundations, the proper aid will be furnished. At the same time he will be informed that since the mission at Velicatá was founded before his brothers took charge of those missions in that peninsula, the requested one thousand pesos cannot be given for that one. Furthermore, since he owes eight hundred and more pesos referred to by Don Fernando Mangino from the value of the utensils received when they took posession of them, they must repay this from the amounts which would be given to him for new buildings, and the corresponding order to this effect is hereby given to the Director. To Don Felipe de Neve, named by Your Excellency, will be given such orders as pertain to him, so that he will facilitate provisions, troops, and other aid which may be needed for the important goal of establishing in Viñadaco or Miñaraco the mission which is to be founded.

Mexico City, November 5, 1774

Areche

The remaining "red tape" items which included a viceregal approval of the financial arrangements and a formal reading of this to Father Francisco Estabillo were completed in Mexico City on November 18, 1774. In the meantime, however, the mission at Miñaraco, named Nuestra Senora del Rosario, had already been founded, and the first entry in the mission books was dated July 31, 1774.[13] This mission was constructed at the site now known as El Rosario de Arriba, slightly east of the center of town and north of the present (1978) main highway. In 1802 the mission was moved to a new site in El Rosario de Abajo at the west end of the settlement and on the south side of the arroyo. It was finally abandoned about 1832.

At about this time, plans were made in Mexico City to assign Alférez Velásquez to exploratory duties north and east of Velicatá in the hope that he would find a seaport more convenient to the northern missions than Bahía San Luis Gonzaga.[14] These plans materialized in formal orders at a much later date. Shortly after the founding of mission El Rosario, exploration were undertaken northward to locate a site for the second of the five missions planned between Velicatá and San Diego. These explorations were considerably delayed while the troublesome

---

[13]Peveril Meigs, *The Dominican Mission Frontier of Lower California*, p. 22; F.J. Weber, *The Missions and Missionaries of Baja California*, p. 54.

[14]García, *José de Gálvez,*" p. 431.

problem of the Franciscan packs was worked on and eventually solved. This problem was, in a way, inherited. The packs in question contained various items, some of them books and personal effects, sent north by the Franciscans when they vacated the missions of Baja California in favor of the Dominicans. Because of apparently unfounded rumors that the Franciscans were looting the missions of the peninsula, these packs were inspected at Loreto, first by José Velásquez acting on orders from the governor, and later by a committee of Dominicans who found everything in order. Later, mission inventories showed nothing missing. These packs were conveyed to Velicatá where they were stored under guard, pending resolution of further difficulties.

This controversy is described at great length and with much detail by Father Francisco Palou, O.F.M. whose sympathies were strongly on the side of the Franciscans (as might be expected).[15] On a superficial reading, this account gives a strong impression that all of the trouble was due to anti-missionary bias on the part of Governor Barri. A more careful perusal shows that, when things were done right or in strict accord with regulations, Father Palou quotes official documents (correctly). However, when something possibly derogatory to the governor is described, the source information is usually second or third hand ("hearsay"). Further, it becomes apparent that the soldiers had one set of orders, and the missionaries had, or believed they had, somewhat different instructions. In several instances, one party to the controversy received definite orders while others involved apparently did not. In consequence, it is most difficult to determine, after a lapse of more than two centuries, whether the difficulty with the Franciscan packs was due to malicious obstructionism on the part of Governor Barri as Palou firmly believed, or to administrative ineptitude on the part of the governor, or to grossly inadequate communication between the various parties concerned. Whatever the causes of the controversy, however, it is clear that relations between the governor and the missionaries during this time were considerably less than cordial.

When José Velásquez assumed command of Velicatá in the spring of 1773, he received custody of the Franciscan packs from his predecessor, and with them the accompanying administrative problems. At this time according to the Dominicans, the packs were embargoed, and they could apparently request, in writing, military aid to prevent their removal

---

[15]H. E. Bolton, "Historical Memoirs of New California," Vol. III, pp. 314-374.

to Alta California. Father Benito Cambón, O.F.M. was sent to Velicatá to ''ride herd'' on the shipment; he remained there as a guest of the Dominicans for some months. Extensive correspondence regarding the packs ensued; the dispute eventually reached Father Serra in Monterey and Viceroy Bucareli in Mexico City. A viceregal decree sent to Governor Barri in May, 1774, stated in part:

> And in the matter of the bales — composed of books, images, cruxifixes, and other ornaments and utensils — which are detained in Loreto, let the Governor of California be ordered not to prevent, but rather to facilitate their dispatch to the missions.

This should have solved the problem completely, but Governor Barri did not issue any enabling orders to detain the packs, but neither did he issue permission requisite to release them. This administrative dilemma is clearly shown in one of many letters from Alférez Velásquez to Father Pedro Cambón. This letter, from the Bolton Collection of the Bancroft Library, follows:

> Very Reverend Father Fray Benito Cambón:
> My dear Sir:
> I have carefully read the second letter which your Reverence has sent me, and I beg you to pardon me for not replying to the point on which your Reverence writes me a second time. But I was convinced that your Reverence, in your wise discretion, would understand that unless I had such an order I had no right to interfere in the matter of whether the loads should go or should not go; in view of this your Reverence will see that I have nothing more to say. As to what your Reverence tells me about Amador, I can say with all truth that he left me no official paper, much less such an order, and if he had left it with me I should be guilty of lying.[16]
>
> Frontier of San Fernando de Velicatá, August 13, 1784. Very reverend father, I kiss the hand of your reverence. Your humble servant,
>
> José Velásquez

[16]This was Pedro Amador, Velásquez' predecessor in command of San Fernando de Velicatá. According to his service record, found for the writer by Dr. William M. Roberts of the Bancroft Library, Pedro Amador was born about 1741, a native of the Pueblo of Veláoculco, of Spanish ancestry and in robust health. This record, prepared at San Francisco in 1790 by Josef (José Darío) Arguello, shows that Pedro Amador began his military service as a private soldier on April 15, 1764. He was promoted to corporal *(cavo)* on June 15, 1785 and advanced to the rank of sergeant on July 20, 1787. He served in the company of the royal presidio of Loreto for twenty-one years and two months; in

It appeared to Father Cambón, correctly, that Alférez Velásquez would not release the disputed packs until he had a specific order to do so. In an attempt to get such an order, he appealed to higher authority — Lieutenant José Francisco de Ortega — stating clearly not only the actions of Alférez Velásquez, but also quoting the order from the viceroy which apparently had not reached Velásquez in official form. With this information at hand, plus his higher rank, Lieutenant Ortega was able to work out a way through this morass of conflicting, misunderstood, and missing orders, while at the same time, by careful documentation, taking steps to avoid a later "backfire" either upon himself or on Alférez Velásquez. Lieutenant Ortega's reply to Father Cambón, duly witnessed and attested, follows:

> Don José Francisco de Ortega, Lieutenant-captain of the Leather-jacket Company of the new presidios of Monterey and San Diego for his majesty, whom God save:
> The document presented by the Reverend Father Fray Pedro Benito Cambón, apostolic missionary for the propagation of the Faith, has been examined by me, and I am convinced of its truth in view of its contents as well as of the decrees issued on the 12th of May by his excellency the viceroy in the royal council of war and the exchequer, and also because there are no orders to the contrary on the part of the goverment of this peninsula, as is explained by Alférez Don José Velásquez, in the replies that are presented to me. I see that in one of them this gentleman says that he does not interfere and ought not to interfere in the question as to whether those packs should go or should not go, which proves that there is no superior

that of Santa Bárbara for two years, one month, and five days; and then for three years, five months and ten days (up to the end of December, 1790) at the presidio of San Francisco. On the expedition for the discovery of the ports of San Diego and Monterey and the erection of the presidios of the same names, he was under the orders of Captain Don Gaspar de Portolá. The evaluation at the end of the service record shows that he had demonstrated valor; his application was adequate; his ability was medium; his conduct was regular; and he was married. An interesting note was appended to the record by Governor Pedro Fages: "He obeys orders although he is without intelligence regarding documents and accounts."

Pedro Amador continued on active duty at San Francisco until some time after 1800. He then retired and died in 1824, probably at San Francisco. In his honor Amador County, California, is reportedly named. A son, José María Amador (1794-1883), also a soldier, served in the campaign against the Mokelumnes in 1819.

This record apparently contains an error or omission, as Pedro Amador was repeatedly referred to as a sergeant and functioned as one for some years before 1773, although his official status, according to his service record, was *soldado*.

order to the contrary because. being in charge of this frontier, he would naturally have such an order if there were one.

Nevertheless, I think it best to send the alférez official notice of this petition, properly authenticated, so that he may at once reply in legal form whether he has had, directly or indirectly, any order to the contrary. As soon as it is ratified by his signature as the word of honor demands, I am ready to furnish the assistance that is asked of me by the reverend father president, providing the necessary escort — for the reverend Father Fray Miguel Sánchez and for those and whatever other packs may belong to the department to which I am going — in the knowledge that by so doing I shall render service to both Majesties — to God, by cooperating to improve the welfare of souls, and to the king by giving evidence of his pious zeal and generosity in liberally opening his royal treasury, and giving the royal and necessary orders for the good of his new and glorious conquest.

I so decree, order, and sign before two witnesses, Manuel Bernal and Juan de Ortega (Lieutenant Ortega's son), soldiers of my company who do not sign because they do not know how. I do this on common paper by military authority and because there is no stamped paper here — much less a royal clerk, as is prescribed by law.

Mission of San Fernando de Velicatá, August 23, 1774. I have given my oath.

Francisco José de Ortega

Alférez Velásquez promptly supplied the requested information "for the third time" in writing, properly witnessed and attested. In his letter of reply, he states "so far as I am concerned, the Lieutenant may in all security give the aid asked for by the father, for insofar as it concerns the rights of my jurisdiction on this frontier there will be no objection." Rather understandably, he requested and received certified copies of the salient correspondence. This rather lengthy action cleared up the problem of the packs insofar as the military and the Franciscans were concerned. The Dominicans, however, still had reservations. According to Palou there had been six orders from the governor to stop the packs from going — but he quotes none of them. Father Miguel Hidalgo at Velicatá claimed that he had received three orders from his father president, Fray Vicente Mora, in Loreto commanding him "under order of secrecy, by no manner or means to permit Father Cambón to take away one thread from the packs that were detained, and in case it should be attempted, to ask in legal form for the aid of the troops." This left Father Hidalgo, the only Dominican then at Velicatá, with a dilemma; so he requested a delay to allow time for his superior (Father Mora) to revoke the order of detainment which he apparently thought the governor had done earlier.

This potential deadlock was broken by the arrival of a courier with the mail. Among a number of letters which do not pertain to the immediate problem was a note from the governor to Alferéz Velásquez: "In regard to the matter of those packs about which I have written, you must not become involved or interfere, nor must any of the troops prevent them from going out, because it is a private matter between those fathers."

Velásquez read this clause from the governor's letter to Fathers Hidalgo and Cambón. Father Hidalgo immediately asked, says Palou, "According to this, if I ask you for aid to prevent those packs from going, you will not give it to me?"

Velásquez replied "No, father, I cannot give it to you, because your reverence now sees the order that I have." Because of the great conflict between the military orders received from the governor by Alferéz Velásquez and the ecclesiastical orders which Father Hidalgo had, or believed that he had, from his superior, Father President Vicente Mora in Loreto, Father Hidalgo requested and received a certified copy of the military orders to justify his non-compliance with those of Father Mora. This cleared the way for the dispatch of the packs northward to Alta California; three loads (all that there were mules for) were immediately sent to San Diego, where they arrived October 28, 1774.

Still there were delays. A request to Captain Rivera y Moncada for mules and escorts to forward the remaining packs from Velicatá to Alta California could not be complied with immediately because the captain was already under orders to make explorations in the San Francisco Bay area; he had neither men nor mules to spare. It was not until January, 1775, that sufficient mules and the requisite military escort became available. On the thirteenth of the month, a small cavalcade set out from the royal presidio of Monterey, southbound, to collect the remaining packs of the Franciscans at Velicatá and some livestock that also belonged to the Franciscans of Alta California. Everything went reasonably well on this expedition and the much-delayed Franciscan packs reached Monterey on June 13, 1775, after delays en route of more than two years. In ecclesiastical charge of this cavalcade was Father Francisco Dumetz, O.F.M., who apparently did everything right the first time.

A number of letters of recrimination resulted from this long squabble over the Franciscan packs. In these, the governor attempted, but not very successfully, to place all blame on the Dominican missionaries. Father Mora, speaking for the Dominicans, made it plain that Governor Felipe Barri was not a suitable candidate for sainthood. A lengthy and bitter war of words was forestalled by the viceroy, who recalled Governor Barri. His successor was Don Felipe de Neve who was appointed to the office on October 28, 1774; he left for his new post the following day and arrived in Loreto on March 4, 1775.[17] Governor Barri sailed from Loreto on March 26 of the same year, to the great relief of all concerned.

With the problem of the Franciscan packs cleared up, Velásquez was again free to guide and guard the Dominican missionaries on their field explorations. The approximate objective, at this time, was location of a site for a mission north of El Rosario, which would constitute the second mission in the chain of five that the Dominicans were ordered to establish between Velicatá and San Diego. These explorations took place during the first quarter of 1775, exact dates being unavailable. Two major explorations were made northward from El Rosario to the vicinity of modern Camalú. On the first, Alferéz Velásquez guided Fathers Manuel García and Miguel Hidalgo, Dominicans, to and through the area. On the second, he accompanied Fathers Miguel Hidalgo and Vicente de Mora to the proposed mission site. The place finally chosen for the mission was twenty-three leagues (approximately 58 m. or 92 km.) north of El Rosario close to the mouth of a steep-walled canyon near the eastern (inland) margin of the coastal plain. This location had been closely approached, and perhaps visited, by José Velásquez during his southerly journey from Monterey with the mail in the summer of 1770. It was subsequently visited by Franciscan missionaries and their soldier escorts in 1771 and early 1772, while they were locating the coastal route from Velicatá northward to San Diego. The proposed new mission was named Santo Domingo by Fathers García and Hidalgo.

---

[17]Felipe de Neve at the time of his appointment was major of the Querétaro regiment of provincial cavalry. He governed the Californias from 1775 to 1782, residing at Loreto in 1775-76, then at Monterey from 1776-1782. During his tenure he attempted with some success to regularize the rather chaotic government of the Californias, codify the regulations and rules, and improve official record-keeping. He was appointed inspector-general of the Provincias Internas in 1782, took part in the later phases of the Colorado River campaigns while en route to his new assignment, and died in what was then Sonora in 1784. See Beilharz, "Felipe de Neve, First Governor of California."

Although the field explorations had been completed to the apparent satisfaction of all concerned, there was still the problem of satisfying the Dominican superiors in Mexico City and the viceroy. To this end, Alférez Velásquez was asked to give his opinion on the site in writing to the Fathers García and Hidalgo:

Very Reverend Fathers:

At the request that your reverences make of me, in which you ask for my opinion of the new site explored by me in company with your reverences, I must say that I agree that the site seems to me to be well suited to the founding of a mission. In the first place it is a day and a half by road from Viñadaco, a very reasonable distance; secondly, it is located at the foot of the Sierra of Cieneguilla where many heathens are located near Valladares, San Telmo, and the Valley of San Quintín; nor is its location far from the South Sea beach (about two leagues) where many heathens gather.[18] As for fields and water the place is very desirable because, as your reverences observed for yourselves, there is an abundance of water, so much so that in some places fording is difficult. And according to the soldiers who first saw the site, there is plentiful water in the dry season, even when there have been no freshets. The farmland is very extensive; there is a single field which I myself have measured, fifteen hundred varas long and three hundred wide. To this there are joined other large fields, so it seems to me that thirty fanegas of wheat could be sown for each field, at the very least. There is

---

[18]Sierra de Cieneguilla is the original name of the high, largely granitic range now officially known as the Sierra de San Pedro Mártir. The range took its ancient name from a marshy spot in the southwestern foothills, reputedly discovered by Linck in 1766 and specifically mentioned by Crespi in his diary of the northward march to San Diego in 1769.

Valladares is a small ranching and mining community northeast of mission Santo Domingo, at Lat. 30°52′20″ N., Long. 115°41′40″ W.: Alt. 2300′ MSL. Near here in 1769 died the interpreter Manuel Valladares of San Ignacio, who was buried by Father Crespi on April 10. The sporadically worked gold mines in the vicinity of Valladares are sometimes almost profitable.

San Telmo is a broad, fertile, well-watered valley about six leagues (15 miles or 24 km.) north of mission Santo Domingo.

San Quintín is on the coastal lowland (old sea floor) bordering on San Quintín Bay, about seven leagues (18 miles or 28 km.) south of mission Santo Domingo. On the west side of the bay and on Isla San Martín (offshore to the west) are some interesting volcanic structures, of possible Pleistocene age.

South Sea beach obviously refers to the Pacific shore.

plentiful timber, much pasturage for cattle in the immediate area. The only fault I find is that strong winds blow in the region, but the surrounding hills protect the site from these winds and allow it to be more temperate. The wind is particularly violent from the northwest.[19]

With this said, it seems to me to be a site very suitable for the founding of a mission, and I sign this at Santísimo Rosario on the second of April, 1775.

José Velásquez

A second request for an opinion on the proposed site of mission Santo Domingo was received from Father President Mora several months later, and Alférez Velásquez' prompt reply to it follows:

The Very Reverend Father President, Fray Vicente de Mora:
My Dear Sir:
Considering the opinion which your reverence deigns to have from me and my soldiers, I may say that having surveyed the site which has been called Santo Domingo in company with the Reverend Fathers Fray Manuel García and Fray Miguel Hidalgo, and for a second time in company with your reverence and the said Father Hidalgo, on both occasions I found that said site has nothing that might hinder its founding. First, it has above it the high and pleasant range called La Cieneguilla in which are lodged many heathens, and they spread along both sides as far as the beach; second, firewood and water — although on this trip I saw less in various places, but where there was some, it was running and the verdancy of the grove on the said arroyo is proof of the abundance of water. Next to said site there are good places for cattle and sheep.

By virtue of this I am of the opinion that the said site is ample for founding a mission.

Santísimo Rosario, July 7, 1775.
José Velásquez

Accompanying this letter were five short certificates from Velásquez' soldiers, each approving the mission site. Signers were Pedro Amador, Claudio Victorio Félix, Sebastián de Arze, Don José Antonio Briones and Guadalupe Almaza. Pedro Amador's brief certificate follows. The others are quite similar, but not identical:

---

[19]These are the typical *katabats* of mountain regions. In clear weather the winds tend to blow downvalley from shortly after sunset to shortly after sunrise.

In view of the opinion requested by the reverend father president in regard to the condition of Santo Domingo, I state that from the experience of having passed it on several occasions, and having seen it always like on the present occasion when we finished inspecting it, it seems to me very suitable for founding the mission.

Santísimo Rosario, July 7, 1775.

Pedro Amador

With this information at hand, work went ahead on founding the new mission which was established on or about August 30, 1775, by Fathers García and Hidalgo. Official approval of the enterprise, however, was not forthcoming until January 20, 1776, as shown by an official letter signed by Felipe de Neve, Governor of the Californias.[20]

Late in 1775, plans that had been under consideration in Mexico City for considerably more than a year were finally completed, and Alférez Velásquez through his governor, Felipe de Neve, received orders to explore across the peninsula toward the northern coasts of the Gulf of California, primarily to find a seaport more convenient to the new settlements than Bahía de San Luis Gonzaga. This expedition was not an isolated episode, but was actually one part of a systematic effort to ameliorate the continuing supply problems of the Californias. As Serra and others had previously noted, transport by sailing ships was at best undependable and was inhibited by a high incidence of scurvy, which the Spanish, at that time, did not understand. Land transportation of supplies, overland from Loreto, was very costly and slow and suffered not only

---

[20]The entire file of correspondence covering exploration for the site of the new mission, opinions regarding the site, and the founding of the mission is found in the Archivo General de la Nación, Californias, Vol. 36, pp. 382-390.

Mission Santo Domingo was first established near the mouth of Santo Domingo Arroyo. Local reports (possibly correct) state that the first Mass there was celebrated in a cave. About 1798 the mission was moved approximately a league upstream to a site which had better agricultural lands and could be more easily defended. Although the Indian population at one time (ca. 1796) reached 350, the mission declined after 1800 and was abandoned about 1839. See Peveril Meigs, "Dominican Mission Frontier," pp. 22-23, 71, 153-154. The mission area is shown in DETENAL map "Santo Domingo," H 11 B 54, 1/50,000, 1974. The later mission is located at Lat. 30°46′40″ N., Long. 115°56′20″ W.; Alt. 280° MSL, approximately. Mission ruins visible today include massive adobe walls and their stone foundations on the north side of the canyon; stone irrigation works are nearby. The mission fields on the valley floor are still cultivated. The ruins of mission Santo Domingo can be reached by a bladed but unpaved road (1978), which leaves Mexican Route 1 (paved) eastward about 7.5 miles south of Camalú.

from chronic lack of mules, but also insufficient forage and a continuing shortage of arrieros. Most difficult part of the main overland route (the Camino Real), insofar as lack of forage was concerned, was the sector between mission San Francisco Borja and mission San Fernando de Velicatá. This route through Yubay, Calamajué, and Santa María de los Angeles is on the northern fringe of the central desert of Baja California. In most seasons of most years forage along this route is inadequate for even a medium-sized mule train. An alternate route, by which supplies from Loreto were brought by sea to Bahía San Luis Gonzaga and thence by mule train through Santa María de los Angeles to Velicatá was established about 1769; but it also passed through lands lacking in adequate forage. A more northerly seaport on the Gulf of California with an inland trail through more fertile lands was much to be desired.

Earlier attempts to reach and supply California from Mexico included the numerous and extensive explorations by Father Kino and his companions about 1700; the voyage of Father Consag (1746); the overland journey of Father Linck (1767); the wanderings of Father Garcés, west of the Gila-Colorado junction (1771 et seq.); and the first Anza expedition, which reached Alta California from Sonora in 1774. José Velásquez who was ordered to make a northeasterly exploration did not find the desired seaport (because none existed). It did result, however, in the first recorded "circumequitation" of the Sierra de la Cieneguilla, now known as the Sierra de San Pedro Mártir. It also achieved the first contact with a number of "heathen" Indian groups, probably the ancestors of the modern Pai-Pai and Kiliwa people who now inhabit the area, and the augmentation of geographical knowledge.

Personnel in the planned expedition consisted of Alférez José Velásquez, commander and military leader; three soldados de cuera: Luis López, Ygnacio Higuera, and Francisco Javier Aguilar.[21] This was too small a party for a journey through unknown lands and amid possibly hostile "gentiles," but because missions Velicatá, El Rosario and Santo Domingo had to be guarded and supplied, there were not enough soldiers or animals available in northern Baja California for a larger expedition.

---

[21]Unlike most military leaders of his time, Velásquez mentioned his soldiers by name. Francisco Javier Aguilar accompanied the 1769 expedition north to Monterey but did not remain in Alta California. After extensive service in northern Baja California, he was promoted to sergeant in 1795 and assigned to command the militia at San José del Cabo from 1796 to 1800.

Proceeding northward, the party left Velicatá on November 17, 1775. On this date, the second Anza expedition, which was bringing the colonists who later founded San Francisco, was westbound down the Gila Valley, near the present site of Mohawk, Arizona. At their closest approach, on November 22, 1775, the larger Anza expedition and the much smaller Velásquez expedition were only about 110 miles apart.

Major record of this expedition is a diary written by Alférez Velásquez. Although he was not blessed with the literary skills of Miguel Cervantes, Velásquez had information to convey and did so rather effectively. The diary, translated, follows:

> DIARY of the expedition made by Alférez Don José Velásquez, by superior order of the Governor of the Californias, Don Felipe de Neve, to the northern coastline of the Gulf of California, carried out in the month of November, A.D. 1775.[22]

> NOVEMBER

> On the 17th day of this month, by order of the Governor, Don Felipe de Neve, I set out to explore the northern coastline of the Gulf of California to see if I could find some shelter therein for his majesty's launches, which take supplies for the soldiers guarding these missions, that would afford closer access to them than that of San Luis Gonzaga. At the same time, I was to make a reconnaissance of a valley which I had formerly seen from a distance and reported to his Lordship.[23]

> I set out from the frontier mission of San Fernando de Velicatá on the said date, accompanied by the soldados de cuera Ygnacio Higuera, Luis López, and Francisco Javier Aguilar. After having travelled for three leagues, we made night camp.

> At sunrise on the 18th we resumed our course along the old road until 9 o'clock in the morning, when we encountered some

---

[22]Archivo General de la Nación, PI Vol. 52, p. 212 et seq. Velásquez calls this report a diary. General style suggests that it was written in its entirety after his return to Santo Domingo.

[23]From further clear descriptions in this report, it is obvious that this valley, "seen from a distance," is today's Valle de San Felipe. Velásquez' statements suggests that he made an expedition in that direction some time prior to the fall of 1775 and that a report on it remains to be found. The same statements also make it clear that Velásquez was not one of the soldiers who accompanied the Linck expedition of 1766 because that party travelled nearly the entire length of the Valle de San Felipe from south to north and returned by almost the same route. E.J. Burrus, *Linck's Diary*.

steep crags and very rocky arroyos.[24] We made night camp in a small valley with much pasturage and water . . . 15 leagues.

On the 19th we followed our course across very rugged sierras. At 10 o'clock in the morning we dropped down into an arroyo with pasturage and running water, bordered with palms and willow trees. This is the beginning of the aforementioned valley which also marks the limits of the spiritual conquest of mission San Fernando de Velicatá.[25] Here we rested for two hours and then resumed our march through this valley and along the slopes of the Sierra de la Cieneguilla (modern Sierra San Pedro Mártir) in a northerly direction. After travelling ten leagues we made night camp.

At sunrise on the 20th we resumed our course through the valley. We crossed three streams of running water and cut across numerous tracks of pagans. We caught no glimpse of them save their little huts because all of them had fled into the sierra. We made night camp after travelling 16 leagues.

---

[24]The "old road" here referred to was almost certainly the trail along the west side of southern Sierra San Pedro Mártir, first used by Father Linck and later followed in part by the Portolá expedition of 1769. Camp on the night of the 17/18 November was probably on the Arroyo Cartabón, not far from the trail between San Fernando and San Juan de Dios.

[25]The party had now crossed the southern end of the Sierra San Pedro Mártir and was now on the east side at the southern end of the Valle de San Felipe. Actual route of the crossing is not made clear, but distances given and terrain descriptions indicate that it was via the interfingering tributaries of the Arroyo del Rosario and the Arroyo Matomí. Most probable route, in consideration of the terrain, was up the Arroyo el Portezuelo (from the west) through a notch in the peninsular divide at its head and down the Arroyo Matomí. This, in its middle course, is separated from the Arroyo Parral (to the north) only by a low gravel divide. In its lower course the Arroyo Matomí is usually dry, joining Arroyo El Canelo a few miles from the Gulf via a maze of shallow distributaries; it empties into the Gulf of California at about Latitude 30'29' N. This route is south of and considerably easier than the crossing used by Father Linck in 1766. There are a number of closely adjacent workable alternative routes in the same area, all of about the same length, difficulty, and physical description. Velásquez' report of the palm canyon, for example, fits Arroyo Matomí and Canyon Parral (about five miles to the north) equally well. Southeast of this line of march is one of the reported locations of the "lost mission" of Santa Isabel, which never existed; also located along this route are one or more "ruby mines," which have produced a very few beautiful, small dodecahedral red garnets and several gold placers, which did not pay very well — as well as a number of turquoise deposits, also not very profitable. Terrain from Velicatá to and slightly beyond the crossing of the peninsular divide is shown in considerable detail on DETENAL maps "Guayaquil," H-11-D-16; "El Metate," H-11-B-86; "Matomí," H-11-B-76; and "Agua Caliente," H-11-B-66. All are to a scale of 1/50,000; all are dated 1974.

·At sunrise on the 21st we continued our journey through the same valley. After passing two watering places we followed along the course of a third and came upon two rancherías of pagans. The women having fled, only the men remained behind yelling and screeching at us from the safety of some high cliffs. These I pacified by means of signs and friendly gestures and presented them with gifts from the supply which I carried them for this purpose. This led them to believe that we were afraid of them.[26] From that point onward, they pressed close behind us, using such insolent and belligerent gestures that we were forced to resort to our weapons in earnest. With unmistakable signs I ordered them to be gone and leave us alone. They scampered to the top of the cliff, and we resumed our march through some low aand dunes that sweep down to the sea. Here the valley comes to an end in a stretch of alkali with the peaks forming a circle around it.[27] Only by the route we took is there a passage through these low sand dunes. We made night camp after travelling 20 leagues.

The whole extent of this valley is bountifully fair with pasture lands and covered with trees such as *palo melesa, uña de gato, mesquite, palo adán* and other kinds of shrubs which we were unable to identify. It has no water save that to be found in all of the arroyos which flow down from the sierra, which is very steep and

---

[26]These Indians were probably Kiliwas, a Yuman-speaking group some of whom still live on the western flanks of the Sierra San Pedro Mártir south of Valle Trinidad. See Peveril Meigs, "The Kiliwa Indians of Lower California." Since the publication of Meigs' work many of the Kiliwas have become Mexicanized, speaking clear simple Spanish, working at a variety of jobs; some acquired respectable mechanical skills and respond to Castilian courtesy. Many of them have an extreme fondness for filled glassware. Because of their adaptability, many of the Kiliwas are likely to lose their tribal identity and to "disappear" by absorption into the general population.

[27]Journey to this point was northward on the west side of the Valle de San Felipe. The various water courses mentioned are streams that flow out of the Sierra San Pedro Mártir. Most of these carry water, most of the time, in the relatively flat part of their courses where the channel is out into bedrock, near and usually west of the steep eastern escarpment of the range. East of this, the water soaks into the sands and gravels that form the floor of the Valle de San Felipe. North of Arroyo Matomí, the various streams that flow out of the sierra join, emptying into the Arroyo Parral in the southern third of the valley and into the Arroyo Huatamote in the central third, which is now known as the Valle Chico and which contains a small dune field in its center. The two main drainage channels, which carry water for a few hours every few years, join on the east side of the valley, becoming the Arroyo Huatamote, and pass through a gap in the Sierra San Felipe, finally emptying into the Gulf of California via a number of distributaries and two inlets between Latitudes 30°50' and 30°52'40" N.

rugged. Along its summits we saw many pine trees, and there must be some oak trees because some of the pagans we saw had acorns.[28] On the 22nd we continued our journey at sunrise through the same passage in the low sand dunes. Some two leagues farther on we discovered a very extensive valley which seemed to crowd the very sea out of the way.[29] Moreover, on the day before, the pagans had given us no opportunity to rest by the water, and this terrain gave no promise of any water; what with the mules about to drop from thirst, I decided to climb to the top of the last hill on our side to set us right about what we would see and to return to the sierra in search of water to satisfy our need. From the top of this hill we saw the mouth of the Colorado River at the very end of the sea. On this side of the peninsula the river becomes more and more beautiful as it spreads through some fair and verdant plains. On the Sonora side there are also some plains visible, and we were able to make out with the naked eye some small sierras that appear as if in miniature at that great distance.[30]

We had no doubt but that this was the very mouth of the Colorado River because we beheld it from a vantage point at a distance of ten or twelve leagues, more or less (actually about sixteen leagues or forty miles). But since the salt water enters the

---

[28]Velásquez' description of the valley indicates that his visit was during a very wet year, much like the fall of 1977. Some years earlier, in late 1930s, the valley floor was almost devoid of vegetation, and so dry that "even the tumbleweed crop failed." Transition from the rain-shadow desert of the valley floor to the montane forests of the upper slopes of the range is extremely abrupt, so that Velásquez' report of pine trees along the summits, and his conclusion about oak trees, are entirely valid. Vegetation and terrain of the higher parts of the Sierra San Pedro Mártir closely resembles parts of eastern Middle Park, Colorado, except that there is no known evidence of glaciation, past or present, in the Mexican sierra.

[29]This broad valley extends across the northern end of the Valle de San Felipe from San Matías Pass eastward to El Chinero, about thirty miles north of San Felipe. Its lower part, near the Gulf, is known as Llano El Chinero. Today it is traversed by a paved road, extending from El Chinero on Mexican Route 5 through Valle Trinidad to Ensenada. The northern third of the Valle de San Felipe contains a large saline playa, surrounded by sand dunes. This area, now known as the Valle de Santa Clara, once contained a large fresh or brackish lake. Preliminary studies indicate that its maximum surface area was about six times that of the modern playa; maximum depth was about 200 feet and outflow was to the southeast into the drainage of the Arroyo Huatamote. Tentative dating of this lake is late Pleistocene, perhaps 20,000 years ago.

[30]The high point climbed by Velásquez was probably the Cerro del Borrego, highest point in the northern part of the Sierra de San Felipe. From this summit (4690') the Colorado delta and the northern part of the Gulf of California are clearly visible, as is

river mouth in a bore that forms an estuary, we feared we would not find fresh water. For this reason, I decided about 2 o'clock in the afternoon to turn back and head due west. By sunset we had succeeded in reaching the sierra.

After the hour of evening prayer, we hurried alongside the bed of a dry arroyo searching for water. Having taken the lead, I fell headlong with the mule and everything into a well hidden pitfall — an animal trap set by the pagans. The soldiers pulled their mules up short in evident fear and alarm. Immediately, Aguilar rushed down to give me a hand and yanked me out of the hole, while the hapless mule was virtually buried alive with saddle, gear, and all. As soon as we had built a fire we pulled out broken pieces of dishes and also the musket; everything was now utterly useless. In order to extricate the mule, which was trembling and in danger, we had to dig a trench along side. While López, Higuera and I dug desperately, Aguilar, with his musket, guarded our rear and the other mules because the camp fires of the pagans were in plain sight. Here we passed the fearsome and never-ending watches of the night. This was some eight leagues from where we had turned back in sight of the Colorado River . . . 11 leagues.[31]

On the 23rd day, we resumed our march at dawn, crossing the very rugged sierra. At about 11 o'clock in the morning, already about to drop from exhaustion and want of nourishment, we found an arroyo with running water which had much snow along its banks. Here we rested and had our fill of the precious water. Fording many arroyos of running water, we continued our journey across this same

the entire length of the Macuata depression which extends between the Sierra de los Cócopas on the east and the Sierra Juárez on the west northward from the foot of the Sierra de San Felipe to the Cerro de la Centinela (Signal Mountain) on the international boundary. The Sonoran sierras appeared "as if in miniature" to Velásquez not only because of distance, but also because of earth curvature, which hid all but the upper parts of the ranges.

[31]This mishap took place along the headwaters of the Arroyo Teraiso, probably north of the east end of San Matías pass. During the journey northward through the Valle de San Felipe, the Velásquez party was traversing the eastern base of the mountains seen by Father Kino and his companions from high points in Sonora three quarters of a century earlier. From the summit of Cerro Borrego Velásquez looked across the parts of the Colorado delta explored by Fathers Kino and González in 1702. DETENAL maps showing the terrain crossed between the Arroyo Matomí and the Cerro Borrego include "Matomí," H-11-B-76; "Agua Caliente," H-11-B-66; "Algodones," H-11-B-56; "San Rafael," H-11-B-45; "Santa Clara," H-11-B-46; "Francisco R. Serrano," H-11-B-35; "Llano El Chinero," H-11-B-36. All are on a scale of 1/50,000; all are dated 1974.

Figure 10. Sand dunes northeast of the Valle de San Felipe. Photo by R.L. Ives.

sierra. At every ford we found rancherías of pagans.[32] On a summit we made night camp after travelling 14 leagues.

At sunrise on the 24th day we resumed our journey through this rugged sierra, all but hemmed in by the numerous pagans who lit smoke signals all about us. We were caught by nightfall in a steep walled arroyo. Here, having commended ourselves to God, we endured another dreadful night after travelling 15 leagues.

On the 25th day we continued our march through this box canyon with much hard labor, clearing great rocks.[33] On one of these, López and Higuera were thrown from their mules not two varas from the brink of a steep precipice. Miraculously, they escaped without injury. In truth, had I been alone rather than accompanied by three soldiers in whom I had great confidence, I would have turned back to San Fernando.

But thanks to the providence of the Most High, we came upon the Camino Real to the new establishments of Monterey at 10 o'clock in the morning. This was at a place between the sites of Santa Ysabel and San Raphael, just above the new mission of Santo Domingo which is 16 leagues distant. We made night camp at San Telmo.[34]

On the 26th day we arrived at this mission of Santo Domingo, where I conclude this diary, and so I sign:

Josef Velásquez (Rubric)

---

[32]Velásquez had crossed the pass of San Matías and was travelling southwest high on the western slopes of the Sierra San Pedro Mártir. Light snowfalls are frequent here during the winter season and most of the watercourses flowing west from the summit contain streams for much of the year in their upper courses. The noted presence of Indians here during the cold season contradicts some anthropological reports. Peveril Meigs, "Dominican Mission Frontier" p. 127, for example, states that the Kiliwas gathered piñon nuts and hunted deer during the warm season but retreated below the mountains during cold weather. Questioning of local Kiliwas, now largely Mexicanized, elicited the information that those who fled the missions (probably about 1830) stayed in the high country all year.

[33]Although nowhere named or located specifically, distances given and terrain descriptions most nearly fit a course about half way through San Matías Pass, then southwest across a rough upland, over a channeled area southeast of Valle Trinidad, and then into the headwaters of Arroyo Seco which was followed to its crossing of the Camino Real. Distances travelled in some of the canyons were about two and a half times airline distances due to deeply-intrenched meanders.

[34]Santa Isabel was near the site later chosen for mission San Vicente. San Raphael was south of it, probably not far from the modern settlement of the same name. San Telmo in the Arroyo San Telmo is about seventeen miles north of Santo Domingo and ten miles inland from the Pacific. It later became an asistencia of mission Santo Domingo.

From where I came, from San Fernando to the Colorado, I travelled more or less from north-northeast to north. After seeing the Colorado, we travelled due west where we met the road to the new establishments; we travelled down (south) to Santo Domingo.[35]

The returning Velásquez expedition arrived at mission Santo Domingo on November 26, 1775. Immediately thereafter, Alférez Velásquez completed his report of the journey and probably also took care of the more pressing items of paper work that had accumulated during his absence from "civilization." After November 30 and before December 8 of that year, he made the journey from Santo Domingo to Velicatá which took two or three days by muleback; presumably he was accompanied by his soldiers. On December 8 he wrote a covering letter for his report which supplies additional information. This letter follows in translation:

San Fernando, December 8, 1775.
Most Reverend Fathers Missionary of the North.
Dear Gentlemen of my highest veneration:
I am exceedingly busy at the moment so that I am unable to write Your Reverences at length, as I would prefer. But this does not excuse me from reporting the information herein contained in at least these few lines. On the 17th of last month I left here by order of my superior officer to explore the north coast and a valley that had been previously seen that lies close to that coast. Through this valley I continued my journey without encountering any obstacle, not even a small hill, until I was within sight of the mouth of the Colorado river. The river looks beautiful as it makes its way through some very lovely valleys, which I viewed from the height of a single hill at the end of my journey. I gave repeated thanks to God for the privilege of beholding those distant lands, so smooth and beckoning because of their greenery. I was able to see other small peaks, and on the Sonora border I saw some small sierras which from their great distance looked tiny.
This valley led us to this opening to the north; it lies between the Sierra de la Cieneguilla (modern Sierra de San Pedro Mártir) and the smaller one on the Gulf side (Sierra de San Felipe), which was

---

[35]DETENAL maps covering the area of the return journey include "Francisco R. Serrano," H-11-B-35; "San Rafael," H-11-B-45; "Potreros," H-11-B-44; "Camalu," H-11-B-53; and "Santo Domingo," H-11-B-54. All are to a scale of 1/50,000; all are dated 1974.

the reason why the Reverend Fathers Consag and Linck made an understandable error. The former made his observations from the sea, and the latter, from the shore; they saw the two sierras super-imposed and believed them to be one and the same. The latter saw only sand dunes and failed to find any pagans. These without exception are very numerous all the way from the frontier of the most recent Christians of San Fernando de Velicatá to the new mission of Santo Domingo where I arrived on the 26th.[36]

I followed a route from north to east both going and returning; I headed west without knowing where I might come out. I met the road to the new establishments between Santa Isabel and San Raphael, about sixteen leagues above Santo Domingo.

Here we celebrated the blessing of the mission church and the baptisms of the first two pagans, who voluntarily offered themselves. One was given the name Andrés, it being the feast day of that saint and the other, that of Domingo, after the sainted founder of Your Reverences' Order, and, of course, of the new mission.[37]

In conclusion, gentlemen, on my entire journey I saw many pines and oaks, abundant pasturage, many arroyos with running water, some snow, and many rancherías of pagans. I include no report on a likely site for a mission because I went in haste and had no time to explore on this matter, but there are suitable places near the mouth of the Colorado. Since the pagans saw us to be only four men, alone, they threatened us in such a way that we were compelled to carry arms in our hands, but thanks to God there were no injuries on either side.

May Our Lord grant your reverences many years of good health, by my earnest desire.

Your most humble servant kisses your hands.

Josef Velásquez (Rubric)

P.S.

I pray and entreat your reverences not to delay forwarding the letters that accompany this one to the lord governor and the reverend fathers, to whom I am forwarding a diary and corresponding map.[38]

---

[36]Velásquez was correct regarding Consag's observations, but very much in error regarding Linck's itinerary, which included long marches in the Valle de San Felipe as well as a crossing of the mountains to the port of the same name. This confusion is additional evidence that Velásquez was not a member of the Linck party. See E.J. Burrus, "Linck's Diary," pp. 66-92 and end map.

[37]November 30th.

[38]Original of this letter is in Archivo General de la Nación, Historia, Vol. 52, pp. 314 et seq. Unfortunately, the map has not been found.

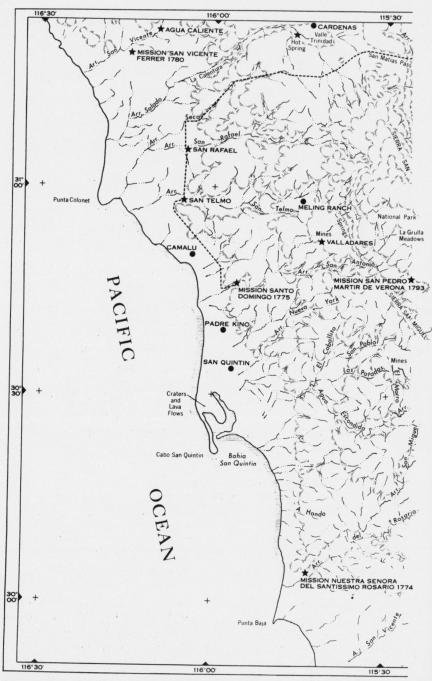

Map 1. Reconstruction of José Velásquez' 1775 route from San Fernando de Velicatá, through the Valley of San Felipe, and around the Sierra de San Pedro Mártir to mission Santo Domingo. Base maps used here are DETENAL sheets Ensenada (H-11-12), San Felipe (H-11-3), Lazaro

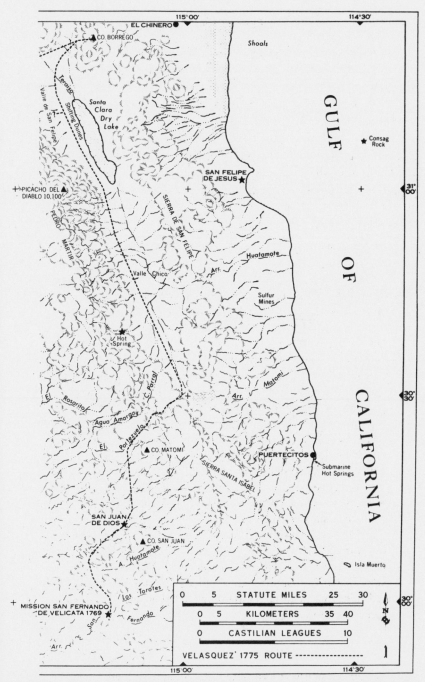

Cardenas (H-11-5, 6), and Punta San Antonio (H-11-9), all 1/250,000, and all dated 1974. Corrections through January 1, 1980 have been noted. Current status of major roads in the map area is shown on DETENAL Tourist Map, "Mexico, Northwest," latest edition.

To replace the Velásquez map, which has not been found, a reconstruction of the route of the expedition to the Valle de San Felipe comprises Map I of this work.

Although Velásquez' reports were seldom mentioned in contemporary California documents and are referred to only in passing in most modern secondary works, they were not "filed and forgotten" in Mexico City but were promptly summarized by the viceroy and sent to the Council of the Indies in Spain whence they were accessible to the king. This procedure is clearly shown by a letter from Viceroy Bucareli to the Minister of the Indies dated March 27, 1776.[39] This letter, in translation, follows:

> Most Excellent Lordship:
> My dear Sir:
> Although in letter No. 2183 I told Your Excellency of the news brought by Father Fray Francisco Garcés from the Colorado river and the good disposition of the several tribes which live there toward receiving the gospel, it seems right to tell your excellency also about other efforts of the missionary friars of the Californias and how they continue to devote themselves to the doctrines that they build up along the tribes, as I am witness to their continuing work.[40]
> I give you the news that Don Felipe de Neve, the present governor of the Californias, ordered Alférez Don José Velásquez to explore the coast north of mission San Fernando de Velicatá on the Sea of Cortés or of California. He saw from a distance the mouth of the Colorado river which he says has its course along some beautiful valleys and fields, smooth and pleasing with its green verdure.
> From the same mountain from which he observed all of this, he was able to see clearly the sierras of the province of Sonora on the shore opposite the Californias.
> He travelled with four (actually three) soldiers who went with him through a fertile valley toward the north between the range which they call La Cieneguilla and another, a small one, on the Gulf side. Father Consag made an exploration of this in the year 1746, affirming that all the land was sandy and had no inhabitants, when in fact there are many.

---

[39]Original is in the Archivo General de Indias. Guadalajara 515 (104-6-17). A copy is in the Bancroft Library.

[40]The work of Father Garcés is summarized in the historical summary.

On his return from this expedition he turned from north to west without any determined route and without knowing where he would intersect the road to the new establishments of San Diego and Monterey. He reached the road between the places of Santa Ysabel and San Rafael, 16 leagues from the mission now being built by the Dominican friars under the name of Santo Domingo.

He affirms that in the lands explored there are opportunities to establish other missions with much fruitfulness because of the numerous villages, flowing water, good pasturage and other worthwhile circumstances. He concludes his report by saying that near the mouth of the Colorado river the heathens were insolent because they saw so few men whom they then insulted and provoked. Only by brandishing their arms were the heathens kept away.

This news, along with what has already been reported concerning the founding of missions along the Colorado river, points out the opportunity of mutual cooperation between the Colorado river missions and those of the Dominican friars, thus insuring that both ends of the roadway and communication with the new establishments will be maintained.[41] This news has given me a new inducement to attempt to resolve seriously the occupation of more land, discovering ignorant tribes that live in the vast expanse between this province and the ports of Monterey and San Francisco, in keeping with my interest in the propagation of the Faith and the adding of other dominions to those that the king now possesses.

This news has not come to me so bare that I should not mention other matters that are particularly agreeable to his majesty, such is the pious desire which animates his royal intentions. This is, that in the new mission of El Rosario de Viñadaco the number of neophytes is growing every day; and in addition to the souls mentioned in the extract forwarded with letter No. 2139, there have been baptized in an event only slightly less than miraculous, two villages — one made up of a hundred souls and the other of seventy-two, both with their respective chiefs, not counting nineteen heathens who presented themselves in the month of September last, asking for baptism. The missionary fathers, Fray Miguel Hidalgo and Fray Pedro Gandiaca (from whose letters this news has been drawn), do not doubt that all the heathen from the catechism school of Viñadaco to the Sierra del

---

[41]History of the two ill-fated missions, La Purísima Concepción and San Pedro y San Pablo Bicuñer on the lower Colorado river is treated in the historical summary. Both were destroyed during the Yuma massacre of 1781.

Norte will soon recognize the mission, and it will continue converting, it may be hoped for copious fruit, which can assure greater progress.

I tell your excellency all the foregoing so that you may deign to give an account to the king, assuring his majesty that I am taking advantage of these opportunities for his successive orders.

May Our Lord guard your excellency for many years. I kiss the hand of your excellency, most reverend secretary.

Knight Commander of Malta, Don Antonio Bucareli y Ursua
(Rubric)
Mexico City, March 27, 1776

Added, on the first page of this document, is the brief notation "His majesty learned of this with particular satisfaction, July 8, 1776."

During the mid-1770s Alférez Velásquez also played a major part in at least two other expeditions into the Sierra de la Cieneguilla. For these we have only indirect evidence; the reports, which were almost surely written, have not been found to date (1978). The first of these expeditions was from Velicatá to the peninsular divide and perhaps a few miles beyond so that Velásquez was able "to see from a distance" the Valle de San Felipe. This expedition took place some time before his major trip to the valley in November, 1775. The northernmost point on this expedition was probably the dissected upland just north of the Cerro de Matomí.

The second expedition, or group of expeditions, went from mission Santo Domingo into the southwest flanks of the Sierra de la Cieneguilla to search for a mission site in that area so that the numerous gentiles there could be converted. As nearly as can be determined, this exploration took place after November, 1775, but before November, 1779. Personnel included Alférez Velásquez, Father José Ayvar, then missionary at Santo Domingo, and some soldiers. Although these explorations disclosed a promising mission site, the projected mission could not be founded as military assistance was refused. Information regarding this exploration is furnished in a letter of complaint, written by Father Nicholás Muñoz of Loreto to Governor Felipe de Neve in Monterey.[42] The letter follows:

Señor Comandante-General:

Nicolás Muñoz of the Dominican Order, apostolic missionary and minister of the royal presidio and mission of Nuestra Señora de

---

[42]Archivo General de la Nación, Californias, Vol. 71, exp. 2.

Loreto, appointed by his provincial vicar, the Reverend Father Preacher Fray Vicente de Mora, president of the missions of California, appears before your excellency, and states as follows:

Having discovered a site very advantageous for the founding of the third mission, among the heathen in the mountains near the frontier of California, as is shown by the reports of Father Josef Ayvar, missionary of Santo Domingo, of the Alférez Josef Velásquez, and of other soldiers who accompanied the officer and the father on the search for the third (site), my Provincial Vicar went to the office of the captain of the province, Don Fernando Rivera y Moncada, to ask for the necessary help to survey the site personally with the idea of establishing the mission without delay on the assumption that it would not be difficult. The captain answered that he had no authority to give such requested help.

The founding of this mission is awaited, along with two others which still remain to be established beyond the present frontier missions. There are two other sites very near the presidio of San Diego de Monterey (sic: this should be Alcalá).

Before my Order went into California the command was given, as with the two foundings that have already occurred, for which purpose the piety and zeal of our august monarch furnished five chests of ornaments for the five missions which were ordered to be established. They probably would have been already established and founded if that spiritual reform and conquest had followed with the fervor with which it began, and it had not been held back by lack of necessary assistance.

In the first year of the coming of the Dominicans into California the mission of Santísimo Rosario was founded; in the second, that of our founder, Santo Domingo; and in both, with the favor of God, spiritual and secular efforts were carried on to the extent possible through the efforts of the missionaries.

The desire for pursuing an enterprise so proper to their vocation and institution must be credited to my companions and brothers ever since they arrived on the peninsula, as I myself am witness. Far from objecting to departure from the old missions, it is not by chance that they have always been prompt to engage themselves in the conversion of these heathens. Many have asked for it eagerly, and not a few of them have remained dissatisfied, complaining to their prelate of not being able to attain it. There has been glaring, unavoidable preference for some over others, as there are not missions of this sort for all.

Our king ardently desires the bringing of those poor little ones to his happy and gentle government, and above all, the conversion of their souls to our holy faith. The meekness of these heathens makes it easy for the sowing of the word of God, and consequently the crop must yield a copious harvest.[43] The ripe wheat is abundant. The zeal of the ministers and the evangelic works do not falter (thanks to God!), from which your grace will infer that the delay in the spiritual conquest does not originate from the oversights of those friars but from lack of help. What is requested depends upon what is to be gained: these souls, and in truth, those of them who have been lost and are being lost in this short time. The missionaries will not be responsible for this, nor for the reverses caused by bad weather from which the missionaries have suffered and are suffering, because they have lacked assistance and right now need the help which I have pointed out to your grace. Even while the miserable Indians, our charge, can never aspire to such benefit from these cited reports, the requested help would lighten my superior's conscience and fulfill his just obligations, which is why I bring up the aforesaid matter, hoping for well-known justice, and for your grace, the most opportune providence on a matter concerning which the king would be much interested, and his religion for the service of God.

Friday, November 23, 1779.

Fr. Nicolás Muñoz

(Rubric)

This letter of complaint did not produce the desired military help, so the Dominicans set about other tasks. The idea of a mission in the southwestern foothills of the Sierra de la Cieneguilla, however, was not dropped, and mission San Pedro Mártir de Verona was eventually founded in the spring of 1794. Subsequently, the mountain range was renamed after the mission. There is no assurance that the ultimate location of the mission either is or is not the site discovered by Father Ayvar and Alférez Velásquez.[44] Mission San Pedro Mártir de Verona was extensively rebuilt in 1801, perhaps at a new location, and continued

---

[43]The natives of La Frontera were not as meek as Father Muñoz then thought. Later, their attacks on the missions kept the area in a state of turmoil. See Peveril Meigs, "Dominican Mission Frontier," pp. 23, 24, 122-123, 125.

[44]Ruins of mission San Pedro Mártir de Verona are located at Lat. 30°47′20″ N., Long. 115°27′50″ W.; Alt. 1540 m. MSL appx. The site is shown on DETENAL map "Santa Cruz," H-11-B-55, scale 1/50,000, dated 1974. These ruins are not accessible by ordinary vehicles. Best access is by road from San Telmo through Valladares to San Antonio, then by trail (about 15 miles) to the mission ruins. A local guide is desirable as the map is not in perfect accord with the terrain.

in operation until about 1846.[45] Mission Santo Domingo was founded on August 30, 1775.

Almost exactly five years later, the next mission in the northern chain, San Vicente Ferrer, was founded on August 28, 1780, by Fathers Miguel Hidalgo and Joaquín Valero. Although the.intervening five years were not marked by outstanding accomplishments, they were not years of idleness for either the missionaries or the soldiers. During this half decade the Dominican missionaries were kept busy maintaining the status quo at mission San Fernando de Velicatá and expanding the establishments at the newly founded missions of El Rosario and Santo Domingo. This involved not only instruction and conversion of the natives, but also establishment of farms and ranches so that ultimately, it was hoped, the missions would become economically self-sufficient. Some time was also spent in exploring new sites for missions and visitas. The soldiers, likewise, were kept busy guarding the three missions, maintaining order among the converts (some of whom were "arrogant and always inclined to do evil"), bringing supplies to the missions, carrying the mail, and convoying supplies and settlers northward from Bahía San Luis Gonzaga to San Diego. During this time, also, Velásquez made his extensive exploration of the Valle de San Felipe and made one or more expeditions into the southwestern foothills of the Sierra de la Cieneguilla to search out a location for a mission there. Hunting for runaway neophytes and returning them to the missions seems to have been a recurring task at this time.

Early in 1780 Alférez Velásquez and seven of his soldiers accompanied Father Miguel Hidalgo, missionary at Santo Domingo, on an expedition northward to a site which they called Santa Rosalía. This was apparently the same valley which had been named Santa Isabel by Juan Crespi when he passed through it in 1769. Velásquez reported as follows:

> Don Joseph Velásquez, alférez of the company of the royal presidio of Loreto, in the name of his majesty, whom may God keep, et cetera.
>
> ### DIARY
>
> of a reconnaissance made by Alférez Don José Velásquez with a corporal and six soldados de cuera, in company with the Reverend

---

[45] A brief summary is found in Zephyrin Engelhardt, *Missions and Missionaries*, Vol. I, p. 628.

Father Rector Miguel Hidalgo, on an exploration for a new mission at the place called Santa Rosalía during the month of January, 1780.[46]

This is to certify that I and my soldiers, Corporal Luis López, Pedro Amador, Joseph Miguel de Uribe, Antonio Jurias, Juan María Romero, Juan López, and Francisco Xavier Alvarado, accompanied the Reverend Father Rector Miguel Hidalgo on an exploration tour to the site of Santa Rosalía. Here a new mission can be established near the royal road to the new establishments of Monterey. The road is almost no distance from the place where the mission should be built. There is the added circumstance that water for irrigation can be easily diverted from the arroyo; the soil is of good quality and there is open country with pasturage that can well maintain all kinds of stock in excess of 1,000 head. It has cottonwood and sycamore timber, much firewood, et cetera.

On the 9th day of the present month we arrived at the site mentioned.

On the morning of the 10th day we set out to explore up the arroyo from the said mission site. After travelling two leagues, we discovered a fine stream of water. Following this stream nearly a league to the northeast, we came upon two plentiful springs of hot water.[47] Besides these hot springs, there is a stream of cold water which comes down from the sierra. From there we turned back because the terrain offered no prospect for a camp site. We named the place San Gonsalvo since it was that saint's feast day.

On the 11th day we set out in a northerly direction. At a distance of two leagues we came upon a beautiful place which we named San Jacinto, another site sufficient to support a mission.[48] There is a marsh with two hot springs at the head of a flat section of land, both fertile and fair; the water from this site finally leaves the plain by means of an arroyo. This latter is decked with sycamores and willows. The stream flows down within easy access of the mission site. One also sees some plains with such an abundance of grazing lands that they could support about a thousand head of cattle.

On the 12th day we set out to explore in a westerly direction. We found tules and an abundance of water. At a distance of two leagues we reached the sea. Midway along this distance, there is sufficient

---

[46]Archivo General de la Nación, California, Vol. 71, exp. 5. This is labelled a diary, but parts of of it were obviously written after Velásquez' return to mission Santo Domingo.

[47]These hot springs are the modern Agua Caliente on the Arroyo San Vicente.

[48]This is the modern San Jacinto, about sixty-two and a half miles north of modern San Vicente. This is close to the epicenter of the 1956 Agua Blanca earthquake.

good land to support another foundation. The arroyo here is bordered by low hills with abundant pasturage which can support three or four hundred head of cattle. From this spot at a distance of two leagues, more or less, there is another site that could serve as a mission rancho; it is known as Santa Rosalía de los Alisos.[49] Although I did not personally explore that far, it is common gossip among the soldiers who go to and come down from San Diego that with the pasturage and water they have seen two hundred head of cattle could be maintained.

On the south side of the mission site, we inspected the place known as Santa Catarina, also called El Salado, which lies on the same Camino Real, distant from the said mission site no more than three leagues.[50] According to what we have seen in the vicinity, it can support a thousand head of cattle. The spring of water at the mission site is abundant due to the amount that flows into it from the north, as we have reported.

This mission site has a great number of heathens according to Corporal Luis López and soldier Pedro Amador. The former has seen forty men with bows in one party; the latter, ninety men. Today we have seen some, and they have shown themselves most affable and gentle.

From Santo Domingo to Santa Rosalía is about 16 leagues.

This is what we have seen.

Frontier of Santo Domingo, January 15, 1780.

Joseph Velásquez (Rubric)
Jph. Mig. Yrive (Rubric)
Juan López (Rubric)
Luis López (Rubric)
Xavier Alvarado (Rubric)
Antonio Hurias (Rubric)
Pedro Amador (Rubric)
Juan María Romero (Rubric)

Worthy of note here is that every soldier who served on this expedition signed the report. When this is considered together with other soldiers' signatures on other reports, and the soldiers' certificates regard-

---

[49]This may be the modern Aguaje los Alisos in the Arroyo San Vicente, five kilometers west southwest from the ruins of mission San Vicente Ferrer.

[50]Arroyo El Salado is the next arroyo south of Arroyo San Vicente. On this arroyo a few miles upstream (east) from the crossing of the Camino Real is the fertile and well-watered valley of La Calentura, today intensively farmed and highly productive. This, reportedly, was a visita of mission San Vicente Ferrer from about 1790 until the end of the mission period.

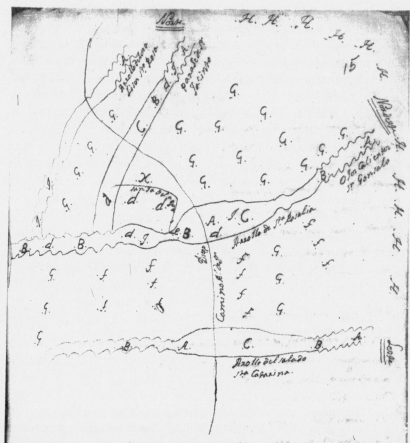

ing the suitability of mission sites, the common belief in the almost total illiteracy of the soldados de cuera would appear to need some rethinking. Accompanying this report is a sketch map in Velásquez' own hand, signed by him, and dated at Rosario, January 15, 1780. This is shown as Figure 11 with the caption translated for easier reading. Although this sketch map would probably not even receive a passing grade in a modern course in cartography (CARTOG. 1 ABC, required of all majors and minors), careful study shows that it conveys the observed information admirably. When this map is used in the field, properly oriented, all major features adjacent to old Santa Rosalía — modern San Vicente — can be located without difficulty. Agreement between the sketch map and the written descriptions is good. When this sketch map is compared to a good modern map of the same area, the agreement is excellent.[51] Thus, it appears that Alférez Velásquez' field reconnaissance here was thoroughly competent.

After the completion of the field work and the writing of Velásquez' report, an ecclesiastical report to the governor was needed. This was written by Father Miguel Hidalgo, O.P., to Governor Felipe de Neve, as follows:

---

[51]Best map currently available is DETENAL map "San Vicente," H-11-B-33, scale 1/50,000, dated 1974.

Figure 11. Alférez José Velésquez' sketch map of the Santa Rosalía site (now known as San Vicente Ferrer), showing location of springs, arroyos and arable lands. Courtesy of the Bancroft Library.

Translation of José Velásquez' caption:
"Plan of the explored site of Santa Rosalía with the arroyos around its circumference, springs of water, arable lands, pastures. Where "A" is marked are sources of water; where "B" is marked is running water; where "C" is marked the water stops; where "D" is marked there are lands for sowing; where "E" is marked is the [proposed] intake of water; where "F" is marked there are plains, mesas, and grassy valleys, serving as meadowland; where "G" is marked is the sierra; where "J" is marked there is timber; where "X" is marked should be the mission site. The Escort of Santissimo Rosario, 17th of January, 1780.

Joseph Velasquez"

Governor Don Felipe de Neve:
My Dear Sir:

Because of your excellency's command I received an order from my superior to survey the site of Santa Rosalía and, after doing so, to report to your excellency concerning its merits and its fitness for a new establishment. In satisfying this order I am addressing to your excellency the enclosed papers. In them I reveal to you the idea which I have formed regarding the stated place and its environs.

A few high points of little import separate the Camino Real from a piece of land whose center and northern end promise a fruitful harvest with a good sowing. The rest is a sandy strip and therefore unfruitful and useless. I do not have sufficient information to make a decision and give you an adequate report regarding the amount of seed that should be sown. It all depends upon how high the water is that is to be gathered for the benefit of the cornfields; only through experience will we be able to resolve this doubt with certainty. I do not consider it very difficult to introduce irrigation water to the area to begin cultivation because of the gentleness of the terrain as well as because of the slight elevation of the little hill whose edge must be skirted by the water to reach the front of the plain. This area offers a chance for the building of the most essential living quarters for the new mission. Everyone can testify to its strength. The premise which persuades us to believe in the site's permanence is that toward the northeast, while we were looking for the source of the water, we have seen several springs, especially two that we called San Gonsalvo. These hot springs add considerable increment to the water that issues from the mountains.[52]

For the necessary roofs and rafters there are some poplars of more than moderate thickness a few steps away. The South Sea is some two leagues distant from the establishment mentioned, and in the intervening distance there are various types of reeds, large streams of water, and strips of land not unsuited for a reasonable seeding.

There is pasturage in all directions, not only on the flat plains but also on the tops of the hills which surround them. One can base a prudent judgement (all things considered) that, being vigilant and helping one another charitably, all kinds of cattle will be able to be

---

[52]The hot springs at San Gonzalo are at modern Agua Caliente. Father Hidalgo changes grammatical subjects several times here. All after "Everyone ————" is a discussion of the water supply in Arroyo San Vicente.

maintained in the vicinity of the mission. The number is not possible for me to estimate with the experience that I have about similar things.

Then your excellency can assign to the mission three ranches. One is San Jacinto, a small plain with a truly pleasant view, bountiful land with some poplars, pasture, and a marsh whose water has a subterranean course as far as a tule swamp where the plain ends. This is two leagues distant to the north. At the north-northwest (as I infer from various statements) there is Santa Rosa de los Alisos.[53] I did not go to inspect it because its small water supply did not raise any hopes of finding anything very useful where it flowed, as some travellers to San Diego stated. Because of its abundant spring Santa Rosalía can be pointed out as one of the major dependencies of the mission system. The remaining one, which lies south of the mission, is Santa Catarina or El Salado. I made no effort to explore all its hidden places and brushy spots; I was satisfied to walk the length of a marsh well supplied with water, but very salty. The ground of the arroyo is also salty, and when the water oozes out, it is very nitrous.[54]

I had the joy of proclaiming the faith to several groups of heathens. It was a delight to see them as they were so joyful and obedient. Not only did they not give us the infection *(lues)* prevailing in all the neighboring region but they also went with us on our survey. Their extreme poverty and unhappiness was unbelievable. We saw a wretched woman dressed in willow bark, her language totally different from that of the Dominican Indians. If His Divine Majesty had not provided an old man who spoke both languages, she would have remained without a name from God; for which reason I asked a priest of the mission to give me a little boy of about ten years, and he granted it to me without any reluctance. He will remain to be taught at the mission until his proper time.

From the frontier (Santo Domingo) it is reckoned to be sixteen leagues to Santa Rosalía.

I remain at the disposal of your excellency; may the Lord Our God grant you life for many years to extend among these the knowledge of the True God.

---

[53]Either Father Hidalgo is confused about this location, or there has been a migration of the placename since 1780. Modern Alisos is about three miles west southwest of San Vicente.

[54]Just upstream (east) of this marshy area is the fertile and productive area known as La Calentura.

Mission of Our Patriarch, Santo Domingo, January 20, 1780.
Your Lordship's hand is kissed by your most humble servant,
Fray Miguel Hidalgo
(Rubric)[55]

Following the field explorations and the reports thereon, mission San Vicente Ferrer was founded at the Santa Rosalía site on August 27, 1780, by Fathers Miguel Hidalgo and Joaquín Valero. Shortly thereafter, perhaps in large part because of its adequate water supply and realized agricultural potential, mission San Vicente became the administrative and military center for the frontier missions. Today, the community which has grown up around the mission site is the shopping and shipping center for a highly productive agricultural district.

On September 20, 1780, Alférez Velásquez was transferred to the royal presidio of San Diego. This ended his tenure as commander at San Fernando de Velicatá, a position which he held for about seven and a half years. During this time much progress was made in the upper part of the peninsula, "La Frontera." Three new missions were founded — El Rosario, Santo Domingo, and San Vicente. A site for a fourth mission was explored, but the mission, proposed for the southwest flank of the Sierra San Pedro Mártir, was not founded until much later.

In addition to explorations for mission sites, Alférez Velásquez conducted an extensive expedition through the Valle de San Felipe, east of the Sierra San Pedro Mártir, on orders from Governor Felipe de Neve. On this journey the low pass between the Sierra de San Pedro Mártir and the Sierra Juárez (modern names) was traversed. New country, on the northwest flank of the higher sierra, was explored. Various other pieces of evidence hint at several other shorter expeditions, but complete accounts have never been found. During this time the long, drawn out administrative dispute over the Franciscan packs was finally resolved to the satisfaction of all the missionaries concerned. No comments on this matter by ex-governors Armona or Barri have been found.

According to some rather vague and contradictory evidence, Alférez Velásquez was replaced at Velicatá by a Lieutenant Diego González. As Lieutenant González was a member of the Rivera party of 1781 through Yuma, he certainly did not spend much time at Velicatá. It seems

[55]Archivo General de la Nación, Californias, Vol. 71, exp. 5.

probable, in the absence of better evidence, that he was assigned to Velicatá, but never reported for duty there. According to available records, Lt. González' only outstanding trait was total incompetence.

During Alférez Velásquez' tenure at Velicatá, both the military and the missionary establishments ran smoothly and in harmony. Written reports of both groups were in close agreement as to both fact and opinion. Neither group complained about the other; there were no reports of missionary misconduct or negligence. Likewise, there were no military deserters reported and no courts-martial. Although it is nowhere specifically documented, there is a strong probability that Alférez Velásquez' excellent record at Velicatá was responsible for his transfer to the more difficult post of San Diego.

SEGUNDO AT SAN DIEGO

When Alférez José Velásquez rode northward into San Diego in the fall of 1780 to report to his new comandante, Lieutenant José Francisco Ortega, he found many changes since his previous visit as a courier in 1770. The combined mission-presidio, which had been a cluster of hastily built huts in 1770, was now two separate establishments. The presidio, on a hillside south of the San Diego river and close to the bay, was walled and roofed. It had become the military headquarters for the southern district of Alta California, including in its care in 1780 not only mission San Diego, but also missions San Juan Capistrano and San Gabriel. The mission was now nearing completion at a new site on the north side of the San Diego river, roughly six miles up the valley (east) of the presidio. Missionary-in-charge was the experienced and competent Father Fermín Francisco Lasuén, O.F.M., who later succeeded Father Serra as president of the Franciscan missions of Alta California.

The political situation in Alta California at this time was not very happy. Almost from the beginning (1770) there had been friction between the missionaries and the military, recorded in great detail in the voluminous writings of Father Francisco Palou, O.F.M., who apparently regarded anyone not a Franciscan as anathema. As a result of this ill-feeling, in part fomented by Father Palou, Pedro Fages was relieved as military commander in 1774. His successor, Captain Fernando Xavier de Rivera y Moncada, was an experienced soldier, who had served long under the Jesuits as comandante at Loreto. He had led one of the land expeditions northward to Alta California and San Francisco bay. Unfortunately, Captain Rivera, who had reentered the military service of New Spain after retirement, was considerably past his prime. Contemporary descriptions indicate that Captain Rivera had prematurely aged and was in ill-health, suffering from fevers and leg pains. Rivera's administration was replete with disagreements, problems, and arguments, which were not all of his own making. The situation was worsened by his strong belief that the proposed mission site on San Francisco bay was unsuitable. Some time after the Indian attack on mission San Diego, November 4/5, 1775, which resulted in the death of Father Luis Jaime, O.F.M., Rivera forcibly removed Carlos, an Indian rebel, from the temporary church building at the mission. Rivera was excommunicated along with the soldiers who aided him. Thereafter, he had about as much influence as a brass magnet. His behavior, at times, was somewhat irrational, and he quarreled with all, including many who could have helped him. Early in 1777 Rivera was transferred to Loreto to serve nominally as lieutenant governor, but with a special assignment to recruit soldiers and settlers for California from mainland Mexico.[1] This assigned duty he performed faithfully.

Don Felipe de Neve, his successor, had been at Loreto for several years, now moved to Monterey where he arrived to assume his official duties on February 3, 1777. Governor Neve was an energetic officer and a competent administrator. He immediately reactivated a number of projects that had been held in abeyance during the tenure of Captain Rivera. As will be detailed later, Alférez José Velásquez, acting in line of duty, took part in some of these. Among his major accomplishments, Governor Neve regularized and codified the government of California under the "Reglamentos," an effort which led to better military and civil records, among other things. Like his predecessors, Governor Neve had trouble with the missionaries who seemed prone to make a "federal case" out of each minor difference of opinion and conflict of regulations. At times, some of the missionaries acted like an unruly junior high school class, "making things tough" for a substitute teacher.

The military forces of California at this time had their own special set of problems. Charged not only with exploration duties which in a more settled region would normally be performed by a civil government or by private interests, the armed forces suffered continually from shortages of personnel, pack and saddle animals, weapons, clothes and, at times, foodstuffs. Although by 1780 Alta California had been occupied for more than a decade, the province was far from self-sufficient. Most foodstuffs, as well as practically all manufactured items, were imported from the mainland of Mexico over long, difficult, and costly sea and land routes.

---

[1]Rivera's complete diary for his tenure as military governor of California has been published by E. J. Burrus. *Diario del Capitán Comandante Fernando de Rivera y Moncada*. There seems to be no documentary evidence that the excommunication against Rivera and his soldiers was ever lifted.

Recruitment of soldiers and settlers was also difficult. As a result, some of the soldiers were recruited from the dregs of frontier society. Their moral standards would be regarded as deficient even in Port Said. These miscreants, by forcing their attentions on Indian women, partially negated the teachings of the missionaries who had high moral standards. In natural consequence, relations between the Spaniards and the Indians were somewhat strained, and many Indians deserted the missions. This problem, according to records reviewed, seems to have been most severe at mission San Gabriel. Misdeeds of these soldiers are fully reported in the various missionary accounts and mentioned at some length in Bancroft's works. There is a strong possibility that several accounts of a single episode, reaching the chroniclers by different channels and at different times, have entered the record as a multiplicity of offenses.

The records of a large number of soldiers, probably a majority, who established families in Alta California — often with Indian wives, do not adequately detail the nature of the frontier society. This is true of missionary and military accounts. Many of these families are still in Alta California and have included in their ranks during the ensuing two centuries, five, six, and even seven generations of "solid citizens." Although the records are far from complete, and sometimes include relatively harmless fictions, many descendants of the pioneer California soldiers are numbered in the upper middle class, economically speaking. Many are engaged in highly skilled trades and professions — master mechanics, engineers, doctors, lawyers, teachers, etc.[2] After the U.S.-Mexican War of 1848, a few of the California pioneer families returned to Mexico. Many of their descendants now occupy positions of responsibility and trust in northern Mexican communities.

Military morale in Alta California was quite poor at this time as is evidenced by repeated desertions. Isolation was an important factor, coupled with a lack of Spanish women on the frontier. Married soldiers, particularly, were unhappy about long separations from their families that would last even years. "Starving time," whenever the ships from

---

[2]Some genealogical data are found in Bancroft's works, but this can now be substantially augmented from documents subsequently found. All of it needs updating, as Bancroft's copy was closed about 1885. Some corrections are also in order, particularly in privately-prepared genealogies, so that *Juana*, the wife of a Spanish soldier in 1780 is correctly described as the daughter of a Chumash sub-chief and not as "a lady of the Spanish nobility." A careful study of the old Spanish-American families of Tucson should also be productive.

San Blas were late (usually), did not help. Poor supply resulted in recurrent scarcities of liquor, chocolate, and tobacco. Suitable clothing was in short supply as were all manufactured items. To worsen an already bad situation, the pay of the soldiers was cut. This reduction in pay was supposedly offset by a lowering of the prices of supplies, but, as the "ceiling prices" were usually less than the cost of production, the net result was a lowered standard of living. Additionally, the financial affairs of the presidios were in a state of turmoil because there were not enough competent *habilitados* (quartermaster-paymaster) to keep accounts straight. When these very real problems are added to the strong anti-military feelings of some of the missionaries, it can be seen that few soldiers in 1780 regarded California as an "earthly paradise on the right hand of the Indies." Most, in all probability, echoed or paraphrased Father Jacob Baegert's unfavorable opinion: "California is the worst place on earth."

The presidio of San Diego in 1780 was the base station for twenty-five soldiers, and perhaps 125 civilians — men, women and children. Not all of these people were physically present at the presidio most of the time. The soldiers were busy carrying mail, transporting supplies, and guarding missions and missionaries, among other duties. The civilians, some of them artisans and craftsmen, were occupied with mission and presidio construction and always troubled with poor service and supply. On arrival at San Diego, Alférez Velásquez' rank almost automatically made him second in command, although he was not so designated in the records until later.

Only a few months after signing in at San Diego, Velásquez was given a series of field assignments directly or indirectly related to the founding of a civilian colony, then known as El Pueblo de Nuestra Señora de los Angeles, now known as the City of the Angels. It was for this planned settlement that Captain Fernando Xavier de Rivera y Moncada was ordered to recruit soldiers and settlers on the mainland of Mexico. Eventually and with much labor, he assembled fifty-nine soldiers, fourteen settlers (many with families), and almost a thousand head of horses, mules and cattle at Alamos, Sonora. This assemblage was divided into two groups: one, commanded by Alférez José de Zúñiga, travelled across the Gulf to Loreto, and thence by mission launches to Bahía San Luis Gonzaga; the second, led by Rivera, travelled northward through Tucson to Yuma. Both were to converge on mission San Gabriel where they would be assigned lands in the new Pueblo de Los Angeles.

Alférez Velásquez was ordered by Governor Neve to go to mission San Fernando de Velicatá to meet the party under Zúñiga and to guide them to San Gabriel. This group arrived at the mission on August 18, 1781, after an uneventful journey. Because some of the children in the party had recently recovered from smallpox, the settlers were required to camp for some time in quarantine about a league from the mission.

The overland party which was led by Captain Rivera y Moncada consisted of forty soldiers, their families, and almost 1,000 head of livestock. Leaving Alamos in early April, 1781, they travelled northward to Tucson, over trails well known and much used. After acquiring an additional military escort here, they continued northward and westward over trails explored and mapped by Father Kino and recently used by the second Anza expedition to California. They arrived at Yuma crossing in late June or early July. The expedition here was joined by a small detachment of soldiers from California; the escort from Tucson was sent back. At the Yuma settlement, on the northern or California side of the Colorado which is opposite the modern city of Yuma, Arizona, the party divided again. Thirty-five men and their families under the command of Alférez Cayetano Limón[3] were sent on to San Gabriel where they arrived without event on July 14, 1781. The remainder of the party which comprised the unmarried soldiers, the squad from California, and the leader, Captain Rivera y Moncada, recrossed the river to the Arizona side where they prepared to stay for some time while the livestock rested, grazed, and recovered from the long journey from southern Sonora.

For some time prior to the coming of the Rivera party, relations between the Spaniards and the Yumas had been deteriorating. The organization of the colony in attempting to combine mission, presidio, and pueblo was far from ideal. Supplies were inadequate, and personal relations between Spaniard and Indian were not good. Many promises were made, but few kept. Nor were gifts forthcoming. The arrival of the Rivera party with its enormous herd of livestock was a "last straw." The animals ate everything in sight, including the Indian crops. Finally, out of all patience, the Yuma people rose in revolt on July 17, 1781, destroying the two missions — La Purísima Concepción and San Pedro y San Pablo Bicuñer — murdering Father Garcés, his three missionary companions and killing Captain Rivera together with forty-six other

---

[3]There is some vague documentary suggestion that Lieutenant Diego Gonzalez was the actual leader of this party. However, because of his total incompetence, he performed no command function and left little record.

Spaniards. The other settlers, mostly women and children, were put to hard labor, but not otherwise molested. This revolt effectively closed the overland route from Sonora to Alta California. Henceforth, it was used only by well-armed parties until some time after the treaty of Guadalupe-Hidalgo (1848).

News of the Yuma massacre reached Tucson rather rapidly by the "Indian telegraph." An escaped captive brought the news to the royal presidio of Altar, Sonora. After a preliminary reconnaisance which apparently resulted in several casualties, Lieutenant Colonel Don Pedro Fages was sent northward from Pitic with a small company of soldiers. He left that presidio, which today is the site of modern Hermosillo, Sonora, on September 15, 1781. Marching rapidly northward, he arrived at the royal presidio of Santa Gertrudis de Altar on September 28, having had minor troubles en route with Indians who were believed to be Seris. At Altar Fages acquired more soldiers and supplies, and his expeditionary force was joined by Captain Pedro de Tueros, commander of that presidio. By long, rapid, and difficult marches, the company, now numbering about 100 Spanish soldiers, crossed the Papaguería in almost a straight line from Altar to Gila Bend, acquiring Indian allies on the way. Progress down the Gila Valley was relatively uneventful, and the punitive expedition arrived at the Yuma Crossing on October 18. Although the Yumas outnumbered the Spaniards by perhaps 30 to 1, several skirmishes were fought. Many captives were rescued and the bodies of the dead were buried, including the remains of Captain Rivera y Moncada. Leaving the Colorado river on October 21, the party retreated to Sonoyta (Sonora), from where the rescued captives were sent on to Altar for debriefing and repatriation.

While the tired and dehydrated animals were recovering in Sonoyta, new orders were received. In obedience to them Fages again took his troop across the Camino del Diablo to Yuma, leaving Sonoyta on November 23. On this second foray, he rescued more captives of the Yumas, buried more dead, found the remains of the four martyred Franciscans, and recovered three of the four mission bells. This accomplished, the expedition returned to Altar, arriving at the frontier post on Sunday, December 30, 1781. The main body of troops camped at Pitic de Caborca (modern Pitiquito) during its layover in Sonora.

News of the massacre reached Governor Neve in Alta California via Alférez Cayetano Limón, who came upon the scene while returning to

Sonora. After convoying the soldier-settlers and their families from the Yuma crossing to California, Limón with his small detachment started eastward over the Anza trail toward Yuma. En route, perhaps at San Sebastián, he heard reports of the massacre from local Indians. Proceeding forward cautiously, he left his supplies in charge of two soldiers and went to the Yuma site where he saw ample evidence of the carnage. Returning westward, he found the two soldiers guarding the supplies dead. Limón had to have engaged in several skirmishes en route during which he and his son, among others, were wounded. On August 30 he brought word of the massacre to Governor Neve at San Gabriel. Then Alférez Limón was sent southward by way of Baja California to carry the unhappy news to Mexico.

At the time the Fages expedition was being readied at Pitic, Teodoro de Croix had advised Governor Neve to assemble all the soldiers he could spare and hold them in readiness for action against the Yumas, when needed. This he did, augmenting the twenty-nine troopers destined for the Santa Barbara garrison with eight or ten men from the presidios of Monterey and San Diego. Alférez José Velásquez led the detachment from San Diego. A brief report by Governor Neve gives the makeup of this special task force.[4] As planned, it consisted of one lieutenant, one alférez, two sergeants, two corporals and forty-six private soldiers. As it worked out, the lieutenant, who may have been Diego González but was not mentioned in the field reports, performed no function; and he may not have been physically present at all. The alférez, José Velásquez, apparently was de facto commander of the task force. The two sergeants were Miguel Rivera y Guevera and Mariano Verdugo. The names of the corporals and private soldiers are not readily available. This special task force functioned for about ten months, and then it was disbanded toward the end of the campaign against the Yumas.

Late in February of 1782, Governor Neve sent Alférez Velásquez, with an interpreter and twelve soldiers, eastward toward the Colorado River to determine if Fages had reached the north bank. If so, he was to coordinate military actions against the Yumas. Although we have no diary of this expedition, a fragmentary and somewhat garbled secondary

---

[4]Neve to Commanding General, Provincial Records MS ii 68, p. 285, dated Nov. 28, 1781.

account of it by Governor Neve supplies useful information.[5] It is certain that Velásquez reached San Sebastián (on San Felipe Creek near modern Harper's Well), but it is not as certain that he reached the Colorado. From the Indians at San Sebastián, he collected a condensed and incomplete account of the Yuma massacre that included mention of:

> black and white men on horseback, armed, who had come four moons ago (including that of March 2). These men crossed the river, went toward the lake, and from there went higher upstream, burning houses, killing some Indians, and freeing some captives. Then they went away. Palma escaped into the mountains.

Date of this visitation can be computed from the Indian information. On the night of March 1-2, the moon was substantially full. Counting back three more full moons, to make a total of four including that of March 1-2), brings us to December 2, 1781, at which time Fages was at Yuma on his second foray. He had arrived November 29 and departed December 13. The acts of the "black and white men," as many of the frontier soldiers were of decidedly mixed racial ancestry, were reported by the Indians of San Sebastián almost exactly as those reported by Fages in his detailed diaries so that the material quoted above is quite surely an Indian account of the acts of the second Fages Expedition at Yuma.[6]

Bancroft, who did not see Fages' diaries, classed this report as an "unintelligible rumor".[7] When the report is compared with the diaries, their substantial identity becomes obvious. It is notable that this report, even though transmitted by "Indian telegraph," twice translated, and paraphrased by Governor Neve or by one of his clerks has retained the major part of its factual content.

During the winter of 1781-1782 there were a number of military conferences in Sonora at which the reports of Fages were considered favorably; future plans were drawn. Eventually it was decided that Fages would journey to California with his troop to join forces with Governor Neve and to attack the Yumas from the west. At the same time a troop

[5]Neve to the Commanding General, San Gabriel, March, 1782, Provincial Records MS ii 76-78, p. 294.

[6]H. I. Priestley, "The Colorado River Campaign 1781-1782: Diary of Pedro Fáges," *Publications of the Academy of Pacific Coast History*, Vol. 3, No. 2, May 1913, pp. 31-56. Further descriptions of these extensive campaigns with additional references are given in the historical summary.

[7]H.H. Bancroft, *Early California Annals*, pp. 367-368.

from Sonora under command of Pedro de Tueros from Altar would march to Yuma to attack the rebellious tribesmen from the east. The date of the combined attack was set for April 1, 1782. In obedience to these orders Fages with thirty-nine soldiers marched northward from Pitic de Caborca (modern Pitiquito) on February 27, 1782. Making rapid progress, he passed through Sonoyta on March 2, crossed the Colorado River on March 11, and arrived in San Gabriel on March 26 after a difficult but uneventful journey.

When Fages arrived at San Gabriel with his troop, Governor Neve was absent, being occupied with work on the many times postponed founding of settlements along the Santa Barbara channel northwest of the mission. Notified of Fages' arrival by courier, Neve returned to San Gabriel and, after considering the situation and his orders, decided that April was no time for a military action at Yuma. As he correctly pointed out, the river was high and difficult to cross at that season. Neve decided to postpone the attack until September 15, when the water would be lower. This created a new problem — the Sonoran troops were waiting on the south bank of the Colorado and would have to be notified of the change of plans. To do this, Fages with ten soldiers from Sonora and ten from Monterey rode east from San Gabriel, leaving on April 2. They contacted the Sonoran troops at Yuma on April 13. A few minor skirmishes with the Yumas ensued, but they were able to begin their return the next day. Because of reported Indian unrest in the mountains east of San Diego, Fages returned to San Gabriel by an entirely new route, turning southwest at San Sebastián. He crossed the Cuyamaca mountains via Carrizo, Vallecito and Oriflamme canyons, and the valley of the San Diego River. Fages was the first European on record to travel directly from Yuma to San Diego. At the presidio of San Diego he met Lieutenant José de Zúñiga, the commandant, and his second-in-command, José Velásquez, who apparently had returned there shortly after his journey toward the Colorado River in March. From San Diego Fages returned to San Gabriel via the Camino Real, a trail most familiar to him. Details of this journey and references to the original documentation are given in the historical summary in this book. Fages then made a trip northward, visiting Santa Barbara, Monterey and San Francisco, before reporting to San Gabriel again where he organized the postponed campaign against the Yumas.

Early in August of 1782 final plans for the attack on the Yumas were completed. In California Governor Neve assembled twenty mounted soldiers including Alférez José Velásquez. He was joined at San Gabriel by Pedro Fages with the thirty-nine men who had accompanied him from Sonora. This complement left the mission on August 21 and Neve followed with his men on August 26. Both contingents travelled eastward on the now well-worn Anza trail. At about the same time in Sonora some 100 mounted men commanded by Captain Joseph Romeu of the royal presidio of Altar set out for the Colorado with instructions to take no action until they contacted Governor Neve at Yuma.

Some days and some leagues east of San Gabriel at the Paraje de Saucito, Neve was met by a courier who brought important orders from Sonora.[8] The new orders changed all the plans for the attack on the Yuma rebels. Effective immediately, Governor Neve was promoted to Inspector General of the Provincias Internas; Pedro Fages was designated to replace him as Governor of California. The actual change of command took place at San Sebastián, a few miles downstream (east) of Saucito where there was ample water and adequate forage. Alférez Velásquez, the only other officer present, certified the change of command:

Don Joseph Velásquez, alférez of the cavalry company of the royal presidio of San Diego of the peninsula of the Californias:
I certify that on the day given below at the place of San Sebastián on the Colorado River Road, Señor Don Felipe de Neve, Colonel of the Royal Troops, was governor of the said peninsula, and on the day set for the general inspection of the veteran troops of the Internal Provinces of New Spain including those of the Californias, he put into possession of his government Señor Lieutenant Colonel Don Pedro Fages, of provisional rank, by virtue of the superior orders of the Commandant General, Cabellero de Croix, of July 12 last of this year. Consequently the aforesaid inspector delivered to him several papers and documents relating to the government, and by his orders I gave recognition of such a provisional governor of the said peninsula of the Californias to the aforesaid Señor Lieutenant Colonel Don Pedro Fages, successor to the troops of the presidios of the peninsula which are included in this detachment. By me there are delivered to Señor Fages the orders that the inspector addresses to all the presidios of the peninsula in order that they may be carried out in the same conformity with the foresaid

[8]Saucito is the place of the little willows, most probably a willow grove that is now overgrown by tamarasks just below Santa Catarina Springs in Coyote Canyon.

act of acknowledgement, and in order that it may be recorded I have signed it. These were the witnesses: Sergeants Miguel Rivera, volunteer of Catalonia, and Mariano Verdugo from the presidio of Monterey; they have signed with me, requiring no proof of greater authority for this act. The situation has been verified so that the new governor may return to the peninsula.

Place of San Sebastián. September 10, 1782.

Joseph Velásquez

Present, Miguel Rivera y Guevera

Present, Mariano Verdugo

This is a copy of the original which I verify. Arizpe, November 4, 1782.

Cristóval Corvalán

(Rubric)[9]

With the technicalities and legalities of the change of command out of the way, Governor Fages went to Monterey via San Diego to assume the duties of his new office. He apparently travelled alone as there is no mention of companions, and the number of soldiers in the Yuma-bound detachment did not diminish after Fages' departure. Neve continued southeastward, arriving at the Colorado River on September 16 and carried on a most desultory campaign for more than two weeks. Results of this were indecisive and disappointing. Perhaps forty Yumas were killed out of an estimated population of 3,000.[10] Spanish losses included four soldiers wounded, none very seriously, and forty-nine horses and mules, some by enemy action. After the departure of Fages, Neve seems to have lost interest in the campaign. The major part of the fighting was done by Sonoran detachments under the command of Captains Romeu and Tueros. Neve terminated the campaign at Yuma on October 3, 1782, sending the California soldiers led by Alférez Velásquez back to the coast, along with California's share of the surviving pack and saddle animals (sixty-five horses and twenty-three mules). Return from San Sebastián was via Carrizo, Vallecito and Oriflamme canyons to Cuyamaca, thence west to the San Diego River and the presidio, as Velásquez stated in a later report. Neve travelled southeastward from Yuma, stopping for a rest at Sonoyta (Sonora) where he prepared a report of the military expedition against the Yumas for Croix:

---

[9] Archivo General de Indias, Guadalajara, 283 [103-5-2]. Copy in Bancroft Library.
[10] J.D. Forbes, *Warriors of the Colorado*, pp. 217-219.

My Dear Sir:

In fulfillment of the higher orders which your grace deigns to confide in me, the command of the expedition intended for the just punishment of the rebellious Yuma tribe, I herewith present the following report.

In the morning of last September 16 I arrived at the Colorado River at the head of a detachment of thirty-nine men which Lieutenant Colonel Don Pedro Fages had led to the Californias. With them were nineteen soldiers, a sergeant, and a subaltern (Alférez Velásquez) from the presidios of the said peninsula.

I located my camp in the ruined Pueblo de la Concepción on the north bank.[11] On the opposite bank I found Captain of Dragoons Don Joseph Romeu encamped; he had arrived (from Sonora) with the troops in his charge. They were composed of 108 men, a captain (Pedro de Tueros) and three alféreces on the fifteenth of the month mentioned above.

On the same day I ordered rafts to be built because no ford had been found. When this was done, Captain Don Joseph Romeu, two alféreces and forty men with one *pedrero* were transferred from the south to the north bank.[12] This task could not be completed until the twentieth because the strong current and the eddy that formed at the landing hindered the course of the rafts. The horses went across with troops at the same time and it was necessary to revitalize both camps with a long rest period.

No Yuma could be captured by the reconnaisance squads which spread out to the north and south as far as two leagues from camp. Consequently we did not get any definite news of the condition of the Yumas. On the 11th of said month the Yumas were sent by Ignacio, brother of Salvador Palma,[13] and the traitor interpreter, Francisco Xavier, to fight the Jalchedune tribe and to rob them of the old lands of Bicuñer.[14] They had established themselves and were

---

[11]This was the settlement associated with mission La Purísima Concepción, atop what is now known as Mission Hill, directly across the Colorado River [north] from the modern Yuma townsite.

[12]This light artillery piece is known as a swivel gun in English speaking countries.

[13]Salvador Palma was a Yuma chief who had been a friend of Juan Bautista de Anza. He is credited, perhaps incorrectly, with leading the attack on the Colorado River settlements on July 17-18, 1781.

[14]Bicuñer was several leagues downstream from La Purísima Concepción and was destroyed at the same time. Exact site of Bicuñer has not been recovered, but it was apparently near modern Algodones, Baja California Norte.

farming new lands which had belonged to other Yumas from Puerto de la Concepción to Bicuñer, adjacent to the land of the Cajuén tribe.

From the 21st to the 23rd in the southern sector, some 600 to 700 Jalchedunes and Cocomaricopas joined; six of their chiefs went to the north camp to bring themselves to me, claiming to be allies in the attack on the Yumas. I told them where the two tribes should be posted as it was my intention to align them on both sides at sunset. I was able to march at ten-thirty that night with the captain of dragoons, two alfereces, two sergeants, three corporals, fifty-three privates and twelve auxiliary Pimas. At two forty-five on the morning tf the 24th I found on the road about four hundred Indians of the two tribes. I was obliged to make a short halt to persuade them to follow on to their appointed destination to prevent their joining or mingling with the troops as they might have done. At three forty-five I continued the march, sending a small squad to see whether the Yumas, Jamajabas (Mohaves), and Camellares were in the ranchería of Bicuñer where they were believed to be. It proved to be abandoned.

I continued toward the Lake of Eulália, but the old road was impassible because it was too brushy. Instead, I followed a road which led me to the land of the Cajuenes. Coming upon some tracks of the enemy, the troops and I followed them.

There was a confused crowd of Jalchedunes and Cocomaricopas at the edge of the dense underbrush; no effort expended seemed sufficient to separate them or to avoid mixing one tribe with another. I succeeded in making some of them advance, but they retreated shortly afterwards and fled from the attacking enemy. We were able to see five horsemen fleeing as soon as they saw the troops, who had halted on a little plain. From there I sent a squad of eight soldiers and twelve Pimas under the command of Alférez Rafael Tovar to scout the ground they were following (I mean the road), fighting on its flank. On this road there followed a part of the Jalchedunes and Cajuenes without going into action, rather they avoided it.

A moment later six shots were heard. At once I went to help the party that was pursuing the enemy in flight. The enemy had sought safety at the river and were crossing a very large muddy lagoon which the foresaid alférez had reported to me as being very near the ranchería from which they were retreating. Confronted with the question of having disobeyed my order, he told me that the enemy had attacked him and that they had hidden themselves in a little woods. But he considered the critical moment lost so that it the would be impossible to attack or inflict injuries on the Yumas and their allies, even though the lake might have been circumvented. Because they had taken refuge in the woods so near the river, obstacles impassible to our troops, they could mock our every effort. At this same time I wanted to detach 400 Indians from the friendly tribes that surrounded us because I had become distrustful of them, having seen certain inconsistencies such as the fact that those who accompanied Alférez Tovar had not shot a single arrow at the Yumas. I decided to return to camp.

There I found that the Jalchedunes had falsely reported that the enemy was coming in great numbers to attack the encampments. Captain Don Pedro Tueros had been obliged to order that the horses be assembled close to both camps and preparations had been made to repel the attackers.

On the 25th two Cajuen chiefs appeared before me. They suggested that as their people passed along the south side of the river we attack the enemy on the morning of the 28th. I had to suspend everything that came first, and I explained what they should carry out that they should return to their tribe to prepare to attack the Yumas. With this understanding the troops were to go to support them. For this purpose Captain Don Joseph Romeu was chosen to lead a detachment made up of an alférez, a sergeant, and forty men with twelve Piman auxiliaries. But the commander, not finding the Indian, Joseph Antonio, at the place pointed out, went on to the ranchería of the Yumas. He attacked and killed many of them as your grace will note from the attached account which relates the special circumstances and events of the action. I can not give a detailed account of the number of those killed, but surely this same fate befell Ignacio, brother of Salvador Palma, who was the most respected of the tribe and commander of all actions of war. Four soldiers came out slightly wounded; three horses were left behind, lost in the lake with harness and equipment. I understood that it was certain that once the troops were withdrawn, the rebel tribe would flee and join Salvador Palma. Accompanied by the old men, some women and children, he had taken shelter in the rough hills of Bicuñer.[15]

Day by day the horse herd was deteriorating. The continuing loss and the deaths of the animals led me to decide that the California troops should be withdrawn together with some of the fresh horses on the 30th of September.

On the 29th I went to the south side of the river where I found a ford that the troops who had been occupying the camp at La

---

[15]These hills are now known as Pilot Knob.

Concepción might cross on the 1st of October. I decided that the united expedition ought to send its troops back to their designated posts, leaving the Colorado on the 3rd of the same month. I did the same the night of the 2nd. However, reflecting on the fact that we had only scant signs that the Yumas had escaped, I decided to pursue them until greater punishment had been inflicted. I returned to dispatch Captains Don Joseph Romeu and Don Pedro Tueros with one alférez, two sergeants, fifty-eight soldiers and twelve Pima auxiliaries. This happened on the 7th; the orders were to attack the enemy if they were found in their rancherías. If not, then they were to surprise them in the land of the Cajuenes at the place of the big house where we had been told they would be found by two Jalchedunes. The Yumas' departure from the river was the only thing that could be ascertained, since the north bank was followed toward the west for some eighteen leagues but not a single Indian was found.

With this assurance, I departed with an escort of thirty men on the 12th of the present month, advising Captain Romeu to do the same the following day with the remainder of the troops and scouts. I figured that he would reach the presidio of Altar between the 26th and the 30th.

Previous expeditions that were made to the Colorado River and the incidents that occurred in them hindered the attainment of favorable results which could have been realized while carrying out the just punishment of the ringleaders and the rebelling Yuma tribe, leaving them subjugated and keeping communication to the river free. Despite the many deaths that were inflicted on the enemy by hostile action, they still faced our expeditionary forces with a sense of trust, and it was this same trust that was the exact means by which we could maintain ourselves among them so as to reach our goal of gathering the ringleaders and capturing them. This was tried on the second expedition without due delay because the enemy was growing suspicious; the only thing we accomplished though the means which we had judged to be useful was to reveal our intentions by the inopportune staging of two ambushes during which we tried to fence them in. But the ringleaders were not together; Palma and Francisco Xavier were located on the south bank, and Pablo and Ignacio on the north one. We did not attain either the capture or death of any of the tribe *(sic!)*.

This happened at the very time that they had delivered the last woman prisoner. We had behaved towards them in good faith, and we recognized that they stood in the greatest fear with no confidence in our making peace although they were asking for it. There are no means available or adequate to attract them, and without such means their capture is impossible. The capture of ringleaders in a countryside where one cannot pursue them because of the shelter it affords is difficult. The troops cannot remain without destroying their horses in a short time because of the lack of pasturage; even where there is some pasture the emptyness and instability of the river banks threaten the loss of the animals. I have experienced this on the north bank where almost immediately the horse herd from California ran into difficulty because although it had much pasturage, there was not much room for exercise.

At a more opportune time, when the expeditionary troop has returned to the presidio of Altar, I will give an account to your grace with the diaries. The events mentioned above caused me to send this information at once; I must add that on the march to the Colorado River forty-five horses and four mules from the remount were lost. Several head of both species were lost and they died there. I distributed the rest, assigning to California sixty-five horses and twenty-three mules. At a convenient time I will send to your grace a formal accounting.

May Our Lord grant many years to your grace.

Ranchería of the Papagos of Sonoitac; October 17, 1782.

Your grace's hand is kissed by his most attentive servant,

Felipe de Neve

To Commandant-General, Cavallero de Croix. [16]

This disjointed and internally inconsistent report, prepared by Felipe de Neve at Sonoyta, appears to be a rough draft prepared by a tired, sick or confused man. Despite its lack of literary quality, however, the report makes it plain that the last Yuma campaign did not accomplish much of importance. After completing his preliminary report of this campaign at Sonoyta, Neve travelled southeastward to Arizpe, then the capital of Sonora, to assume his duties as Inspector-General of the Provincias Internas. Although he almost certainly stopped over at the royal presidio of Altar, no record of this has been found. He was promoted to commandant-general of the Provincias Internas on February 15, 1783, and spent the remaining months of his life wrestling with the problems of an overextended, undermanned, and inadequately supplied frontier. Neve died November 3, 1784, at what is now Flores Magón, Chihuahua.

---

[16]Original report is in Archivo General de la Nación, Guadalajara 283 [103-5-2]. Copy in Bancroft Library. In making the translation sentence structure has been rearranged to improve clarity.

Neve's criticism of earlier operations at Yuma is characteristic of his later years. While an officer of the Provincias Internas, he wrote many denunciations and criticisms, unfortunately basing some of them on incomplete, obsolete, or erroneous data. One of the principal targets of his spleen was Juan Bautista de Anza who deserved better treatment.[17] Not long after his return to the presidio of San Diego with his troop from the Yuma campaign, Alférez Velásquez was ordered south with thirteen soldiers to escort and guard supply trains coming north from mission San Vicente. The Indians of that area, who were apparently "good Christians" only when watched closely, had repeatedly harassed and attacked the mule trains bringing supplies up the peninsula. On this specific assignment the Velásquez party was attacked by heathens who set fire to the grass where the men camped and started grass fires in front of the advancing party. Although documentation is not as detailed as might be desired, this kind of trouble was fairly standard between San Vicente and San Diego. At one time, the attacking Indians killed a Spanish corporal. Governor Neve had plans to reroute a portion of the trail, apparently putting Alférez Velásquez in charge of the exploration. Before the plan could be carried out, however, Neve was promoted and transferred. Trouble in this section of the Camino Real was not greatly reduced until the Dominicans founded missions San Miguel (1787) and Santo Tomás (1791).[18]

In May, 1783, Alférez Velásquez received orders from his commanding officer, Lieutenant José de Zúñiga of San Diego, to reconnoiter the country east of San Diego to locate a possible southern route to the Colorado River as suggested by Father Lasuén. Such a route involved a crossing of the Laguna and Cuyamaca Mountains, a northern extension of the granite-cored Sierra de Juárez of Mexico with some crests rising over 6,000 feet only thirty-five miles from the seacoast. Complicating travel in this area are the steep fault scarps on the east sides of the ranges, separating them from the below-sea-level desert, now known as the Imperial Valley. A trail of sorts connecting Yuma with San Diego via San Sebastián was known to the Spaniards prior to 1783, parts of it

---

[17]E.A. Beilharz, *Felipe de Neve: First Governor of California*, (San Francisco: California Historical Society 1971), p. 158 et seq.

[18]H.E. Bolton, "In The South San Joaquín Ahead of Garcés," *California Historical Society Quarterly*, Vol. X, No. 3 (Sept. 1931) pp. 211-219.

having been traversed by Fages in 1772.[19] He used the trail twice in 1782, travelling from San Sebastián to San Diego. Alférez Velásquez used it again in the fall of 1782 while returning from the Yuma campaigns. Various missionaries and soldiers had also travelled parts of this trail in the course of their official duties.

The more direct route from San Diego to the Colorado River envisioned by Father Lasuén was not actually established until the early years of the twentieth century. Then, by use of industrial explosives and powered earth-moving machinery a road was built from San Diego to Yuma. This, with many rebuildings and reroutings, has become modern Interstate Highway 8 which connects San Diego with Casa Grande, Arizona. A few miles to the south in Mexican territory, a similar road was constructed from Tijuana to San Luis del Río Colorado. With further work, this has been extended eastward through Sonoyta and now connects Baja California del Norte with the road system of mainland Mexico. A railroad, the San Diego and Arizona Eastern, was also constructed in this area and connects San Diego with El Centro in the Imperial Valley. Both roads and the railroad are continually in need of extensive and costly repairs due to flood damage. Although the rainfall in parts of the area averages only about five inches a year, several years' quota may fall in a single day. With steep grades and little vegetation runoff is extremely rapid and powerful enough to convert reinforced concrete structures to piles of rubble in a matter of minutes. Because of repeated flood damage to the right-of-way the San Diego and Arizona Eastern Railroad has been inoperative for more than two years (prior to 1979) and has been abandoned for economic reasons.

Alférez Velásquez' expedition into the San Diego back country was the first official attempt to explore a direct trail over the coast ranges to Yuma. Approaching the Cuyamaca Mountains from the southwest, he traversed the summit area nearly to the eastern escarpments. Looking down upon familiar trails coming in from the east, he decided that the proposed route was not feasible and returned to San Diego via the Cuyamaca Lake area and the San Diego River. The diary of his journey, forwarded to Governor Fages by his commander, Lieutenant José de

---

[19]See historical summary for further details and references; also H. E. Rensch, "Fages' Crossing of the Cuyamacas," *California Historical Society Quarterly*, Vol. XXXIV, No. 3, (Sept. 1955), pp. 193-208. Because of the excellence of Fages' original narratives the various independent studies of his itineraries are in very close agreement.

Zúñiga, and which accompanied the map of the mountain area east of San Diego, reads as follows:

1783, June 22, San Diego

José de Zúñiga to Fages, concerning a reconnaissance of a route to the Colorado River by Alférez Don José Velásquez. His return. Includes a diary of his journey and the plan of the mission of San Diego:

He reports that Alférez Don José Velásquez set out from that port on the 30th of last May to reconnoiter the way to the Colorado River through that part of the country which the Reverend Father Fermín [Lasuén] had observed, and his return on the 3rd of June. Furthermore the accompanying diary adds a statement of the effective forces and lists the utilization of the troops during the present month. Here is the diary to which reference has been made:

In compliance with the order which my Commandant Don Joseph de Zúñiga gave me on May 30th last to reconnoiter the way which, by report of the Indians, was said to be convenient for crossing over the sierra, I set out from this royal presidio at sundown on the same day.

We went by way of the ranchería of Las Choyas and slept after travelling four leagues, which I note in the margin.[20]

The 31st, at sunrise, we resumed our march by a good road. We rested near the village of Natoma: 8 leagues.[21]

Leagues

4

8

5

4

21

At three in the afternoon the march was resumed by a poor road with [steep] grades and rocks. We slept at the place called "La Madera," according to the Indians: 5 leagues.

---

[20]This village of Indians was along the bay shore west of the Camino Real and apparently extended from just north of Chollas Creek to a point somewhere south of the Sweetwater River. Location is shown on Pantoja's map of 1782, reproduced in Bancroft, *Early California Annals*, p. 456. Remaining archeological evidence suggests that this site was occupied for many centuries.

[21]Natoma, according to distances given, was somewhere near the head of the Otay Valley, perhaps three miles northwest of modern Dulzura. Aboriginal inhabitants of this area seem to have lost or abandoned a large number of metates.

This place is a small valley; its middle part, a plain surrounded by higher portions, and on two borders it has piñon pine trees. Although this might be good timber, it could not be brought out because of the distance and the bad road.[22]

There we came upon a ranchería. Its chief told me where the pass or path was for descending on the other side. He pointed out that there were two ways, one by the north and the other by the southeast. I asked him if he wanted to give me a guide to follow the latter path. He and two others, to whom I gave gifts, got ready quickly, and on the first of the month we resumed our march through very hilly and rough country. We bore toward the north. At four leagues we met the descent by the same route that comes from San Sebastián, near the up-grade to Cuñama, as will be seen by the plan on page 74.[23]

Having recognized beyond any doubt where we were, I did not want to descend because I well remembered that when I came from San Sebastián (fall, 1782), I had wanted to climb up this same grade and could not.

When I had decided to turn back, I asked the heathen Indians if they knew whether there was any other trail to the south. They answered, "No," whereupon I determined to turn back. I asked the soldiers by what way they wanted to return. They all answered, "By San Luis, so as not to go over again the distance and bad ground we had covered." I realized that they were right because from the presidio to the crest of the sierra by the way we took is twenty-one leagues, rather more than less, and from the said crest to here (presidio of San Diego) by the San Luis route would be fourteen or fifteen leagues at most.[24]

---

[22]This is an excellent, terse description of the modern Corte Madera Valley. Topography is shown on the U.S. Geological Survey map "Descanso," 1/24,000, 1960. The small lake in the bottom of the Corte Madera Valley is recent and man-made and was not there in 1783.

[23]The phrase "as seen by the plan on page 74" is not part of the original text, but was inserted by a contemporary copyist. Route was northeast from La Madera and the party was in the McCain Valley area where the smaller streams drain into the Carrizo Gorge.

[24]Route from the McCain Valley area to Cuñama [modern Cuyamaca] was northwest along the eastern edge of the Laguna Mountains. Course very nearly approximated the modern Sunrise Highway. Along this route are a number of vantage points, particularly near the Laguna radar station from which an excellent overview of the Carrizo Gorge and of the trail to San Sebastián can be obtained.

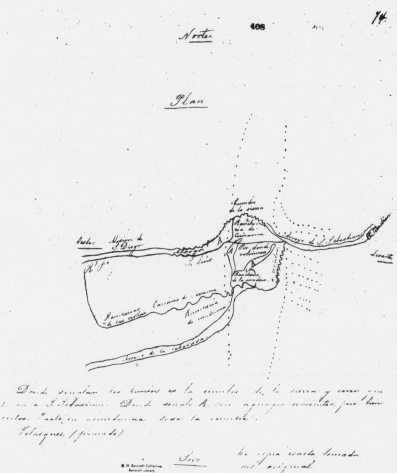

Figure 12. Velásquez' 1783 map of the San Diego back country. This is the first known map of this area. Here, the San Diego River is shown as Arroyo San Luis; Cottonwood Creek (a tributary of the Tijuana River) is shown as Arroyo de la Caballada; Cuyamaca Rancho as Cuñama; the Oriflamme Canyon — Carrizo corridor to the desert as Arroyo de San Sebastián; and the Carrizo Gorge is indicated by "Al registro."

Velásquez' original caption, translated, is:
"Where the dots show is the crest of the sierra and the hill which comes down to San Sebastián. Where the "A" indicates there are running streams, but very short. Pasturage is abundant on all the crest.
    Velásquez (signed)
                        This is an exact copy
                        made from the original"

Having returned, we rested near the village of Cuñama. Seeing a mountain gap toward where the sun sets, I asked the Indians if it was good to descend to San Luis. They answered that it was. About three o'clock in the afternoon we set out after our rest, and at sundown we stopped at the end of San Luis Box Canyon.[25]

On the next day we took the road and about ten o'clock we reached San Luis where we rested until two o'clock. Then we set out and arrived at the presidio about seven in the evening.

In all the journey through the sierra we saw several rancherías of Indians, very mild mannered and friendly. Water was very scarce, pasturage in abundance.[26]

Velásquez' sketch map (Fig. 12) which accompanied the trip report is, at first glance, a somewhat puzzling document. Some study discloses that the sketch actually consists of a plan (ordinary map) and a profile (cross section) drawn on the same sheet. Furthermore, the route indicated by Velásquez is that of the trail he was ordered to investigate, not the route which he followed in many places. Because Velásquez' map contains little distortion and includes a number of identifiable key points, a transparency of it can be projected, to scale, on a modern topographic map facilitating site identification.[27] Utilizing this interpretation, the map becomes a source of information rather than an enigma.

Route of the expedition, as indicated by the report and in part by map, was westward from the presidio of San Diego, around the west end of Presidio Hill, then southward to the ranchería of Las Chollas, whose location, shown on Pantoja's 1772 map, has since been confirmed by archaeology. Thence, the party crossed the very low divide between Sweetwater drainage and the Otay drainage and ascended the Otay Valley (eastward) to its head, near which was the ranchería of Natoma (misrendered as Madama by the map copyist).[28]

---

[25]Cuñama Ranchería in 1783 was not far from the later established Rancho Cuyamaca, which is now within Cuyamaca State Park, San Diego County, California. This area is mapped on the U.S. Geological Survey Quadrangles "Cuyamaca Peak," 1/62,500, 1960; and 1/24,000, 1960. The San Luis Box Canyon of the San Diego River is now occupied by the waters of the El Capitán Reservoir.

[26]Both the diary (actually a report) and the map carry the designation Archivo General de la Nación, Californias, 71, 14. Both are contemporary official copies.

[27]The map used for this purpose is the U.S. Geological Survey Map "San Diego," 1/250,000, 1960. Due to rapid urban growth and new highway construction, the cultural features of this map are obsolete.

[28]The site of Natoma is based on course and distance, backed up by some archaeological evidence. Tevanna, shown on the map but not mentioned in the report,

From Natoma, the expedition crossed the divide between Dulzura Creek and Pine Valley Creek, passing near modern Honey Springs and through Bratton Valley. In Pine Valley Creek Velásquez found running water. The area is now a part of Barrett Reservoir. A somewhat arduous traverse of another local divide brought the party to La Madera where they camped for the second night. With Indian guides they proceeded eastward and northward, crossing Cottonwood creek near modern Morena Reservoir, and came to Tecate Divide which separates the Pacific drainage from the Imperial Valley drainage, near McCain Valley — a suitable route for equestrian travel to the desert.[29]

The return journey to San Diego was made along the precipitous east rim of the Laguna Mountains, thence across the Cuyamaca Upland, through the Indian settlement of Cuñama, and then down the western slope of the range to San Luis Box Canyon, now occupied by El Capitán Reservoir. From there along familiar trails they descended the valley of the San Diego River, passing through San Luis, which is near modern Lakeside, past the mission, and arrived safely at the presidio of San Diego. A reconstruction of Velásquez' route, drawn on a modern topographic base, comprises MAP II.

In October of 1783 Velásquez received orders from Governor Fages to explore the region near the mouth of the Colorado, to search for a ford, to recover stolen horses, and to keep a careful diary of the

---

was probably one of five or more adjacent sites near modern Jamul. The La Madera ranchería was about a mile east of the modern reservoir in the center of Corte Madera Valley. Field studies now in progress (1979) should clarify these ancient site locations.

[29]Carrizo Gorge is a mountain defile which rises near the International Boundary south of Jacumba and descends northward for some twenty miles to the old site of Tres Palmas near the junction of Carrizo, Bow Willow, and Vallecito Creeks. The upper (southern) third is a relatively broad, flat-floored valley; the lower third is a gravel-floored valley supporting a forest of smoke trees *Dalea spinosa* in its southern part. The central third, rock-floored and sloping steeply northward, is not traversible by ordinary four wheeled vehicles. Intermittent springs are present north of the Route 8 crossing, but this water is arsenical; at the south end of the smoke tree forest the seeps are laden with fluorine (60 ppm or more). The tunnels, fills, dugways and trestles of the now inoperative San Diego and Arizona Eastern Railroad are visible high on the east wall of the gorge.

From Fages' use of place names and descriptions in his 1781 diary of the journey from Yuma to San Diego, it appears that Tres Palmas and all places east of it were familiar to him, while sites west of that point were new. From this it may be concluded, perhaps correctly, that Fages entered the Imperial Valley on his 1772 journey from San Diego via Carrizo Gorge.

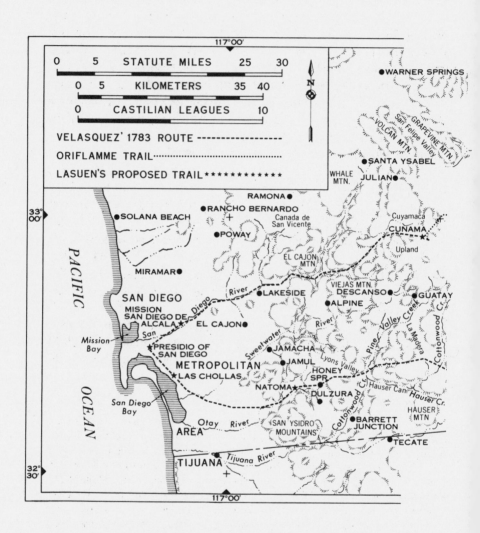

Map 2. Summary topographic map of the San Diego back country, showing reconstruction of José Velásquez' 1783 route, Father Lasuén's suggested route to the Colorado crossing, and the already-known Oriflamme trail, mapped and described by Pedro Fages in 1782. Certain cultural features, such as roads, railroads, reservoirs and military installations, which were not present in 1783, are not shown here. This map is compatible with U.S.

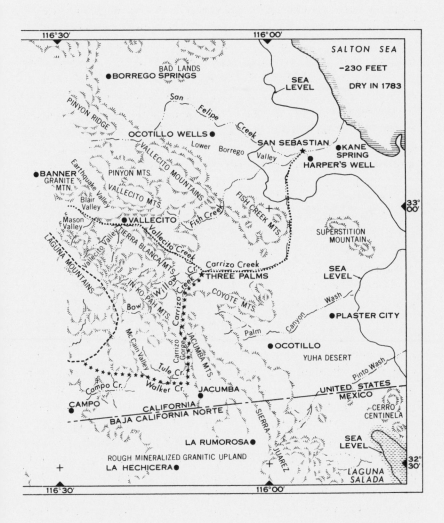

Geological Survey sheets Santa Ana (NI-11-8, 1969), Salton Sea (NI-11-9, 1969), San Diego (NI-11-11, 1970), El Centro (NI-11-12, 1969); and DETENAL sheets San Diego (NI-11-11, 1974) and Mexicali (NI-11-12, 1974); all 1/250,000. Map corrections through March 1, 1980 have been noted. Current status of major roads in this map is shown in the Rand-McNally *Road Atlas of the United States*, latest edition.

journey.[30] There is no evidence or suggestion that this journey was ever made, and no contemporary reason was given for the apparent cancellation of the orders. A probable cause was the rather widespread Indian unrest along the California coast at this time. This journey was eventually made, in April, 1823, by Father Félix Caballero whose route crossed the trails travelled and mapped by Father Kino more than a century earlier.[31]

Following the reglamentos established by Governor Neve, the service records of most, if not all, the officers and sergeants stationed in California were prepared in December, 1783. That of Alférez Velásquez *(Appendix A)* was compiled in large part by his commanding officer, Lieutenant José Zúñiga, who described him as sixty-six years old in robust health and with a record of thirty-three years of military service. Also mentioned, in addition to his major expeditions of which we have good documentary records, are a number of entradas made in search of Christian fugitives. "On four occasions they made war on him, and he came out wounded in one of them." Further details of these manhunts are unfortunately lacking.

Captain Nicolás Soler, adjutant inspector of the presidios of California, had a somewhat different opinion. He stated on his service record that "the age of this weary officer demands his retirement because he is useful only for fatigues in the field and has little confidence in deliberating by himself." Just what caused Soler to give this harsh evaluation is hard to determine because nothing in Velásquez' performance, either before or after December, 1783, gives any indication that he was "burned out," slow, or unable to make decisions. Governor Fages disregarded Captain Soler's remarks, however, and Alférez Velásquez continued on active duty at the presidio of San Diego. Although they had little immediate effect on Velásquez' duties, several changes took place in the mission administration about this time. Father Junípero Serra, President of the Alta California missions since 1769, died at Monterey on August 28, 1784, at nearly seventy-one years of age. He was succeeded as president by that assiduous critic of things

---

[30]Archivo de California, Provincial Records, III, 188-190.

[31]Father Caballero's diary (in translation) is given in L.J. Bean and W.M. Mason, *Diaries and Accounts of the Romero Expeditions in Arizona and California*, pp. 11-13. This work also describes several other attempts to reopen the Colorado crossing and to establish mail service between Sonora and California. Helpful terrain information has come from explorations by Carl Lumholtz and Alberto Celaya; see Carl Lumholtz, *New Trails in Mexico*, reprinted by Glorieta, 1971, pp. 254-286.

governmental and military, Father Francisco Palou, who apparently did not want the position. About a year later, in September of 1785, Father Palou departed for Mexico City and was replaced by Father Fermín Francisco Lasuén, who ruled quietly, diligently, and ably until his death at Monterey on June 26, 1803, at the age of about eighty-three.[32]

After several early crises the supply situation in Alta California improved slowly with the establishment of a local livestock industry. Local agriculture developed particularly near mission San Gabriel as did very limited local manufactures. The cost of supplying Alta California, however, remained high, and the slowly growing colony was still inconvenienced by delayed supply ships from San Blas and by Indian attacks on the mule trains travelling northward in Baja California. To reduce these problems and inconveniences Governor Fages favored an overland supply route from Sonora and devoted considerable effort to locate a Colorado River crossing away from the territory of the still-disaffected Yuma Indians. One effort in 1783 was cancelled, probably because of Indian unrest on the coast. In 1785 the governor organized another attempt to reopen the trail to Sonora. This one he led personally, choosing Alférez José Velásquez as second in command and diarist of the expedition. At this time, Velásquez was about sixty-eight years old and had been recommended for retirement by Adjutant Inspector Captain Nicolás Soler. However, his services at San Diego were satisfactory, and Velásquez was still one of the most experienced soldiers in the Californias.

---

[32]A complete Serra bibliography would fill a medium-sized book. Pertinent works about Serra include Francisco Palou, *Relación Histórica de la Vida y Apostólicas Tareas del Venerable Padre Fray Junípero Serra,* and Maynard Geiger, *The Life and Times of Junípero Serra, O.F.M.* Father Lasuén, unfortunately, lacked a contemporary biographer. An able evaluation of Lasuén and his work is contained in C.E. Chapman, *A History of California,* pp. 364-382. Since the publication of Chapman's work many documents and records concerning Lasuén have been found, but a definitive biography of Father Fermín Francisco Lasuén, O.F.M., is still awaited.

Although the multiple problems of divided authority, conflicting orders, differing objectives and slow communications continued throughout the Spanish period in Alta California, the political climate changed markedly for the better with the accession of Father Lasuén to the mission presidency. The almost continual quarrels between Father Serra and various governors, so thoroughly reported by Father Palou, ceased. The previous hostility between the president and the governor was replaced by mutual respect, if not by close friendship. There is a strong possibility that the troubles between the president and the governor in Serra's time were fomented and exacerbated, either intentionally or inadvertently, by Father Palou and his writings.

Figure 13. Mouth of the Carrizo Gorge, a view looking south from the Bow Willow Trail, southwest of the ancient site of Tres Palmas. Photo by R.L. Ives.

The party assembled at San Vicente, northernmost Dominican mission in Baja California, travelled eastward through the valley of La Calentura, crossed the peninsular divide, descended to the Colorado delta area, travelled northward along the east face of the Sierra de las Cocopas to the Imperial Valley, and then turned westward, arriving at San Diego by familiar trails. Velásquez' diary of the expedition, which will be presented later, had an interesting and precarious history. The original which was sent to Monterey was officially copied in a journal, and at a later date the journal containing this diary with more than 140 other volumes of historical documents was kept in the federal customs house in San Francisco. During the earthquake and fire of April 18-19, 1906 the entire collection was destroyed, as were a number of paintings and other records. Most fortunately, one of Bancroft's writers had made a hand-written copy of the diary and from this copy the following translation has been made:[33]

1785, April 27 — San Diego

Josef Velásquez. Account of the journey which Governor Fages made through the frontier, crossing the sierra and visiting certain Indian tribes. A diary which Josef Velásquez kept by order of the Governor, Don Pedro Fages, of the survey of the frontier which his lordship made personally, crossing the sierra, exploring from the mouth of the Colorado River to the Gulf of California, passing through the territories of the tribes of Camillares, Cucupaes, Guijecamaes, Cajuenes, and Yumas, and having seen this, his return back across the said sierra, arriving at this presidio.

ON THE EIGHTH day of the current month, his lordship ordered that Sergeant Mariano Verdugo should go ahead with the horse herd and some loads of supplies to wait for us at the watering place of La Calentura.[34] His lordship (Fages), two soldiers, and I, set out the same day toward the south along the Camino Real of the missions for two leagues. Leaving the camino, we turned southeast and went downward through a pass. We came to an arroyo which

---

[33]Bancroft Library C-A 3 BL 189.

[34]After almost two more centuries of use, with minimal maintenance, the road east from La Calentura still needs "to be fixed up a little." It is currently (1979) impassible by ordinary four-wheeled vehicles. Velásquez' trail from San Vicente to La Calentura follows about the same course as the modern good road. The valley of La Calentura, watered by the underflow of the main stream, has been agriculturally productive since late mission days and is currently intensively farmed.

took us upward to the east and to the said watering place about five leagues. Once there, his lordship directed that I should take six soldiers and two Indian interpreters to repair the trail if necessary; we had the requisite tools. He ordered that if I encountered any heathens I should let them know that we would not harm them, but rather that we would be friends to whom I would give presents. He had given me some packages of seeds for that purpose. That same evening I marched up the arroyo four leagues to the east. We made camp in the same arroyo on the eighth and ninth (of April).

[THE NINTH] Immediately at dawn I resumed the march. Soon we came to the beginning of a grade which had to be fixed up a little. I left a note for the said señor (Fages) to tell him to water the animals there. I continued on up the grade and then followed a small arroyo down from the summit. Near its end there was pasture and water where I left a cross made from sticks to show the señor that this was the place to spend the night, as he had told me to do. Along the banks of the stream we saw some deep pits which the Indians had made to catch deer, so I directed that willow branches be set up as a warning sign lest the horses fall in. A little earlier I had left a note for the señor so that he would stop where the cross was found, but for fun the soldiers made a cross among the branches at the pits which caused a certain ambiguity, on account of which he stopped halfway between the two crosses. Today I probably travelled six leagues.

[THE TENTH] Preparations having been made as ordered by his lordship, I resumed my march over the somewhat brushy ground until we came out on a very beautiful plain with pasture and water; it also had a hot spring.[35] When I arrived here, a smoke was seen. I sent a guide who was with me to summon the Indians, if there were any. Returning, he told me that there were no people there but that he would go on to the village which was at the corner of the plain and would talk to them. I sent him on his way, giving him some beads for the chief. After a short while we followed the trail of this guide. In the middle of the plain we met two natives who on meeting us went

[35]This is the modern Valle Trinidad. The hot spring is at the extreme western edge of the valley just south of the main arroyo. The intermediate stop with "pasture and water" was El Encino. In 1796 José Joaquín Arrillaga twice travelled approximately this same route and described the same features clearly. See Froy Tiscareno and J.W. Robinson, *José Joaquín Arrillaga-Diary of His Surveys of the Frontier — 1796*, pp. 31, 50-51. DETENAL maps covering the journey from San Vicente to Valle Trinidad include: "San Vicente," H 11 B 33; "Punta Colonet," H 11 B 43; "Lazaro Cardenas," H 11 B 34; "Francisco R. Serrano," H 11 B 35; all 1/50,000; all dated 1974.

Figure 14. The fertile valley of La Calentura, view looking east (1977). Photo by R.L. Ives.

ahead of us toward the village. When we arrived there I asked for the chief. Those who were there told me that he had gone hunting but that they already sent for him. After giving them presents I asked them where there was a good way to get through the sierra and to go down to the river. They answered that there were three ways, pointing out to me one to the north, a second toward the east, and another toward the southeast. The first was very steep and horses could not get down it; the second was better, but rocky; the third was fairly good, but there was no water.[36]

Having heard this, it seemed best to reconniter the second, that going in the right direction. I asked them for a guide and they answered that there was one who knew the way well. They called him. When he came to me I saw that he was dressed as a woman. When I said that I did not want to take a woman, they answered that he was a man.[37] With that I gave them presents and resumed our march toward the southeast.

At the end of this plain we made camp for the night; we had probably covered seven leagues.

At first daylight I sent back two soldiers to tell the governor what had been happening and to tell him where I had gone to explore. His lordship slept at the place of the crosses located in the plain of the hot spring. He made night camp at the edge of it where the trail rounded a little hill. He sent me a corporal and four soldiers with an order that we should get together without fail the next day. They found me in a narrow arroyo with running water with some little pools where the Indians bathed. This meeting took place at midday because I had already left the place where we had spent the night on that same plain; we were slowly traversing a rather rocky, narrow arroyo, and at three leagues I came upon the water hole.

---

[36]The northernmost route was through the Portezuelo de Jamul, a gap in the Sierra de Juárez that leads downward into Arroyo Agua Caliente and to the Laguna Salada. The modern "road" through this gap is not recommended for travel in any ordinary vehicle. To the east the route described led to Arroyo Grande and eventually to the south end of Laguna Salada. The wheel track on this route can be traversed by high-center vehicles, preferably with four-wheel drive. The southeast route was San Matías Pass, leading to the San Felipe Desert. It is now traversed by a good paved road connecting Ensenada on Mexican Route 1 with El Chinero on Mexican Route 5.

[37]The guide was a male transvestite. These were apparently numerous among the California Indians in the late 1700s. Fages comments upon them, most unfavorably, in another document. See H. I. Priestley, "A Historical, Political, and Natural Description of California by Pedro Fages," *Catholic Historical Review*, January, 1919, pp. 486-509; April, 1919, pp. 71-90. Reprinted, Ramona: Ballena Press, 1972. Specific reference is to p. 33 of reprint.

Without pausing I went to look at the summit and decided on the right trail, returning to the watering place for a siesta. That afternoon I ordered the corporal and his party to go forward at once to open up the road as far as it had been examined.

We slept on the same slope.

AT FIRST LIGHT ON THE ELEVENTH, I continued toward the east to explore where a way could be cleared. When I discovered the descent from the sierra, I sent the corporal and one soldier to tell his lordship that a way had been found, but that I had not found water and, according to the guide, that it was still far away. Also, if it seemed good to him, he might find water where we had been before, and in the afternoon we might find a better water hole farther ahead.[38] The governor, however, had not received my information and had already come in search of me. He turned back where he met the corporal because he misunderstood what I had told him, thinking that he should wait for me at the watering place. After the way down was cleared as well as possible, I returned to meet his lordship at the watering place, arriving after dark.

AT DAWN ON THE TWELFTH, his lordship ordered us to go ahead with the three Indians and four soldiers. When we reached the end of the cleared path we followed an arroyo. On leaving this there appeared to us some hills and a pass, very rocky and thorny. Having halted, his lordship ordered me to go as far as the pass to learn if any water was nearby as the guide said, and if it was good, to make a smoke signal.

Having scouted and seen that it was not far to water, I made a smoke signal and went promptly to meet his lordship because where he had stayed it was still necessary to clear the way upward. When I arrived where the clearing needed to be done, his lordship was already on his way down. Seeing him coming, we dismounted and began to open the road. His lordship also helped us throw stones aside. By this labor we reached the watering place, which was a small, narrow arroyo with only a little running water, but there was enough for all the horses to drink.

We probably travelled five leagues.

After we had rested and eaten, his lordship ordered me to go out with four soldiers and three Indians to scout the country. We were not to go so far as to be detected by a village which the guide told us lay this side of the hill. I scouted as far as a very wide arroyo that cut

---

[38]Velásquez was here scouting out a trail across the peninsular divide near the junction of the Sierra Juárez and the Sierra San Felipe, a region of rough, rocky hills, narrow tortuous canyons, and problematical water supplies.

across the way. Here I turned back to tell his lordship that I had cleared a stretch of road that I had surveyed.

ON THE THIRTEENTH, we continued our march toward the east and reached the arroyo mentioned above.[39] A short way within it a pagan Indian was seen at a distance, whom we conjectured to be a lookout. He came into view after we crossed the shoulder of a hill above the arroyo. The guide was instructed to talk to him. As soon as the lookout was spoken to, he stopped and came over to the lord governor who gave him a present and asked him where he lived. He said that his village was a good distance down the arroyo. We moved forward following the arroyo and soon began to see several villages on both sides of it; we counted nine of them. On the average, there were twenty-eight or thirty houses in each.[40]

The guide stopped, saying that there was no more water farther on, whereupon his lordship ordered that a halt should be made. We finished eating, and he then ordered me to go with my party to scout the watering place of which the guide told us. Continuing down the arroyo, I came to a tank of rain water at one side of a little ravine, but I saw it was impossible for the horses to drink from it.[41] I climbed a hill from which I saw that the sierra was coming to an end and discovered a plain or level stretch where the Colorado River runs.[42] When I asked the Indian guide where there was water, he answered ''where the hills end, before the plain.'' At the same time I saw a great deal of smoke where the Indians said it would be, two leagues off. Asked what that smoke was, the guide replied that it was a village and that they sowed wheat there.[43] With this comforting news I descended into the arroyo where the governor was already waiting and gave him the information. He decided to wait for the

---

[39]This large canyon was almost certainly Arroyo Grande, which rises in the extreme southern part of the Sierra Juárez, flows northeast, and empties into the southeastern end of the Laguna Salada.

[40]These Indians may have been Pai-Pais. Some members of this group still live in the eastern canyons of the Sierra Juárez, and others visit the area seasonally to gather piñon nuts and for other purposes.

[41]This arid region has many small natural rock tanks *tinajas* in which rain water collects and remains for weeks, months, and sometimes years. The low mountains north of Arroyo Grande are known today as the Sierra de las Tinajas.

[42]Velásquez was looking northeastward across the flood plain at the junction of the Laguna Salada and the Colorado delta.

[43]The manuscript specifically reads trigo (wheat). This may be an error for maiz (corn). However, as wheat was introduced to the Yuma area not later than about 1776, its culture nine years later, and only sixty miles southwest of Yuma, is entirely possible.

Figure 15a. The Trinidad hot spring. Photo by R.L. Ives.

Figure 15b. Warm pool fed by the Trinidad hot spring. Photo by R.L. Ives.

horses and the packs. When they arrived, he ordered me to have the sergeant caution the men to drink water and follow after us. This done, we slowly resumed the march down the arroyo. Although we had expected to leave it in two hours, it was quite otherwise because there were so many narrow turns that nightfall overcame us.

We came out onto the plain without finding water; the guide was at fault. The trail forked; one fork led to the east and the other to the northeast. We took the latter to avoid entanglements with delta channels closer to the mouth of the river. His lordship ordered two soldiers to remain behind to allow the horses to eat some bushes we found. Where we stopped, the governor made a beautiful fire so that those behind could come on by the light because the trail could hardly be seen due to the darkness of the night.

On this day we probably travelled fifteen leagues.

ON THE FOURTEENTH as soon as it was light, I noticed a little range of hills near the river; I had passed near its foot before.[44] We resumed our march on a line toward the north. Having passed over the plain, some low dunes lay across our path. Once these were passed, we found a very wide alkali flat, very muddy, from which we learned that there the tide ebbed and water came from underground. We crossed over this difficult alkali flat and found the point of the range. We were comforted by the thought of drinking water because I had seen a little good water here before, but not finding any, we were obliged to stop without water.

When the heat of the sun had subsided, as we were already near the river, his lordship decided that I should go ahead to see if water could be found in a field of reeds, which I had seen before, well

---

[44]This statement is not compatible with any known journey by Alférez Velásquez. The hills which he noted were the Cerro El Mayor, a southern extension of the Sierra de los Cocopas. His nearest previous documented approach to this was on November 22, 1775, when he climbed the Cerro Borrego, or a closely adjacent high point, some forty-five miles distant to the southwest. This statement may hint at a journey to the Colorado delta by Velásquez some time before 1785 for which no documentation has yet been found. The expedition here was crossing the mouth of the Laguna Salada depression parts of which are below sea level. This formerly received inflows of water from the Río Hardy when the Colorado was in flood and from the Gulf of California during extreme spring tides. Despite these inflows, however, the basin was usually dry, for the average annual potential evapotranspiration is approximately 140 inches, while the average annual precipitation is less than five inches. In recent years the basin has received a fairly steady inflow from the Río Hardy through a man-made canal. This is some of the most barren land in North America. Had Jacques Cartier visited the region, he would have included it among "the lands that God gave to Cain."

away from the river. For this purpose he gave me some beads and ten men to accompany me.

Having marched a little way over the plain near the range mentioned above, I saw some Indians on a little hill. Here I stopped and called them through the interpreter. They came in a friendly fashion. After giving them some strings of beads, I asked them if there was water among the reeds. They answered that there was some in the wells, but that in their village there was much water easily obtained, and pasturage.[45]

On receiving this information I told them to lead on. About a cannon shot away a large crowd of people were coming, more or less five hundred, some armed and some not, with three others on horseback riding about among them as if preparing for a skirmish. When I saw this, I pretended that I was about to give them some beads, but I told them that anyone who came armed would get nothing but the lance. All this was to keep them occupied while my soldiers remounted. As soon as they told me that they were ready, I went ahead looking for water, keeping the Indians ahead of me without allowing them to mingle with our men. Those that persisted in approaching too close, I charged with my horse, and so I continued to drive toward the water. I had noticed before that those who were armed were displeased and drew apart. The three on horseback were Juilica men.[46] I remained only with the Cucupaes who had their village on this shore of the lagoon. As soon as I saw water, I made the Indians draw to the side. We watered the horses one by one.

When this was completed, the Indians came to me with gifts of squash, beans, fish and different kinds of meal. I said that they should keep them until the great chief, who was coming behind us, should arrive and that they should go to meet him with water, which they did. I soon saw the lord governor coming. He was following me, not holding back, so as to give assistance where it might be needed. He travelled into the midst of everything. When I saw him, I went to meet him, telling him what was taking place. Then we withdrew a short distance into the plain. There we halted; then he went with eight men and the interpreter to talk with the Indians of the village. He ordered me to send the horse herd along and said that he would not leave until the horses had finished drinking. The watering

---

[45] These Indians were Cocopas, a subgroup of the California Yumas who live in the Colorado Delta region and practice agriculture. See E. W. Gifford, "The Cocopa," *Univ. of Calif. Publications in Archaeology and Ethnology*, Vol. 31, No. 5, 1933; and A. A. Williams, *Travelers Among the Cucupa*.

[46] A small group of Yuma Indians who lived near the mouth of the Colorado River.

completed, he withdrew to the camping place, telling me that the Indians had given him many little presents. They urged him to rest there two or three days. To all this he had answered "yes," but he gave orders that all should sleep with their horses saddled. Secretly he ordered me to pack up at dawn. Before daylight we were to begin the march along the edge of the plain close to the sierra to avoid getting ourselves into some lagoon or estuary and to pass the many villages which might be there to judge from the great number of smokes we saw.

After this order was given and we were at rest, at the beginning of prayers, some old Indians came with women who carried a basket of seeds and some jugs of water. The governor, in his turn, gave them trinkets and told them to return to their village to sleep. They might come again the next day.

This day we made nine leagues.

THE FIFTEENTH, before daylight, everything was ready. The governor ordered the horse herd and the pack animals to move out. With eight soldiers strung out toward the north, we proceeded along the edge of the sierra staying clear of several villages from which we hid because they might have been frightened to see us.

About eight o'clock in the morning we came upon an estuary of salt water from which we understood the tide came up this far. Since the estuary was bordered with luxuriant reeds, mesquite bushes, pigweed, and other pasturage plants, it follows as a consequence that, although the water is salty, the land is beautiful. This was even more evident as we saw that the Indians sow up to the very foot of the sierra itself, narrowing the roadway.[47] It was necessary for four soldiers to pass over the narrow place, then the horse herd and the pack train in single file. The lord governor, the soldiers, and I held back, taking care to get everything across. But the Indians were treacherous and they took advantage of this opportunity, thinking

---

[47]This location is now known as Río Hardy. The Colorado delta is an enormous flood plain. Tidal bores from the Gulf of California, sometimes exceeding thirty feet in height, bring salt water many miles up the river and its numerous distributaries. See F.B. Kniffen, "The Natural Landscape of the Colorado Delta," *Univ. of California Publications in Geography*, Vol. 5, No. 4, 1932; and Godfrey Sykes, *The Colorado Delta*. The expedition here was travelling north near the west bank of the Río Hardy with the Sierra Mayor immediately to the west. DETENAL maps covering the journey from Valle Trinidad to Río Hardy include: "Francisco R. Serrano," H 11 B 35; "Agua Caliente," H 11 B 25; "Salinas Ometepec," H 11 B 37; "Guardianes de la Patria," I 11 D 85; "Plan de Ayala," I 11 D 86; "Sierra Cucupa," I 11 D 75; and "Guadalupe Victoria," I 11 D 76; all to scale of 1/50,000, all dated 1974.

Figure 16. The Rio Hardy, a distributary of the Colorado, at its closest approach to the Sierra Mayor. This is approximately the head of tidewater. Photo by R.L. Ives.

that we were afraid. Two Indians climbed the heights above us and began to shout, shooting arrows and throwing stones. But as they could not hurt us, we paid no attention to them.

This defile passed, in a short distance we came upon another estuary of excellent water. It too came close to a hill which stood out from the sierra. Here I saw a beautiful mesa, perfect for the purpose of founding a mission; it commands those lovely plains with pasturage and water. The sierra was farther back and not too high, and there was abundant firewood and much moist land for sowing crops. As if these were not enough, there are good sources of water. For building houses, stone is at hand; lumber can be brought from the river although it is six or seven leagues distant, more or less, but over flat land. These are the lands of the Cajuenes. It is well known that they are the enemies of the Yumas, although neighbors, which was affirmed by having seen what I am going to tell.

After marching two leagues beyond the estuary mentioned, we encountered a dead Indian on the path. As the sun was getting hot and as it was already almost noon, and with damp ground, his lordship decided to stop. He sent me to climb a nearby hill to see if I could find where the lake of Santa Olalla might be, as the diary of Señor Anza mentions.[48] Having climbed the hill, looking around, I could not see any plains beyond the cottonwood groves of the river. I could only tell where the river came from — first, because I saw the ribbon of sand dunes reaching out toward the hills of San Pedro y San Pablo which are close to the river; second, because from where we had slept there was a line of smokes as far as the Yumas, who are also near the said little hills. Looking farther, I saw that from where we were toward the north the land was very sterile, and the view of the river was much less pleasant. A short league to the south among the trees there appeared to be a little lagoon.

After I descended, I told the lord governor all that I had seen. He ordered me to inspect the aforementioned water to see whether it could be drawn for the men. On reaching it I found a lovely lake of good water, which from a distance had appeared small to me. On its shore was a village which the Yumas had attacked. Although I saw no dead bodies there, I did see the trail where the defenders had come out fighting. Then at the distance of a musket shot I began to see dead men. These were only in the road and along the sides

---

[48]The location of Santa Olalla, discovered and named by Juan Bautista de Anza on February 12, 1774, is not known with any certainty, as the site has been obliterated by repeated changes in the course of the Colorado River. Most probable location is near the old Paredones channel about fourteen miles southwest of Pilot Knob.

between the small hills where there were many buzzards. I saw seven bodies, not counting those seen by the soldiers driving the horse herd. The Yumas had come on horseback. From the looks of the trail twenty of them had passed. They had been running and killing as far as the foot of the sierra. Because they could not get their horses up the hill, they had uprooted the seeded gardens and destroyed the property of those who had fled, as I saw by the trail when I went up the hill.

As soon as I had finished watering our animals, I returned to tell the lord governor I had found water. Then he sent the sergeant to water the horse herd. This done, he ordered us to saddle and pack up, and we marched toward the northwest, hurrying a little because he wanted to see from a high point before dark what I had described to him. We came to the foot of a hill. Leaving the mules there, we climbed on foot up to where he could make out the little hills and the dunes that I had reported. Since the governor had laudable understanding, he took charge and decided on which direct road we were. During these deliberations the soldiers overtook us, and we likewise saw the horse herd coming. When we descended the hill, it was becoming too dark to travel so he had us make fires from time to time in order that those behind might find us more easily. We stopped in this plain about ten o'clock at night.

Today we travelled about seventeen or eighteen leagues.

THE SIXTEENTH at dawn we resumed the march to the northwest over flat land with such a strong wind that we could hardly travel. We rested in front of the hill of Santa Rosa de las Lajas, looking for the watering place found in the diary of Don José Moraga.[49] I could not find it. The governor ordered me to search for another watering place and to make a smoke signal if I found one. By three in the afternoon he had marched as far as San Sebastián without having seen smoke. Not having found water and considering that he had already explored the route and that it was getting dark, he

---

[49]The hill of Santa Rosa de las Lajas is the modern Signal Mountain, known in Mexico as the Cerro de la Centinela. Fages and Velásquez were travelling northwest across the extreme southern part of the Imperial Valley in the area now known as the Yuha Desert. The watering place referred to is Yuha Spring about two miles southwest of modern Yuha Well. It is hard to find and has been dry most of the time since about 1900. Lt. José Joaquín Moraga commanding the third division of the second Anza expedition passed through this area on December 15 and 16, 1775. He also had trouble with inclement weather. During the journey northward from Río Hardy the Fages-Velásquez expedition passed within a day's march of the farthest west points reached by Melchor Díaz (1540), Juan de Oñate (1605), Father Kino (1701-1702) and Father Garcés (1773). They were now substantially on the Anza trail of 1774-1776.

moved ahead with two soldiers. But they lost their way, passing beyond the arroyo with the watering place. Then his lordship prepared to proceed a little farther to the banks of that arroyo where there were some fires. He left one of the soldiers stationed where they had separated; the other he sent to make a short cut to the watering place. His lordship remained alone, poking the fire, by whose light we all came together.

When they finally unloaded and unsaddled, he ordered the sergeant to take the horses to pasture, to water if any was found, and if water was not found this night, it would be located the next morning. None of us knew where we were, thinking that this was not the arroyo of San Sebastián — especially when I asked the man who had searched the route along which the arroyo ran, he answered "to the south," which was most confusing to me, so I told the governor that this was not San Sebastián. His lordship affirmed that it most surely was.

[THE SEVENTEENTH] At dawn a water hole was found.[50] Water was given to the horse herd and more was drawn for us, whereupon I begged pardon of his lordship for my stubbornness the preceding night. He then ordered that the sergeant should remain with the horse herd, pasturing it at the watering place until we were ready to leave. He issued strict orders that no soldier should approach the village. He took this same precaution during the entire journey.

Yesterday we travelled ten or eleven leagues.

When we brought up the horse herd, we skirted a hill and began the march westward. There were some arroyos that lay across the trail. After prayers we found the place called La Palma with water and pasturage.[51] When we stopped, we sensed the presence of heathens on the opposite bank of the arroyo. In view of this, his lordship gave me orders that at dawn six men and I should surround the village and call its chief because on one occasion when the governor had passed by this place horses had been stolen.

By this evening we had made four leagues.

---

[50]The expedition approached San Sebastián from the south- southeast, travelling over the broad alluvial area between the Superstition and the Fish Creek Mountains. They apparently became confused in the darkness by the maze of brush-filled arroyos near San Sebastián water hole. Fages had previously visited the area once in 1772 and several times in 1782 during campaigns against the rebellious Yumas. Velásquez had been to and through the area twice in 1782.

[51]La Palma was apparently the same as Tres Palmas visited by Fages in 1782 and probably in 1772. It was near the junction of Carrizo, Bow Willow and Vallecitos Creeks, and was later the site of the Carrizo Stage Station.

Figure 17. The Sierra de las Cocopas as seen from the east. The expedition travelled across the flat delta deposits in the foreground. Photo by R.L. Ives.

THE EIGHTEENTH, at dawn, I surrounded the village and found no one in it except a woman with a child. She made signs to point out a range of small hills nearby. We scanned with our eyes and saw people on the top. Whereupon I returned, reporting to his lordship what was happening. Then he ordered us to load and saddle up. He ordered three soldiers with two sluggish beasts to go ahead. We followed behind, then the pack animals, and finally the horse herd, all going toward the west.

Soon after starting, the sergeant counted the horses and found one missing. He went back to recount, which gave the Indians time to drive another horse off and kill it with jara blows.[52] While he was counting, about thirty Indians appeared. When the soldiers learned of the missing horse, they hunted for it diligently. The trail could not be found because the Indians, who had led it off, covered its tracks. While they the soldiers were hunting for it, the Indians followed them in a friendly fashion, calling them to their village to give them food. The soldiers would not pay attention to them. Finally, they saw a horse's footprint where the Indians were trying to cover the trail. The followed the trail diligently until they found the horse dead from the blows. Seeing this, the Indians ran up the hill. The soldiers immediately returned.

We reached the San Felipe Valley about eleven or twelve in the morning, six or seven leagues from where we had slept.[53] The sergeant came last and told us about the Indians who had killed the horse. The sun had already set and some heathens, who had come to visit us, had already gone when his lordship ordered me to take twelve soldiers and the interpreter. Since night had fallen, we were to march silently, each one taking a well-trained horse. We left our mules tied up a long way from the village; the horses were saddled very quietly. We had been ordered to surround the village of these rascals and, when it became light, to speak to them through the interpreter. He would order the chief to be bound, and whoever appeared to be his second man was to be told to come with him because the great chief wanted to talk to them. For the rest of those who seemed to be most guilty, he would order that they be given six lashes, letting them know that it was for the damage they had done before and on this occasion. To the others — women and children, he would give presents of beads.

---

[52] A *jara* was a primitive lance, consisting of a sharpened pole, used effectively as a weapon by the Indians.

[53] This valley was visited and named by Fages in 1782. It was later the site of a military depot and a stage station. Today, known as Vallecito, it is a county park.

All this was carried out to the letter, but having surrounded the village when it became light, we found only empty houses. Straining eyes to all sides, we saw a fire about a musket shot away at the foot of a hill to the north; the hill was much cut by ravines and surrounded by the plain. As the fire was so near, I considered that if the Indians were not spoken to, they would think that we were afraid; it is unimaginable that the Indians could believe this about the king's troops.

In the end we hurried to surround the hill; I called the interpreter to tell them not to be frightened and that I wanted to talk to them without making any trouble although our arms were in hand. The Indians rushed to the crest of the hill and began to run away. Running toward an Indian soldier, Corporal Olivera raced his horse at high speed. As I was going around the hill to place the men, the corporal shouted to me, "Señor, they are running away, what shall I do?" I stopped and ordered the corporal and another to fire on those who were on the hilltop.

When the shots rang out, one of the Indians fell; the rest threw themselves into the gullies. Seeing this, I ordered the interpreter to speak to them. Their answer was that they did not want to talk. They kept on lashing out with jaras, wounding two horses. I ordered the corporal to keep up a steady fire. After a short while I ordered the interpreter to tell them, for the third time, that they must make peace and that I would not do them any harm. They answered "No," that they would not. In attempting to flee they were blocked by the soldiers behind the hill, but the Indians did wound a soldier. When we opened steady fire on them, some fell, and they returned to the gullies.

One of them fought more than all the rest. For the fourth time I gave an order to speak to this one, who was pointed out to be the chief. He answered the interpreter that he would not surrender, that he did not know how to die. Some soldiers called to him, making signs that they would not do anything at all to him. His answer was to throw darts, whereupon I ordered the soldiers to fire until he was killed. All became silent. The remainder, with the women and children, were hidden in ravines. I ordered the interpreter to assemble them while I inspected those who came out wounded, but there were only three, none serious.

This done and the people already assembled, I asked one of them who had killed the horse. By a sign he pointed to where the dead chief was. When asked who had killed a soldier in this same arroyo in which they were, he replied he did not know. Noticing that the women were talking in signs, I asked the interpreter what they were saying. He replied that they were saying that the chief had collected men together, and they had killed people including a soldier. This was Hermenegildo Flores who had deserted last year from the presidio. It was while I was going toward the summit that I heard the news that they had killed him, and I had to report this to the presidio.[54]

Returning to the Indian women who were at the beginning of the arroyo, I asked them through the interpreter who had killed a Christian man and a Christian woman of the mission of San Diego. They answered, "the dead chief." When asked who had killed an Indian from San Sebastián who had served as a guide on the trip which I made there, they answered that "those yonder" had killed him.

It is a common rumor that these same Indians had killed another soldier, a deserter, a long time ago. The interpreters of the mission of San Diego, according to information of those from the sierra, consider the Nuzes as spies or bandits, and these are the same kind.[55] The soldier, Solis, heard a woman, half-Spanish half-Indian, say that they had killed the late Flores, from which it was inferred that it was God's will and that they have paid what they owed.

When this was done, I gave all of them beads and withdrew to inform the governor of what happened. He felt that I should have left the village undisturbed. However, when I gave him my reason and explained what was said by the Indians, he agreed. The Indians of San Felipe, who sometimes visited his lordship, told him that those of Jurín were bad.

ON THE NINETEENTH we travelled west, passing villages and talking with good Indians who came out unarmed to meet us and to give the governor mescal. We rested at the foot of the grade in the afternoon. When we had repaired a section of the mountain grade, we went on. We arrived at the summit at the village of Cuñamac; the governor talked to the chief.[56] Among other things, he mentioned

---

[54]José Hermenegildo Flores had apparently deserted from the San Diego presidio in 1779 and fled to the Colorado River. Later Flores, who was actually an Indian, returned to the desert mountain region east of San Diego. In May, 1784, Velásquez learned of Flores' whereabouts from the San Diego Indians. Soldiers were dispatched, but they were unable to find him. Some discrepancies in the various accounts hint that there may have been two deserters with similar names. See J.D. Forbes, *Warriors of the Colorado*, pp. 225.

[55]The manuscript here is unclear. It appears that the Nuzes are the Indian inhabitants of Jurín, which is probably the same place as the Jurín mentioned later.

[56]This was the large Indian village on the rolling upland at the crest of the Laguna Mountains. From this the name Cuyamaca is derived. Fages and Velásquez apparently

the heathens of Jurín, what they were like, and talked about those who had killed the soldier Flores.

After all the troops passed, we went downward to rest some distance away from the village in a little arroyo where there was pasture and water. That night the governor did not sleep because a thick fog rolled in; water collecting on the treeleaves fell like a heavy shower so that all his clothing was soaked; the same happened to the rest of us.

This day we travelled about four leagues.

AT DAWN ON THE TWENTIETH I pressed forward and fixed the way down where his lordship overtook me. We continued the march without stopping except for a rest in San Luis Box Canyon, finally sleeping at this presidio.[57]

We had covered sixteen or seventeen leagues.

With the arrival of the expedition at the presidio of San Diego the official diary ends because the chronicler, Alférez José Velásquez, left the party with the men and animals borrowed for the expedition. He resumed his duties as the second-in-command of the post. The remainder of the cavalcade continued north over the Camino Real en route to their regular duty stations. At Santa Barbara Corporal Olivera left the party to resume his assigned duties at the presidio.[58] Governor Fages and Sergeant Verdugo continued north to Monterey.[59]

---

followed the former's 1782 route up Vallecito Valley to Mason Valley, then up Oriflamme Canyon to the summit, and thence into the central part of the Cuyamaca Rancho State Park.

[57]This is now occupied by the waters of El Capitán Reservoir. Maps covering the journey northward and westward from Río Hardy include DETENAL sheets "Sierra Cucapa," I 11 F 75; "Guadalupe Victoria," I 11 D 76; both 1/50,000, dated 1974: Army Map Service sheet "El Centro," NI 11 12, series F 501, Edition 1, 1/250,000: U.S. Geological Survey quadrangles "Salton Sink, California," 1/500,000, 1908: "El Centro," 1/250,000, 1969; "Salton Sea," 1/250,000, 1969; "San Diego," 1/250,000, 1970; "Santa Ana," 1/250,000, 1969. Quadrangles to scales of 7.5' and 15' are available for most parts of the area within the United States, and are listed in *Index to Topographic Maps of California* published every few years by the U.S. Geological Survey.

[58]Ignacio Olivera was corporal at Santa Bárbara in 1785. He was later promoted to sergeant and died at Santa Bárbara in 1794.

[59]Mariano Verdugo, a veteran of the first expedition to Alta California in 1769, was a sergeant at Monterey from 1781 to 1787. Then he moved to Los Angeles where he served as alcalde from 1790 through 1793, and again in 1802. Verdugo Canyon, east of the metropolitan center, is named for him.

Map 3. Topographic map of northern Baja California Norte southern California, and adjoining parts of Sonora and of Arizona, showing reconstructed route of the Fages-Velásquez expedition of 1785 from mission San Vicente eastward to the Colorado Delta, then northward to San Sebastián water hole in the Imperial Valley of California, thence across the Laguna Mountains, via the Oriflamme Trail, to the presidio of San Diego. Major changes in land use and status since 1785 are indicated. Base maps used

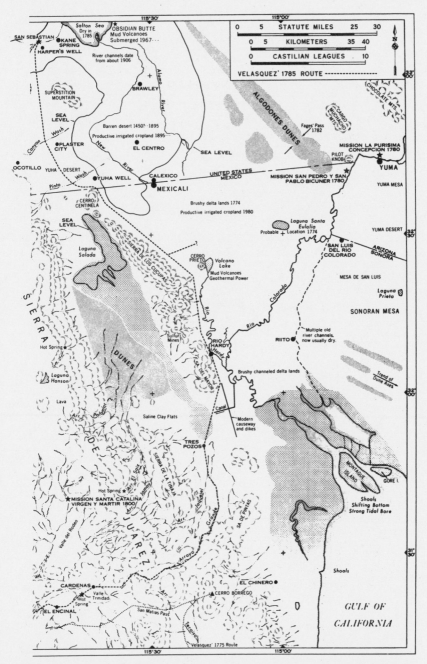

Salton Sea (NI-11-9, 1969), San Diego (NI-11-11, 1970), El Centro (NI-11-12, 1969); and DETENAL sheets San Diego (NI-11-11, 1974), Mexicali (NI-11-12, 1974), Ensenada (H-11-2, 1974), San Felipe (H-11-3, 1974), and Lazaro Cardenas (H-11-5, 6, 1974). Map corrections through June 1, 1980 have been noted. Current status of major roads in the map area is shown in the Rand-McNally *Road Atlas of the United States*, latest edition, and on DETENAL tourist map "Mexico, Northwest," latest edition.

In December, 1783, Captain Nicolás Soler, adjutant inspector of the presidios of California, in preparing Alférez Velásquez' service record, recommended that he be retired because of age and indecision *(Cf. Appendix A)*. No evidence of these failings has been found in the record prior to 1783, and it is most difficult to reconcile this judgement with Velásquez' adequate, if not excellent, performance as second-in-command at the presidio and diarist of the expedition to the Colorado delta. Perhaps this recommendation was another of Captain Soler's many errors of judgement.

After his return from the Colorado delta expedition, Velásquez resumed his regular duties at the presidio of San Diego. In addition to the normal camp routine of drilling soldiers, maintaining the presidio in a state of supposed military readiness, supervising the guard at the mission and the presidio, and caring for the million and one problems endemic at an understaffed and undersupplied frontier post surrounded by not always friendly natives, a major concern of Velásquez was the apprehension of army deserters and runaway mission neophytes. There is no record of the number of searches for deserters and runaway Indians, but desertion was a serious and continuing problem in California at this time.

In October of 1785 Velásquez suffered an injury to his hand. Which hand was injured, how the injury occurred, and how serious the injury appeared to be initially are not told by surviving records. Despite this incapacity, Velásquez in late October led a party of soldiers northward from San Diego in pursuit of a deserter. By the time the troop reached San Gabriel, his hand had become badly infected and he was hospitalized. His condition worsened, and he was given the last rites of the church. On All Soul's Day, November 2, 1785, Alférez Velásquez died at the age of sixty-eight years. Cause of death, as indicated by the scanty clues available, seems to have been a massive systemic infection of a type popularly known as "blood poisoning."

Fray Miguel Sánchez of mission San Gabriel recorded Velásquez' passing in the mission records:

1785, November 3: San Gabriel, *14th de razón*.
Fray Miguel Sánchez. Minister. Alférez Joseph Velásquez.
Buried today in this church the body of Don Joseph Velásquez, alférez of the presidio of San Diego, who died yesterday.[60]

---

[60]San Gabriel, Libros de Misión, Ms. 8, item 3. The notation *14th de razón* apparently indicated that this was the fourteenth burial of a Spaniard *(gente de razon)* at the mission.

Governor Fages was informed of Velásquez' passing as follows:

1785, November 13. Santa Bárbara.
Felipe de Goicoechea to Pedro Fages.
On a shipment from his office and the death of an alférez:
He says that by the official letters that Lieutenant José de Zúñiga sent, he will advise what has happened in San Gabriel. He says . . . that he also knew . . . of the death of Alférez José Velásquez in San Gabriel where he had sent his company and that the cause was an injury to one hand, which injury he had before leaving this presidio . . . There is no other news.[61]

The official certification of death was made by Lieutenant José de Zúñiga, Velásquez' commanding officer:

1785, December 1. San Diego.
José de Zúñiga certifies that Alférez José Velásquez died the 2nd of November in the mission of San Gabriel; he was buried in the church of this mission according to its missionaries, Fray Antonio Cruzado and Fray Miguel Saenz (Sánchez), who affirmed it.[62]

Because Alférez Velásquez apparently had no living relatives, Lieutenant Zúñiga was spared the nightmare duty of writing a letter to his next of kin.

As a result of incomplete mission cemetery records, which only go back to 1910, the location of the grave of Alférez José Velásquez at mission San Gabriel remains unknown.[63] There is neither marker nor inscription. Study of the historical record almost two centuries after Velásquez' death indicates that the epitaph — EUGE, SERVE BONE ET FIDELIS — would be admirably suited.[64]

[61]Provincial State Papers, Benicia, Military, Ms. V, 160.
[62]Provincial State Papers, Benicia, Military, Ms. VII, 2. at the mission.
[63]Provincial State Papers. Benicia, Military, MS, VII, 2.
[64]Personal communication from mission San Gabriel, April 5, 1979. Apparently no record of graves was kept at mission San Gabriel prior to 1910.
[65]Latin text from Aloisius Gramatica, Bibliorum Sacrorum Iuxta Vulgatam Testamentum, Secundum Matthaeum, 25:21. Spanish text in E.N. Fuster and Alberto Colunga (eds), Sagrada Biblia, San Mateo 25:21. English text in C.C. Ryrie, (ed), The Ryrie Study Bible: King James Version, Matthew 25:23

APPENDIX A

JOSÉ VELÁSQUEZ'
MILITARY SERVICE RECORD

It was not until about 1781 that official military service records in New Spain were prepared and kept with any consistency. Prior to that time records were apparently prepared by individual officers to accompany their requests for promotion, reassignment, etc.[1] In 1781, Governor Felipe de Neve of Alta California, in his famous Reglamento, ordered, the preparation in standard form of the service records of all officers and sergeants on duty in California. In accord with these orders, Lieutenant José de Zúñiga, commanding officer of the royal presidio of San Diego, prepared the official record for Alférez José Velásquez.[2] This record is provided below in translation. The printing on the original form is here italicized.

The Alférez D. José Velásquez — *HIS AGE* sixty six years — *HIS COUNTRY (BIRTHPLACE)* San Ildefonso de Ostímuri — *HIS CHARACTER* honorable — *HIS HEALTH* robust. *HIS SERVICES AND CIRCUMSTANCES ARE AS STATED.*

DATES ON WHICH HE BEGAN EACH ASSIGNMENT

ASSIGNMENT	DAY	MONTH	YEAR
Soldier	1	January	1751
Corporal	1	May	1768
Sergeant	2	April	1771
Alférez (Ensign)	2	February	1773

---

[1]An "old style" service record, that of Captain Juan Bautista de Anza (1767) is presented in Kieran McCarty, "Desert Documentary," pp. 5-7. A collection of later service records (1817) is contained in the same work, pp. 111-132.

[2]This information was obtained from a photostat of the original document supplied by the Bancroft Library. The document carries the identification Guadalajara 286 (103-5-5): Chapman 4909.

TIME SERVED AND DURATION IN EACH ASSIGNMENT

ASSIGNMENT	YEARS	MONTHS	DAYS
Soldier	17	4	
Corporal	2	11	19
Sergeant	1	9	13
Alférez (Ensign)	10	10	18

TOTAL TO END OF December 1783
33[3]

REGIMENTS IN WHICH HE SERVED

In the cavalry company of the presidio of Loreto, 29 years, 9 months, and 26 days, and at the presidio of San Diego the remainder of the total (3 years, 2 months and 4 days to December 31, 1783).

CAMPAIGNS AND ACTIONS OF WAY IN WHICH HE SERVED.

In the expedition for the discovery of San Diego and Monterey, at which latter point he made the second entry, since it was not found on the first. With only one servant he crossed the new establishments, taking the (packets of) letters to Mexico, with the news of the occupation of Monterey. He remained ten years on detached service on the frontier with the heathen Indians of Old California, during which he made many journeys to their villages and into the Sierra in search of recent Christian fugitives. On four occasions they made war on him and he came out wounded in one of them. And in the past year, 1782, he went into the Sierra and to the place called San Sebastián, and he made a campaign under the orders of the Commanding General Don Felipe de Neve against the rebelling Indians of the Colorado River.

José Zúñiga
(Rubric)

---

[3]Lieutenant Zúñiga had some trouble with his arithmetic here. Although the total service was 33 years, as stated, the columns add up to only 32 years, 11 months and 20 days. The error seems to be in the time served as corporal. Subtraction shows that this should be 2 years, 11 months and 29 days, not the two years, 11 months and 19 days stated in the record.

NOTES OF THE COLONEL

N.B. This is Lieutenant Zúñiga's evaluation of Alférez José Velásquez.

VALOR	sufficient
DILIGENCE	he has it
ABILITY	moderate
CONDUCT	regular
CONDITION [marital status]	widower
Zúñiga	(Rubric)

INFORMATION OF THE INSPECTOR

N.B "Inspector" here has been crossed out, and "adjutant" inspector inserted.

Age has wearied this officer. His retirement is requested because he is useful only for fatigues in the field, and has little confidence in deliberating by himself.

(Rubric)

This rubric is almost certainly that of Captain Nicolás Soler, adjutant inspector of the presidios of California.

APPENDIX B

PERSONNEL MENTIONED
IN PEDRO FAGES' DIARIES
OF THE COLORADO RIVER CAMPAIGNS

ANTONIO, JOSÉ. Yuma Indian, son of Salvador Palma.

ARBIZU, ALFÉREZ MANUEL ANTONIO, remained in military service after the Colorado River campaigns, becoming captain at Altar in 1796. A close, and probably younger relative, Manuel Ignacio de Arvizu, had a distinguished military career in Sonora from 1779-1803; see H.F. Dobyns, *Spanish Colonial Tucson*, p. 204, Note 9.

BARRANECHE, FATHER JUAN, O.F.M. (Yuma martyr), see H.H. Bancroft, *Early California Annals*, pp. 362-363, Note 12; Douglas Martin, *Yuma Crossing*, pp. 49-52, 63-70.

BENÍTEZ, MARÍA JOSEFA, rescued Yuma captive, 10 years old.

CASTRO (Corporal of Buenavista). Because Castro was a common name in the Sonoran military service in 1781, as it still is, this corporal cannot be further identified with certainty.

CENIZO, FATHER ENRIQUE, O.F.M. (Chaplain of expedition) was born at Dávila, Salamanca, Spain, about 1733. He took the habit *(tomo el avito)* at the age of 25 in 1758. He had been a religious for eleven years when he left Spain in 1769. (AGI, Guad. 369, Bancroft Library Film). He apparently suffered from ill health after his arrival in the New World. After spending some time at Pátzcuaro, he next appears on the record as a military chaplain at Santa Gertrudis de Altar, and from there in 1781 he accompanied the Fages Expedition to Yuma. He was *capellan propietario* at Altar and unable to perform some of his duties because of illness *(por enfermedad* April 6, 1791). Data from archives of Altar, Sonora, courtesy of Rev. Dr. Kieran McCarty, O.F.M.

CROIX, TEODORO DE, Commandant-General of Provincias Internas, see note 25, Historical Summary, p. 15.

DÍAZ, FATHER JUAN, O.F.M., (Yuma martyr) see H.H. Bancroft, *Early California Annals*, pp. 362-363, Note 12; Douglas Martin, *Yuma Crossing*, pp. 49-52, 63-70.

FAGES, PEDRO (Commander of Expedition), see Note 28, Historical Summary, p. 18.

FRANCO, JUAN (Sergeant) stayed in the military service after the Colorado River campaigns; his name appears on the record as first ensign of the Tucson garrison in 1794. He was promoted to Lieutenant on May 9, 1794, and retired with that rank on June 8, 1797. Dobyns, *Spanish Colonial Tucson*, p. 107, 204, Note 5.

GARCÉS, FATHER FRANCISCO (Yuma martyr), see Note 10, Historical Summary, p. 3.

JAVIER, FRANCISCO, Jalicomaya Indian. Jalicomaya is apparently the same tribal group as Hakyikamais who lived along the Colorado in the mid 18th century, midway between the Gila-Colorado junction and the river's mouth. See internal index in Jack Forbes, *Warriors of the Colorado*.

MORAGA, IGNACIO, Sergeant of Altar, retired as captain at Altar sometime prior to 1797. His son, Salvador Moraga, who was born in 1776, and enlisted in 1797, was promoted to carbineer in 1807, and to first corporal of the company in 1816 (see detailed service records in McCarty, *Desert Documentary*, pp. 115-116). Probable close relationship between the various Moragas who served honorably in Sonora and in California is not made entirely clear by available records.

MORENO, FATHER MATÍAS, O.F.M. (Yuma martyr), see H.H. Bancroft, *Early California Annals*, pp. 362-363, Note 12; Douglas Martin, *Yuma Crossing*, pp. 49-52, 63-70.

NEVE, FELIPE DE, Governor of California. Born in Bailen, Spain; birthdate uncertain. After some military training and experience there, he came to the New World, appearing first in the records of Mexico in 1766 as a recruiter for the newly formed Querétaro Regiment of Provincial Cavalry. By 1774 he had attained the rank of major and also served as alcalde of Querétaro. On October 28, 1774, he was appointed governor of California to replace Felipe de Barri. Neve arrived at Loreto, Baja California, March 4, 1775. The capital was soon moved to Monterey by official orders dated April 19, 1776. Neve moved northward shortly thereafter and arrived in Monterey February 3, 1777. As governor, Neve encouraged and supported the founding of several communities, chief among which were Santa Bárbara, San José, and Los Angeles.

He prepared a *Reglamento* which led to the improvement of previously chaotic military records. He had continual difficulties with the missionaries, due in part to the unclear delineation of authority, jurisdiction, and responsibility. In early September, 1782, while riding eastward to the long postponed attack on the rebellious Yumas, he was overtaken by a messenger bearing official messages. These messages contained Neve's promotion from governor to Inspector General of the Provincias Internas. The messages also contained Pedro Fages' promotion to the governorship of California. The transfer of office took place at Saucito, near Santa Catarina spring in Coyote Canyon, on September 10, 1782. Neve, after some rather indecisive military actions at Yuma, travelled eastward through Sonoyta to Arispe.

As Inspector General, he founded the Villa de los Seris (near modern Hermosillo) and wrote a number of intemperate criticisms of the Yuma enterprises in which he blamed Juan Bautista de Anza for what had gone wrong. Neve was later promoted to Commandant-general of the Provincias Internas. He died August 21, 1784, at what is now known as La Colonia Flores Magón, Chihuahua. See H.H. Bancroft, *Early California Annals*, pp. 237-238, 296, 363, 393, 405, 446-448, 608.

NORIEGA, JUAN, Sergeant, appears on the 1818 roster at Tucson. We cannot be sure that this is the same man who was a sergeant at Altar in 1781-82.

PACHULA, Indian chief at San Sebastián.

PALACIOS, MIGUEL, Sergeant. An officer named Palacios (no other identification) was in command of the presidio of Tucson on April 1, 1805. Here again we have an identity problem.

PALMA, IGNACIO. Yuma sub-chief, brother of Salvador.

PALMA, SALVADOR, Chief of Yumas. See Note 16, Historical Summary, p. 6.

RIVERA, MIGUEL, Sergeant. No additional information available.

RIVERA Y MONCADA, CAPTAIN FERNANDO JAVIER. Killed at Yuma. Captain Fernando Javier de Rivera y Moncada was born near Compostela, Mexico, about 1725. He entered the military service in 1742 and was immediately assigned to Baja California. In 1750, at the death of Captain Bernardo Rodríguez Lorenzo, he was named his successor as captain of the presidio of Loreto. He took an active part in Ferdinand Consag's famous expeditions of 1751 and 1753. He also accompanied Wenceslaus Linck's lengthy expedition of 1765 and supplied a military escort for Linck's famous 1766 exploration to the San Felipe area although he did not personally accompany it. During the Jesuit expulsion of 1767 acting under the orders of Gaspar de Portolá, he helped assemble the Jesuits for their journey to Europe and took an active part in the transfer of Jesuit properties to the Franciscans. During the northward march (1769) which resulted in the founding of San Diego, Rivera was military leader of one of the land parties.

Before the new arrivals at San Diego had recovered from their saddle sores and scurvy, Rivera became a member of a military party that set forth northward, July 14, 1769, to discover the port of Monterey. Missing the seaport, the expedition travelled beyond it to the San Francisco area, and finally returned to San Diego on January 24, 1770. Here, supplies being scarce, Rivera was sent south with forty men to get supplies from the missions of Baja California. Rivera retired to the mainland, apparently in 1770, and planned to spend the rest of his life on a farm near Guadalajara. His plans for retirement did not work out. In 1773, after a conference between Viceroy Bucareli and Father Serra, Rivera was appointed military governor of California to replace Pedro Fages with whom Serra found much fault. Late in 1773 Rivera left for his new post, travelling via Guadalajara, Tepic, and Sinaloa, to recruit some fifty or so settlers en route. Sailing across the Gulf of California from the mouth of the Yaqui, he arrived in Loreto in March, 1774. Thence, he rode horseback the entire distance from Loreto to Monterey, more than 1200 miles by the then-extant trails, where he arrived on March 23, 1774. From that date until he was relieved on February 3, 1777, Rivera occupied an "impossible" position with multiple unsolvable problems — too few soldiers, bad morale, rebellious Indians, inadequate supplies, not enough animals for transportation, no pay, ill-defined authority and responsibility and many stubborn missionaries, who had no authority and ill-defined responsiblity. During this period, planned extension of the mission system was slowed by lack of soldiers and supplies; it was interrupted by the Indian raid on mission San Diego de Alcala, Nov. 5, 1775, in which Father Luis Jaime and others were killed. Rivera, accompanied by Juan Bautista de Anza who had just arrived at San Gabriel with settlers from Sonora, visited the scene and attempted to restore some sort of order. As a result of his efforts to recapture an Indian miscreant, who had sought ecclesiastical asylum in the church at San Diego de Alcala, Rivera was excommunicated, on somewhat shaky grounds, by Father Vicente Fuster, O.F.M. Rivera's somewhat irrational behavior in his conferences and correspondence with Anza (late April and early May, 1776) can be better understood when it is realized that he was not only profoundly upset by his possibly unjust excommunication, but also that he was suffering from fever, dizziness, and a pain in his thigh. This physical condition probably was the result of an earlier, poorly-set leg fracture by which, incidentally, his bones were identified in late 1781 after his death at the hands of the Yumas. He notes in his diary for April 13, 1776: . . . *no venía en estado de leer por el dolor*. Despite Rivera's opposition, on rather good military grounds, the San Francisco colony was established in late summer and fall of 1776 with Lieutenant José Joaquín Moraga in active command. Early in 1777 both Californias were combined into a single administration with Monterey as the capital. Don Felipe de Neve, formerly governor of Baja California, was assigned as governor of the enlarged province, and Rivera, despite his repeated requests for retirement, was assigned as military commander of Loreto, Baja California. Among his many duties was the recruitment of additional soldiers and settlers for Alta California. In late 1780 and early 1781, Rivera, now on the mainland and in compliance with his orders, had recruited many soldiers and settlers needed for the new settlements in Alta California. The settlers were sent by sea to Loreto — one group went north by sea under the command of Alférez Ramón Lasso de la Vega, to Bahía San Luis Gonzaga; the second group followed overland under the command of Lieutenant José Zúñiga. From the San Luis Bay both groups rode overland through San Diego; all arrived safely at mission San Gabriel by August 18, 1781. Meanwhile, Captain Rivera on the mainland, accompanied by 42 soldiers and 961 horses and mules, rode north toward the Colorado crossing. At Tucson, he acquired an additional temporary military guard, commanded by Lieutenant Andrés Arias Caballero. At the Yuma crossing, Rivera was met by some soldiers from California, commanded by Sergeant Juan José Robles. The Tucson contingent was sent back. Most of the others in the party were sent on to San Gabriel under the command of Lieutenant Diego González and Alfereces Cayetano Limón and José Dário Arguello. This group, consisting of thirty-five soldiers, thirty families, and some members of the Sonoran escort, arrived at San Gabriel on July 14, 1781. Rivera, with his small remaining troop and nearly a thousand horses and mules, went into camp on the Arizona side of the crossing. The tired and hungry livestock ate everything in sight, including the Yuma crops. Beginning on July 17, 1781, the Yuma people went on a rampage, destroying the two mission settlements — La Purísima Concepción and San Pedro y San Pablo Bicuñer — killing or capturing all the Spaniards in both settlements, and later, crossing the river, exterminated the small military group under Captain Rivera y Moncada despite a valiant but hopeless defense.

ROMERO, MIGUEL ANTONIO, Yuma captive from Buenavista.

ROMEU, CAPTAIN JOSEPH ANTONIO. From Altar. One of a number of competent and experienced soldiers who came to the New World from Spain after about 1760. These soldiers were entirely separate from the better known Catalonian Volunteers, under the command of Captain Agustín Callis and Lieutenant Pedro Fages. Joseph Romeu was born at Valladolid, Spain, probably in the 1740s. He came to the New World and to Sonora in time to develop close personal friendships with many of those who served in the Elizondo campaigns against the Seri rebels. He probably served in these campaigns, but he is nowhere mentioned in numerous available documents concerning the Seri wars. Before 1780 he was serving at the royal presidio of Santa Gertrudis de Altar with the rank of captain. Romeu took a very active part in the Colorado River campaign (1781-82). As a result he was recommended for promotion from captain of dragoons to lieutenant colonel by Teodoro de Croix (Croix to Gálvez, Arispe, November 20, 1782; AGI Guadalajara 283).

In this letter of recommendation the services of Captain Pedro de Tueros were also favorably mentioned; commendations were aslo made for Raphael Tovar, Manuel Arvizu, and Diego López. Tovar was listed as a sergeant by Fages, and Manuel Arvizu was an alférez. Sergeant Diego López, apparently a member of the Altar company, was not listed by Fages. From 1781 to early 1791, Joseph Romeu continued at Altar, commanding the post at times. He was then appointed governor of California to succeed Fages. Romeu received the "keys of office" at Loreto, Baja California, from Lieutenant Governor José Joaquín Arillaga on April 16, 1791. In ill health with symptoms suggestives of cardiac ischemia, Romeu rode slowly northward, arriving in Monterey October 13, 1791. There he died April 19, 1792. See H.H. Bancroft, *Early California Annals*; Priestley, *Colorado River Campaigns*; and AGI Guadalajara 283.

SAMBRANO, MARÍA JULIANA, rescued Yuma captive. Her new born daughter was mentioned but not named in Fages' diary.

TOVAR, GASPAR, Sergeant, see note on Romeu above.

TOVAR, RAFAEL, Sergeant, see note on Romeu above; it seems likely that Gaspar and Raphael are the same person.

TUEROS, PEDRO, commander of the presidio of Altar. Rendered as Fueros in many accounts. Tueros was an experienced frontier soldier. He was probably born and educated in Spain. He first appears in the records of New Spain in 1772 when he was the fiscal commissioner at the placers of Cieneguilla near Caborca. In this capacity he wrote and excellent report (1772) which was verified and endorsed by Francisco Antonio Crespo, governor of Sonora, in 1774. Later, with the rank of captain, he served at the presidio of Altar as post commander. After March, 1778, he was commandant at arms of Sonora. He took a very active part in many frontier military engagements, specifically including the Colorado River campaigns. His services were commended in 1782 and he was appointed governor of Coahuila in that year. See McCarty, *Desert Documentary,* pp. 19-24; also Dobyns, *Spanish Colonial Tucson,* pp. 68, 198; and Priestly, *Colorado River Campaigns,* passim.

VELÁSQUEZ, JOSÉ, second-in-command of San Diego.

ZÚÑIGA, JOSEPH DE, commander at San Diego. Zúñiga was born in Mexico in 1755. He enlisted as an officer trainee October 18, 1772. After extensive service on the Texas frontier, he was commissioned as alférez August 26, 1778, and promoted to lieutenant April 21, 1780. The next year he conducted a division of Rivera y Moncada's colonists from Guaymas to Loreto and Bahía San Luis Gonzaga by sea. Then he led the column overland via San Fernando Velicatá to mission San Gabriel. José Velásquez was designated guide from Velicatá to San Gabriel. On September 28, 1781, Zúñiga was assigned, as lieutenant, to command the presidio of San Diego, which position he occupied for more than eleven years. During his tenure there, relations with the Indians, with his superiors, and with the missionaries were cordial. During much of this time he served as the quartermaster/paymaster and — a rare accomplishment for Alta California at that time — kept his accounts in perfect order.

On May 19, 1792, he was promoted to captain and assigned to the presidio of San Agustín de Tucson as commander. After a period of detached duty at Monterey, he finally arrived at Tucson in 1794. The next year from April through May he led an expedition from Tucson to Zuñi and back. His full report on conditions at Tucson (1804) is one of the best surviving records from that time. During his tenure at Tucson, Zúñiga served as the adjutant inspector of the military province of Arispe with the rank of lieutenant colonel. After 1810 the records of José de Zúñiga are elided with those of Ignacio de Zúñiga. Who remained active until after 1842, or 87 years after the birth of José. See Dobyns, *Spanish Colonial Tucson*; Jack Holterman, "José de Zúñiga," *Kiva*, Vol. 22, No. 1 (Nov. 1956); George Hammond, "The Zúñiga Journal," *New Mexico Historical Review*, Vol. VI, No. 1 (Jan. 1931); and McCarty, *Desert Documentary*, pp. 86-92.

APPENDIX C

THE GARCÉS STATUE

Plans for a statue of Father Hermenegildo Francisco Garcés, at the scene of his martyrdom, were apparently first conceived about 1926 by Father Tiburtius Wand, O.F.M. (Born, Aureus Wand, Heiligenstadt, Germany, June 3, 1884; died, Santa Barbara, California, April 8, 1962), then stationed at Yuma. With a donation of $2,000 from a prominent Yuma citizen, Mr. Charles D. Baker, negotiations were begun with a prominent German sculptor, Mr. Joseph Fleck, for the creation of the statue.

The sculptor, Joseph Fleck, was born January 10, 1884, at Mellrichstadt, Bavaria, Germany, into a family already noted for its sculptors. He studied in the academies of Florence and Rome, and, during a long and productive life, created statues that now stand on all of the five inhabited continents. Joseph Fleck died October 1, 1970. His studio, in Fulda, Germany, is now operated by his son, Rudolf Fleck, also a sculptor.

While Joseph Fleck was creating the statue, Father Wand was transferred from Yuma, and Mr. Charles Baker died, leaving the completion of the project in the hands of Rev. Nicholas Perschl, O.F.M. (born, Francis Xavier Perschl, in St. Paul, Minnesota, on December 3, 1887; died, Phoenix, Arizona, June 16, 1969), and Brother Wendelin Hottinger, O.F.M. (born, Unteralpfen, Freiburg, Germany, May 12, 1854; died, San Luis Rey, California, November 23, 1936). Upon these two diligent and productive workers devolved the tasks of preparing the base for the statue, its shipment and erection, and arrangements for the dedication. Base for the statue contained petrified wood, hauled from a distance of forty miles. Father Perschl and Brother Hottinger personally made forms, poured cement, and built a small octagonal garden about the base for the statue.

When completed in Germany, the statue was sent by rail to the Atlantic coast, then shipped by sea via the Panama Canal to San Pedro, California, and thence sent by rail to Yuma. With the assistance of heavy hoisting machinery lent by the U.S. Bureau of Reclamation, the statue was moved from the rail car, carried up Mission Hill, and firmly mounted on the prepared base. The formal dedication, October 21, 1928, was, according to Father Perschl's autobiographical notes:

. . . a gala affair. A crowd of over 3,000 attended. Father Fidelis
Voss, O.F.M. brought a group of Apaches from far away Apache-
land. Other missionaries accompanied their Pimas, Papagos, etc.
Old-time Sisters of St. Joseph who had worked in Yuma across the
river also enhanced the festivity by their presence. Bishop [John
Joseph] Cantwell [of Los Angeles] blessed the statue and gave a
wonderful speech. He was followed in turn by Bishop Juan Navarrete
[born, Oaxaca, August 12, 1886] Archbishop for Northern Sonora,
Mexico, who gave a Spanish speech. This too was a masterpiece.
Finally Dr. Frank G. Lockwood, Dean of the University of Arizona,
pinch-hitting for Professor [Herbert Eugene] Bolton who was unable
to attend, gave a masterful speech comparing the two great missionaries of the Southwest, Kino and Garcés. It left no doubt in the
minds of the listeners that Garcés fully deserved to have a memorial
erected in his honor on the spot where he shed his blood for his faith
and in the exercise of his missionary calling. To climax it all a "big
feed" was given by the Indians.

Inscription of the bronze plaque on the base of the statue reads:

BORN APRIL 12, 1718
DIED JULY 19, 1781
FRAY
HERMENEGILDO FRANCISCO
GARCES
DARING EXPLORER, ZEALOUS
MISSIONARY AND UNFAILING
FRIEND OF THE YUMA INDIANS
PADRE GARCES FOUNDED THE
YUMA INDIAN MISSION AND
NEARBY GAVE HIS LIFE
FOR THEIR SOULS
HIS FAITH WAS UNSHAKABLE
HIS HOPE WAS TRANQUIL HIS CHARITY JOYOUS
HIS ZEAL TRIUMPHANT

The statue is located in the courtyard of St. Thomas' Indian Mission,
atop Mission Hill, directly across the Colorado River from the Yuma
Territorial Prison. Official location is in NW 1/4 of NW 1/4 of Section

36, Range 22, East, Township 16 South, California Coordinate System, Zone 6, clearly shown on the U.S. Geological Survey 7.5' Quadrangle Yuma, East (1965). The boundary between Imperial County (California) and Yuma County (Arizona) passes through Mission Hill. St. Thomas' Indian Mission is easily accessible by paved roads from Yuma (Arizona) and Winterhaven (California), and will become more accessible late in 1978 when the new bridge across the Colorado River is completed.

Data sources include Yuma County Historical Society; Yuma Daily Sun (editions of October 21 and 22, 1928); Oblasser Library, Mission San Xavier del Bac; Rev. Dr. Kieran McCarty, O.F.M., Tucson, Arizona; Franciscan Archives, Oakland, California; German Consulate, Phoenix, Arizona; U.S. Consulate General, Frankfurt au Main, Germany; Fulda Historical Society; and Mr. Rudolf Fleck, Fulda, Germany.

APPENDIX D

MISSIONS OF BAJA CALIFORNIA

MISSION NAME	ORDER	FOUNDED/ ABANDONED	PHYSICAL STATUS
San Bruno	Jesuit	1683-1685	Stone ruins
Loreto	Jesuit	1697-1822	Stone, rebuilt
San Javier	Jesuit	1699-1817	Stone
Liguí	Jesuit	1705-1721	Tile Floor
Mulegé	Jesuit	1705-1828	Stone
Comondú	Jesuit	1708-1827	Stone ruins

Father Juan María Salvatierra, S.J. died July 18, 1717
José Velásquez was born some time during the year 1717

La Purísima	Jesuit	1719-1822	Stone ruins
La Paz	Jesuit	1720-1749	No ruins
Guadalupe (Sur)	Jesuit	1720-1795	Stone foundation
Dolores	Jesuit	1721-1740	Adobe ruins
Santiago	Jesuit	1724-1795	No ruins
San Ignacio	Jesuit	1728-1840	Stone
San José del Cabo	Jesuit	1730-1840	No ruins
San Miguel (Sur)	Jesuit	1730-1737	No ruins
Todos Santos	Jesuit	1734-1854	Adobe, rebuilt
San Luis Gonzaga	Jesuit	1737-1768	Stone
La Pasión	Jesuit	1737-1768	Stone ruins

José Velásquez enlisted January 1, 1751 at Loreto, Baja California

Santa Gertrudis	Jesuit	1752-1822	Stone
San Borja	Jesuit	1762-1818	Stone
Calamajué	Jesuit	1766-1767	Adobe ruins
Santa María	Jesuit	1767-1769	Adobe ruins

Jesuit expulsion, 1767-8

San Fernando	Franciscan	1769-1818	Adobe ruins

Mission field of Baja California ceded to the Dominicans in 1773.

El Rosario	Dominican	1774-1832	Adobe ruins
Santo Domingo	Dominican	1775-1839	Adobe ruins
San Vicente	Dominican	1780-1833	Adobe ruins

Yuma massacre, July 17, 1781
José Velásquez dies at mission San Gabriel, Calif. Nov. 2, 1785

San Miguel	Dominican	1787-1834	Adobe ruins
Santo Tomás	Dominican	1791-1849	Adobe ruins
San Pedro Mártir	Dominican	1794-1806	Stone foundation
Santa Catalina	Dominican	1797-1840	Adobe ruins
Descanso	Dominican	1814-1834	No ruins
Guadalupe (Norte)	Dominican	1834-1840	No ruins

The foregoing list is expanded from the tabulation in Walt Wheelock and H.E. Gulick *Baja California Guidebook* p. 18. Locations of the Jesuit missions of Baja California are shown on a map by Jane Bendix in P.M. Dunne *Black Robes in Lower California*. Routes to the missions or their ruins are described, as of 1975, in Wheelock and Gulick, and successive locations of the missions, when they were moved, are given in the same work.

MISSIONARIES AND MISSIONS IN BAJA CALIFORNIA — 1751

MISSIONARY	MISSION
Juan Armesto	Loreto
Miguel del Barco	San Javier
Jacobo Baegert	San Luis
Juan Bischoff	Santiago
Fernando Consag	San Ignacio
Jacobo Druet	Purísima
José Gasteiger	Guadalupe
Lamberto Hostell	Los Dolores
Francisco Inama	La Paz
Francisco López (brother)	Loreto
Juan Mugazábal (brother)	Loreto
Pedro Nascimben	Santa Rosalía
Carlos Neumayer	San José del Cabo
Jorge Retz	Santa Rosa (Todos Santos)
José Rondero	San José Comondú

JESUIT MISSIONARIES OF BAJA CALIFORNIA

NAME	NATIONALITY	BORN	ARRIVAL	DEPARTURE	DIED	AGE	PLACE
Arnés, Victoriano	Spaniard	1736	1764	1768	1788	52	Rome
Armesto, Juan	Spaniard	1713	1748	1752	1795	82	Bologna
Badillo, Francisco M.	Spaniard	1719	1752	—	1783	64	—
Baegert, Jakob	Alsatian	1717	1751	1768	1772	65	Neustadt
Barco, Miguel	Spaniard	1706	1744	1768	1790	84	Bologna
Basaldua, Juan	Mexican	1675	1702	1709	—	—	—
Bischoff, Johann	Bohemian	1710	1752	1768	after 1769	—	Bohemia
Bravo, Jaime	Spaniard	1683	1705	—	1744	61	Loreto
Carrasco, Lorenzo	Mexican	1695?	1727	—	1734	39?	Santiago
Consag, Fernando	Croatian	1703	1733	—	1759	56	Santa Gertrudis
Copart, Juan B.	—	—	1684	—	—	—	—
Diez, Juan José	Mexican	1735	1766	1768	1809	74	Ferrara
Druet, Jacobo	Italian	1698	1732	—	1753	55	—
Ducrue, Franz Benno	German	1721	1748	1768	1779	58	Munich
Echeverría, José	Spaniard	1688	1730	—	1756	68	—
Escalante, Francisco	Spaniard	1724	1756	1768	1806	82	Jaén
Franco, Francisco I.	Spaniard	1738	1764	1768	1807	69	Bologna
García, Andrés	Spaniard	1686	1737	—	1764	78	—
Gasteiger, Joseph	German	1702	1745	—	1754	52	Guadalupe
Goñi, Mathías	Spaniard	1648	1683	1685	1712	64	Mexico
Gordon, William	Scot.	1677	1730	—	—	—	—
Guillén, Clemente	Mexican	—	1714	—	1748	71	Loreto
Guisi, Benito	Italian	—	1711	1712	1713	—	lost at sea
Helen, Everard	German	—	1719	1735	1757	—	—
Hostell, Lambert	German	1706	1745	1768	1773	67?	Dusseldorf
Inama, Franz	Austrian	1719	1750	1768	1782	63	Vienna
Kino, Eusebio F.	Italian	1645	1683	1685	1711	66	Magdalena
Link, Wenceslaus	Bohemian	1736	1762	1768	1790	54?	Oelmutz?
López, Francisco	Mexican?	—	—	—	—	—	—
Luyando, Agustín	Mexican	—	1730	1730	—	—	—
Luyando, Juan	Mexican	1700	1727	1734	1757	57	Tepotzlian

This listing is slightly condensed and modified from a tabulation in Burrus (ed) *Informe del Estado de la Nueva Cristianidad de California* (Madrid: Porrua, 1962) p. 310.

JESUIT MISSIONARIES OF BAJA CALIFORNIA

NAME	NATIONALITY	BORN	ARRIVAL	DEPARTURE	DIED	AGE	PLACE
Masariegos, Francisco	Mexican	1685	1740	1740	after 1753	—	Sinaloa
Mayorga, Julián	Spaniard	1669?	1707	—	1736	67?	Comondú
Minutili, Gerónimo	Italian	1669	1702	1705	after 1712	—	Sonora
Mugazábal, Juan	Spaniard	1682	1704	—	1761	79	Loreto
Nápoli, Ignacio	Italian	—	1721	1732	1744?	—	—
Nascimbén, Pedro	Venetian	1703	1745	—	1754	51	—
Neumeyer, Carlos	German	1707	1745	—	1764	57	Todos Santos
Osorio, Francisco	Mexican	—	1725	1727	—	—	—
Peralta, Francisco	Mexican?	—	1709	—	1711	—	—
Piccolo, Francisco	Sicilian	1650	1697	—	1729	79	Loreto
Retz, George	German	1714	1748	1768	1773	59	Trier
Rondero, José	Mexican	1718	1745	1751	1768	50?	Ixtlán
Rotes, José María	Mexican	1732	1750	1768	1799	67	Bologna
Salazar, Julián	Mexican	1728	—	1768	1790	62	Zeca
Salvatierra, Juan	Italian	1644	1697	—	1717	73	Loreto
Schwartz, —	German?	—	—	—	—	—	—
Sistiago, Sebastián	Mexican	1684	1718	1747	1756	72	—
Sotebajar, Tomás	—	—	—	—	—	—	—
Sotelo, Manuel	Spaniard	1736	1761	—	—	—	—
Tamaral, Nicolás	Spaniard	1687	1717	—	1734	47	San José del Cabo
Taraval, Sigismundo	Italian	1700	1730	1750?	1763	65	Santiago
Tempis, Antonio	Austrian	1703	1736	—	1746	43	Bohemia
Tirsch, Ignacio	Bohemian	1733	1762	1768	after 1769	—	—
Trujillo, Gaspar	Mexican	1704	1744	1748	1775	71	—
Trujillo, Joaquín	Mexican	1726?	1744?	1748?	—	—	—
Ugarte, Juan	Honduran	1660	1700	—	1730	70	San Javier
Ugarte, Pedro	Honduran	—	1704	1710	—	—	—
Ventura, Lucas	Spaniard	1727	1757	1768	1795	66	Bologna
Villavieja, Juan	Spaniard	1736	1766	1768	1816	80	Cadiz
Wagner, Franz	German	1706?	1737	—	1744	58	Comondú
Zumpziel, Bernard	German	1707	1739	1748	—	—	—

This tabulation is based on Gerard Decorme, *La Obra de los Jesuitas Mexicanos,* Vol. II, p. 543. This has been corrected and augmented by the insertion of later information, much of it derived from researches by Rev. Drs. Ernest J. Burrus, S.J. and Charles W. Polzer, S.J.

FRANCISCAN MISSIONARIES IN THE CALIFORNIAS 1769-1785

NAME	NATIONALITY	BORN	ARRIVAL	DEPARTURE	DIED	AGE	PLACE
Amurrio, Gregorio	Spaniard	1744	1773	1779	—	—	—
Barreneche, Juan	Spaniard	1749	1779	—	1781	32	Yuma
Cambón, Pedro	Spaniard	1738	1771	1792	—	—	—
Caveller, José	Spaniard	1740	1771	—	1789	49	San Luis Obispo
Crespí, Juan	Spaniard	1721	1769	—	1782	61	San Carlos
Cruzado, Antonio	Spaniard	1724	1771	—	1804	80	San Gabriel
Díaz, Juan	Spaniard	1736	1780	—	1781	45	Yuma
Dumetz, Francisco	Spaniard	1734	1771	—	1811	77	San Gabriel
Figuer, Juan	Spaniard	c. 1742	1772	—	1784	42	San Diego
Fuster, Vicente	Spaniard	1742	1773	—	1800	58	San Juan Capistrano
Garcés, Francisco	Spaniard	1738	1780	—	1781	43	Yuma
García Riobo, Juan	Spaniard	1740	1782	1786	—	—	—
Giribet, Miguel	Spaniard	1756	1785	1800	1804	48	Agramont
Gómez, Francisco	Spaniard	1729	1769	1771	—	—	—
Jayme, Antonio	Spaniard	1740	1771	—	1775	35	San Diego
Juncosa, Domingo	Spaniard	1740	1771	1774	—	—	—
Lasuén, Fermín	Spaniard	1736	1773	—	1803	67	San Carlos
Mariner, Juan	Spaniard	1743	1785	—	1800	57	San Diego
Moreno, Joseph	Spaniard	1744	1780	—	1781	37	Yuma
Mugartegui, Pablo	Spaniard	1736	1774	1789	—	—	—
Mugia, Joseph	Spaniard	1715	1773	—	1784	69	Santa Clara
Noboa, Diego	Spaniard	1742	1783	—	1798	56	—
Noriega, Matías	Spaniard	1736	1779	—	1798	62	—
Palou, Francisco	Spaniard	1723	1773	1785	1789	66	Querétaro
Parrón, Fernando	Spaniard	c. 1728	1769	1771	—	—	—
Paterna, Antonio	Spaniard	1721	1771	—	1793	72	Santa Bárbara
Pena Saravia, Tomás	Spaniard	1743	1772	1794	1806	63	Mexico City
Pieras, Miguel	Spaniard	1741	1771	1794	1795	54	Mexico City
Prestamero, Juan	Spaniard	1736	1773	1774	—	—	—
Sánchez, Miguel	Spaniard	1738	1774	—	1803	65	San Gabriel
Santa María, Vicente	Spaniard	1742	1775	—	1806	64	San Buenaventura
Serra, Junípero	Spaniard	1713	1769	—	1784	71	San Carlos
Sitjar, Buenaventura	Spaniard	1739	1771	—	1808	69	San Antonio
Somera, Angel	Mexican	1743?	1771	1772	—	—	—
Uson, Ramón	Spaniard	1737	1772	1774	—	—	—
Vizcaíno, Juan	Spaniard	1728	1769	1770	—	—	—

This tabulation is derived in major part from Maynard Geiger, *Franciscan Missionaries in Hispanic California, 1769-1848*. Discussion of additional data, some of it highly discrepant, with the late Father Geiger was found most helpful.

APPENDIX E

PORTOLA'S ACT OF FORMAL POSSESSION OF THE PORT OF MONTEREY

Don Gaspar de Portolá, captain of dragoons of the regiment of Spain, governor of California and commander-in-chief of the expeditions to the ports of San Diego and Monterey, located at 33 and 37 degrees (north) latitude, in accordance with the royal decree:

Be it known by this present letter that in this presidio and at the port of Monterey on June 3 of this year, in fulfillment of the orders in my possession given me by the Most Illustrious Inspector General, Don Joseph de Gálvez, member of the royal and supreme Council and Chamber of the Indies of His Majesty, as appears in the decree given me naming me commander-in-chief of the said expedition, by virtue of his viceregal powers, and noting among the articles of the decree one which I must duly execute immediately upon my arrival at the said port of Monterey, that I should take formal possession in the name of His Catholic Majesty. I ordered the officers of the land and sea to convene and requested the reverend fathers to be also present in observance of the same orders, and I ordered the troops to stand by armed.

Informing them of my orders and having chosen the moment for their fulfillment, I proceeded to take possession in the royal name of His Majesty in accordance with the instructions outlined by the decree. I performed the ceremony of throwing earth and stones in the direction of the four winds and proclaiming possession in the royal name of His Catholic Majesty, Don Carlos III (whom may God preserve), by recognizing as his property the said port of Monterey and all other lands which by right and title thereto pertain. Having raised the triumphant standard of the cross as the first object of interest of the Catholic, Christian, and pious zeal of His Majesty, I manifested this through the orders given by my superiors. This interest becomes all the more evident from the generosity with which he has opened the royal treasury for the purpose of garnering the evangelical harvest and which is provided for the benefit of the innumerable pagans of this fair land.

In witness whereof and for evermore, I affix my signature as do the officers as witnesses. And bearing in mind that the maritime officers, according to their calling, recognize more about ports than the officers of the land, I wish that they also be witnesses in order to insure more authenticity. They are the captain of the bark called *El Príncipe*, which is at the said port commanded by Don Juan Pérez and whose pilot is Don Miguel del Pino, together with others of the land expedition.

Port of Monterey, June 3, 1770

Gaspar de Portolá (Rubric)

Don Juan Pérez, Captain and pilot of His Majesty's packet boat named the *San Antonio*, alias *El Príncipe*, and Don Miguel del Pino, Lieutenant Captain and second pilot of the same packet boat, hereby solemnly swear that Governor Don Gaspar de Portolá has taken possession, in the name of his Catholic Majesty, of the Port of San Carlos de Monterey, and of its lands. This said port is the very same one mentioned in the history of the voyage of Don Sebastián Viscaino and in the sailing directions of the pilot Don José Cabrera Bueno. And so that it may be of record wherever required, we hereby affix our signatures at the same port on the 3rd of June in the year 1770.

Miguel del Pino (rubric)

Juan Pérez (rubric)

As Lieutenant of the Compañía Franco de Voluntarios de Cataluña, assigned by His Majesty to this Kingdom of New Spain, I hereby certify that the commander-in-chief of this expedition, Don Gaspar de Portolá, has taken possession of the Port of Monterey and its lands on the day mentioned, in the name of His Catholic Majesty. And because, according to the History of the Californias, the voyage of Sebastián Viscaino, and the sailing instructions of Cabrera Bueno, he has found the landmarks both on land and sea, without any exception, I sign this that it may be of record wherever required, today, the 11th of June of 1770.

Pedro Fages
(rubric)

This material is translated from Archivo General de la Nación, PI Vol. 76, pp. 76-77. A similar version, containing the same basic information, is found in the Bolton Papers (Bancroft Library, C-B 840, item 90, folder 33), and is presented in translation in Bolton. *Historical Memoirs of New California*, Vol. II, pp. 291-292, 384, n. 163.

APPENDIX F

TAR SPRINGS
OF SOUTHWESTERN CALIFORNIA

Extensive field work, augmented by a study of available literature, indicates that there are considerably more than 1,000 tar springs, tar swamps, and tar pits in the Los Angeles-Ventura area of southwestern California. Most of these are small, unspectacular, and of little commercial value. In fact, a tar spring in an urban area, or amid intensively cultivated fields, is an expensive nuisance. A reliable, early geologic report on these tar springs is E.W. Hilgard, "The Asphaltum Deposits of California," in *Mineral Resources of the United States*, 1883-1884, (Washington, Government Printing Office, 1885) p. 938-948. Although nearly a century old, this report is surprisingly complete, and even mentions (p. 939) "petroleum springs (that) indicate their position off shore at several points."

From north to south, the four tar springs mentioned in the José Velásquez report are:

1. At Carpinteria. This tar spring was discovered by the Portolá expedition on August 17, 1769. Geographical location is Lat. 34°23'16" N.: Long. 119°30'48" W.: Alt. 20' MSL, approximately. This area is shown on the U.S. Geological Survey 7.5' Quadrangle "Carpinteria," dated 1952, photo-revised 1967; and on the centerfold map in Carpinteria Magazine/Visitor's Guide, 1977-78. The tar spring is best reached by driving to the south (seaward) end of Eighth St. (Carpinteria), then crossing the railroad tracks. The spring is on a low bluff just above the beach, which is now set aside as Carpinteria Beach State Park. South of the tar spring in the surf is a large mass of tar-cemented conglomerate, of no great geological antiquity. There are a number of other very small tar springs and seeps in the general area. The main tar spring at Carpinteria has produced many interesting and valuable Pleistocene plant fossils.

2. Approximately 2.6 miles east-southeast of Camarillo. This tar spring was discovered by the Portolá expedition on its return journey from San Francisco Bay, probably on January 14, 1770; it is mentioned in Pedro Font's diary for February 23, 1775. Geographical location is Lat. 34°12'29" N.: Long 118°59'32" W.: Alt. 120' MSL, approximately.

This area is shown on the U.S. Geological Survey 7.5' Quadrangle "Newbury Park," dated 1950, photo-revised 1967. The main tar spring is located on a flat area at the foot (west end) of the Conejo Grade on Ventura Boulevard, south of the main road and east of Conejo Creek. There are a number of other very small tar seeps in the area, and several small caved-in pits remain from unsuccessful attempts at commercial production of asphalt.

3. At the south foot of the Santa Monica Mountains, between the Río Porciúncula, now Los Angeles River, and Ballena Creek, now Ballona Creek. This large expanse of tar swamps was discovered by the Portolá Expedition on August 3, 1769. Geographical position of the center of the tar seep area is Lat. 34°04'25" N.: Long. 118°19'36" W.: Alt. 240' MSL, approximately. This area is mapped in the U.S. Geological Survey 7.5' Quadrangle "Hollywood," dated 1966 and revised in 1972. The tar springs originally covered somewhat more than 1200 acres and contained forty or more springs and seeps of tar, as well as a number of sources of water. Boundaries of the area, in terms of modern culture, are Gardner Street (west), Rosewood Avenue (north), Harvard Boulevard (east), and Third Street (south). This area overlaps in considerable part the old Salt Lake Oil Field now abandoned.

As the City of Los Angeles grew westward, the headwaters of Ballona Creek were diverted into storm sewers and buried drains, and the tar springs and seeps were buried by later construction. This burial, however, did not shut off the upwelling of tar, and flows into catch basins, sewers and cellars are a continuing local problem. Tar seeps also undermine street paving and are a recurrent nuisance on lawns and sidewalks. An excellent engineering summary of this problem, with a map and photographs, is C.A. Richards, "Engineering Geology Aspects of Petroleum in the Urban Environment," in *Geology, Seismicity and Environmental Impact, Special Publication,* Association of Engineering Geologists, October, 1973, pp. 391-399.

4. Along the course of Oil Creek. This group of tar pits is better known as the La Brea Tar Pits, taking its name from a later surrounding land grant. These were discovered by the Portolá expedition on August 3, 1769. Geographical position of the center of this group of tar springs is Lat. 34°03'45" N.: Long. 118°21'24" W.; Alt. 180' MSL, approximately.

This area is mapped on the U.S. Geological Survey 7.5' Quadrangle "Hollywood," dated 1966 and revised in 1972. The La Brea Tar Pits originally covered somewhat more than 234 acres. Most of the area has been set aside as Hancock Park, and the numerous tar pits there are a continuing source of excellent Pleistocene mammalian fossils. The area of the La Brea Tar pits substantially overlaps that of the now-abandoned Salt Lake Oil Field. Clear description of the Rancho La Brea tar pits and of their paleontological importance is found in Chester Stock, *Rancho La Brea; A Record of Pleistocene Life in California*, Los Angeles Museum, Publication 1, 1930, 82 pp.

First known description of the interesting and sometimes spectacular gas bubbles in the La Brea tar pits (Fig. 9) is found in Duflot de Mofras, *Exploration des Territoires de l'Orégon, des Californies et de la Mer Vermeillo, exécutée pendant les années 1840, 1841 et 1842*, 2 vols. with atlas of 26 sheets, maps and plans; Paris, Published by Order of the King, 1844, Vol. II, p. 337.

The records and itineraries of the Portolá expedition indicate that Corporal José Velásquez was present at the discovery of each of these tar sources, and that on his courier journey south from Monterey, he was visiting sites 1,3, and 4 for the fourth time, and site 2 for the third.

There is another small tar source south of the Santa Monica Mountains that was almost certainly known to the Spaniards, but is not clearly described in available accounts. This is located at Lat. 34°03'45" N.; Long. 118°17'00" W.; Alt. 259' MSL. approximately. This area is shown on the U.S. Geological Survey 7.5' Quadrangle "Hollywood," dated 1966, revised 1972. This area of about 32 acres is roughly co-extensive with modern Lafayette Park, at the intersection of Wilshire Boulevard and Hoover St. Los Angeles. Just northwest of this is the former site of Bimini Hot Springs, which were a minor resort from about 1870 to about 1930, and are now obliterated by urban construction. This area is just south of the largely-abandoned Los Angeles oil field.

Geologic studies indicate that all tar seeps immediately south of the Santa Monica Mountains have a similar origin. Petroleum from moderately deep structures percolates upward through steeply-dipping and truncated Miocene beds into a thin, relatively flat-lying cover of poorly consolidated Pleistocene beds (mostly sand), and thence to the surface. The more volatile components of the petroleum evaporate at and near the surface, leaving behind the thick and viscous tars, which were known to the Spanish as *brea*. There is some evidence that the rate of upward percolation of petroleum to the tar springs is influenced both by earthquakes and by withdrawal of oil from adjacent production structures.

Check-observations for this appendix to enable updating of field notes to May, 1978, were furnished by the U.S. Geological Survey, Flagstaff, Arizona and Menlo Park, California offices; the Carpinteria Chamber of Commerce (Sandi Augerot); the Ventura County Public Works Agency (Donald A. Betlach); the Los Angeles City Department of Public Works, Bureau of Engineering (Art Dennis); and the Los Angeles Chamber of Commerce.

BIBLIOGRAPHY

Here are listed, in alphabetical order, all of the printed works referred to in the text. Documents and maps are referenced by foot-notes at the place of their occurrence in the text. Internal bibliographies in many of the cited works will be found pertinent and useful.

Aguierre, Amado. *Documentos Para La Historia de Baja California.* Mexico, D.F.: University of Mexico, 1977, Document 18.

Alegre, F.J. *Historia de la Provincia de la Compañía de Jesús de Nueva España.* See edition by E.J. Burrus, and Felix Zubillaga. Rome: Institutum Historicum S.J., 4 vols. 1956, 1958, 1959, 1960.

Almada, F.R. *Diccionario de Historia, Geografía, y Biografía Sonorense.* Chihuahua: Ruiz Sandoval, 1952.

Anonymous. *Carpintería Magazine/Visitor's Guide,* 1977-78. Carpintería Chamber of Commerce, 1976.

Arricivita, Juan D. *Crónica Seráfica y Apostólica del Colegio de Propaganda Fide de la Santa Cruz de Querétaro en la Nueva España.* Mexico, D. F. 1972.

Aschmann, Homer. *The Central Desert of Baja California.* Berkeley and Los Angeles: University of California Press, 1959: reprinted, Riverside: Manessier, 1967.

Baegert, Johann Jacob, S.J. *Observations in Lower California by Johann Jakob Baegert.* Translated by M.M. Brandenburg and C.L. Baumann. Berkeley and Los Angeles: University of California Press, 1952.

Bancroft, Hubert Howe. *Early California Annals.* New York: Bancroft, 1889.

_____. *History of Arizona and New Mexico.* San Francisco: The History Company, 1889.

Bannon, John F. *The Spanish Borderlands Frontier.* New York: Holt, Rinehart and Winston, 1970.

Bean, L.J. and Mason, W.M. *Diaries and Accounts of the Romero Expeditions in Arizona and California.* Los Angeles: Ward Ritchie, 1962.

Beilharz, E.A. *Felipe de Neve, First Governor of California.* San Francisco: California Historical Society Special Publication No. 49.

Bolton, Herbert E. *Kino's Historical Memoir of Pimería Alta*. Cleveland: Clark, 2 vols. 1919.

——————. *Historical Memoir of New California*. Berkeley: University of California Press, 4 vols. 1926.

——————. *Fray Juan Crespi, Missionary Explorer*. Berkeley: University of California Press, 1927.

——————. *Anza's California Expeditions*. Berkeley: University of California Press, 5 vols. 1930.

——————. *Outpost of Empire*. New York: Knopf, 1931.

——————. ''In The South San Joaquín Ahead of Garcés.'' *California Historical Society Quarterly*, Vol. X, No. 3: September, 1931, pp. 211-219.

——————. *Rim of Christendom*. New York: MacMillan, 1936.

Brandenburg, M.M. and C.L. Baumann. See Johann Baegert.

Brandes, Ray. *The Costansó Narrative of the Portolá Expedition*. Newhall: Hogarth, 1970.

Brinckerhoff, Sidney B, and Falk, Odie B. *Lancers for the King*. Phoenix: Arizona Historical Foundation, 1965.

Burrus, Ernest J. *Kino's Plan*. Tucson: Arizona Historical Society, 1961.

——————. *Informe del Estado de la Nueva Cristianidad de California*. Madrid: Porrua, 1962.

——————. *Kino and the Cartography of Northwestern New Spain*. Tucson: Arizona Historical Society, 1965.

——————. *Kino Escribe a la Duquesa*. Madrid: Porrua, 1965.

——————. *Kino Writes to the Duchess*. Rome: Jesuit Historical Institute, 1965.

——————. *Wenceslaus Linck's Diary of His 1766 Expedition to Northern Baja California*. Los Angeles: Dawson, 1966.

——————. *La Obra Cartográfica de la Provincia Mexicana de la Compañia de Jesus*. Madrid: Porrua, 2 vols. 1967.

——————. *Ducrue's Account of the Expulsion of the Jesuits from Lower California: 1767-1769*. Rome: Jesuit Historical Institute, 1967.

——————. *Wenceslaus Linck's Reports and Letters 1762-1778*. Los Angeles: Dawson, 1967.

——————. *Diario del Capitán Comandante Fernando de Rivera y Moncada*. Madrid Turanzas, 2 vols. 1968.

_____. "Rivera y Moncada, Explorer and Military Commander of Both Californias, in the Light of His Diary and Other Contemporary Documents," *Hispanic American Historical Review.* Vol. I, No. 4, November, 1970, pp. 682-692.

_____. *Kino and Manje, Explorers of Sonora and Arizona.* Rome: Jesuit Historical Institute, 1971.

_____. *Juan María Salvatierra.* Los Angeles: Dawson, 1971.

Cabrera Bueno, J.G. *Navegación Espectaculativa y Práctica.* Manila, 1734.

Chapman, Charles E. *A History of California.* New York: Macmillan, 1921.

Chappe d'Auteroche, J.B. *Voyage en California pour l'observation de Passage de Venus sur le disque du soleil, le 3 Juin, 1769.* Paris: Jombert, 1772.

Coues, Elliott. *On the Trail of a Spanish Pioneer.* New York: Harper, 2 vols. 1900.

Crosby, Harry. *The King's Highway in Baja California.* Salt Lake City: Publisher's Press, 1974.

Cuevas, Mariano. *Monje y Marinero — La Vida y Tiempos de Fray Andrés de Urdaneta.* Mexico, D.F.: Editorial Layac, 1962.

Cullimore, Clarence. *The Martyrdom and Interment of Padre Francisco Garcés.* Bakersfield: Kern County Historical Society, 1954.

Dampier, William. *A New Voyage Round the World.* Edited by Albert Gray. London: Argonaut Press, 1927, pp. 177-181.

Decorme, Gerard, S.J. *La Obra de los Jesuitas Mexicanos.* Mexico D.F.: Porrua 2 vols. 1941.

Denis, A.J. *Spanish Alta California.* New York: Macmillan, 1927.

Dobyns, Henry. F. *Spanish Colonial Tucson.* Tucson: University of Arizona Press, 1976. Donohue, John A. *After Kino, Jesuit Missions in Northwestern New Spain, 1711-1767.* Rome: Jesuit Historical Institute, 1969.

Dunne, Peter Masten, S.J. *Black Robes in Lower California.* Berkeley and Los Angeles: University of California Press, 1952.

_____. *Jacobo Sedelmayr.* Tucson: Arizona Historical Society, 1955.

_____. *Juan Antonio Balthasar.* Tucson: Arizona Historical Society 1957.

Englehardt, Zephyrin, O.F.M. *Missions and Missionaries of California*. Chicago: Franciscan Herald Press (Second Edition) 2 vols., 1929.

Engstrand, I.W. *Royal Officer in Baja California; Joaquín Velázquez de León*. Los Angeles: Dawson, 1976.

Ewing, Russell C. "'The Pima Uprising of 1751-1752: A Study of Spain's Indian Policy," Unpublished Doctoral Dissertation, University of California, 1934.

_____. "The Pima Uprising of 1751," in *Greater American Essays in Honor of Herbert Eugene Bolton*. Berkeley: University of California Press, 1945.

Forbes, Jack D. *Warriors of the Colorado*. Norman: University of Oklahoma Press, 1965.

Fuster, E. N. and Alberto Colinga, Editors. *Sagrada Biblia*. Madrid: Editorial Católica, 1969.

Galvin, John. *A Record of Travels in Arizona and California*. San Francisco Howell, 1960.

_____. *The First Spanish Entry into San Francisco Bay*. San Francisco: John Howell, 1971.

Geiger, Maynard, O.F.M. *The Life and Times of Junípero Serra*. Washington: Academy of American Franciscan History, 2 Vols. 1959.

Gerhard, Peter. *Pirates on the West Coast of New Spain, 1575-1742*. Glendale: Clark, 1960.

Gifford, E.W. "The Cocopa," *University of California Publications in Archaeology and Ethnology*, Vol. 31, No. 5, 1933.

Gramatica, Aloisius. Editor. *Bibliorum Sacrorum Iuxta Vulgatam Clementinum*. Bonis Auris, 1913.

Graves, Clifford "Don Pedro Prat," *Journal of San Diego History*, Vol. 22, No. 2, Spring, 1976.

Hammond, G. P. "The Zúñiga Journal, Tucson to Santa Fe: Opening of a Spanish Trade Route, 1788-1795," *New Mexico Historical Review*. Vol. VI, No. 1, January, 1931.

Hilgard, E. W. "The Asphaltum Deposits of California," in *Mineral Resources of the United States, 1883-1884*. Washington: Government Printing Office, 1885.

Hittell, T.H. *El Triunfo de la Cruz*. San Francisco: California Historical Society Special Publication No. 38, undated.

Holterman, Jack. "José Zúñiga," *The Kiva*, Vol. 22, No. 1, November, 1956.

H.O. Publication 84. *Sailing Directions for the West Coasts of Mexico and Central America*. Washington: Government Printing Office, 1954.

Ives, R.L. "The Bolas de Plata Discovery of 1736," *Rocks and Minerals*, Vol. 10, 1935.

_____. *"Sedelmayr's Relacion of 1746,"* Bureau of American *Ethnology*, Bulletin 123, 1939, pp. 99-117.

_____. "The Quest of the Blue Shells," *Arizoniana*, Vol. 2, No. 1, Spring, 1961, pp. 3-7.

_____. "Kino's Route Across Baja California," *The Kiva*, Vol. 26, No. 1, April, 1961, pp. 17-29.

_____. "Dating the 1746 Eruption of Tres Vírgenes Volcano, Baja California del Sur, Mexico," *Bulletin*, Geological Society of America, Vol. 73, No. 5, May, 1962.

_____. "The Manila Galleons," *Journal of Geography*, Vol. 43, No. 1, Jan. 1964.

_____. "Retracing the Route of the Fages Expedition of 1781," *Arizona and the West*, Vol. VIII: Spring and Summer, 1966.

_____. "From Pitic to San Gabriel in 1782: The Journey of Don Pedro Fages," *Journal of Arizona History*, Vol. IX: Winter, 1968.

Lumholtz, Carl. *New Trails in Mexico*. New York: Scribner, 1912; reprinted Glorieta: Rio Grande Press, 1971.

Martin, Douglas. *Yuma Crossing*. Albuquerque: University of New Mexico Press, 1954.

Mathes, W. Michael. *First from the Gulf to the Pacific*. Los Angeles: Dawson, 1969.

Meigs, Peveril. *The Dominican Mission Frontier in Lower California*. Berkeley: University of California Press, 1935.

Merk, Augustinus. Editor. *Novum Testamentum*. Rome, 1951.

Mofras, Duflot de. *Exploration des Territoires de l'Oregon, des Californies et de Mer Vermello, exécutée pendant les années 1840, 1841 et 1842*. Paris: Published by Order of the King, 2 Vols., with atlas of 26 sheets, maps and plans, 1844.

McCarty, Kieran, O.F.M. *Desert Documentary*. Tucson: Arizona Historical Society, 1976.

Navarro García, Luis. *José de Gálvez y la Comandancia de las Provincias Internas*. Sevilla: Escuela de los Estudios Hispano-Americanos, 1964.

Nentuig, Juan, S.J. *Rudo Ensayo*. Translated and edited by Eusebio Guitéras, Records American Catholic Historical Society of Philadelphia, Vol. 5, No. 2, 1894.

Nuttall, Donald A. Pedro Fages and the Advance of the Northern Frontier of New Spain, 1767-1782. Unpublished Doctoral Dissertation, University of Southern California, Los Angeles, 1964.

Ortega, José and Balthasar, J.A. *Apostólicos Afanes de la Compañía de Jesús Escritos por un Padre de la Misma Sagrada Religión de su Provincia de Mexico*. Mexico, D.F.: Editorial Layac, 1944.

Palou, Francisco. *Relación Histórica de la Vida y Apostólicas Tareas del Venerable Padre Fray Junípero Serra*. Mexico: 1787.

Polzer, Charles W. *A Kino Guide: His Missions — His Monuments*. Tucson: Southwestern Mission Research Center, 1968.

_____. *Kino Guide II: His Missions — His Monuments*. Tucson: Southwestern Mission Research Center, 1982.

Pourade, R.F. *The Call to California*. San Diego Union-Tribune, 1968.

Priestley, Herbert I. *The Colorado River Campaigns, 1781-1782: Diary of Pedro Fages*. Academy of Pacific Coast History, Publications III, May, 1913.

_____. *A Historical, Political and Natural Description of California by Pedro Fages*. Ramona: Ballena, 1972.

Rensch, H. E. "Fages' Crossing of the Cuyamacas," *California Historical Society Quarterly*. Vol. 34, No. 3, September, 1955.

Richards, C.A. "Engineering Geology Aspects of Petroleum in the Urban Environment," in *Geology, Seismicity and Environmental Impact*, Special Publication, Association of Engineering Geologists, October, 1973.

Robles, V.A., Editor. *Diario y Derrotero de la Caminando, Visto y Observado en la Visita que Hizo a los Presidios de Nueva España Septentrional*, Report of Brigadier Pedro de Rivera's Inspection Trip to Northwestern Mexico in 1726. Mexico, D.F.: Secretaria de la Defensa Nacional, 1946.

Roca, Raul. *Paths of the Padres Through Sonora*. Tucson: Arizona Historical Society, 1967.

Rohder, Regis, O.F.M. *Mission San Antonio*. Jolón: Franciscan Fathers, undated.

Rowland, Donald W. The Elizondo Expedition Against the Indian Rebels of Sonora. Unpublished Doctoral Dissertation, University of California, 1931.

Rudkin, C.N. *Observations on California*. Los Angeles: Dawson, 1956.

Ryrie, C.C., Editor. *The Ryrie Study Bible: King James Version*. Chicago: Moody, 1978.

Sánchez, Joseph P. The Catalonian Volunteers and the Defense of Northern New Spain, 1767-1803. Unpublished Doctoral Dissertation, University of New Mexico, Albuquerque, 1974.

Schurz, W. L. *The Manila Galleon*. New York: Dutton, 1939.

Servin, Manuel P. *The Apostolic Life of Fernando Consag*. Los Angeles: Dawson, 1968.

Smith, Fay Jackson, John L. Kessell and Francis J. Fox, S.J. *Father Kino in Arizona*. Phoenix: Arizona Historical Foundation, 1966.

Stock, Chester. *Rancho La Brea; A Record of Pleistocene Life in California*. Los Angeles Museum, Publication 1, 1930.

Sykes, Godfrey. *The Colorado Delta*. Washington and New York: Carnegie Institution of Washington and American Geographical Society, 1937.

Thomas, A.B. *Teodoro de Croix and the Northern Frontier of New Spain*. Norman: University of Oklahoma Press, 1941.

Tiscareno, Froy, and J.W. Robinson. *José Joaquín Arrillaga — Diary of His Surveys of the Frontier, 1796*. Los Angeles: Dawson, 1969.

Treutlein, Theodore E. *Missionary in Sonora*. San Francisco: California Historical Society, 1965.

Venegas, Miguel, S.J. *Noticia de la California*. México, D.F.: Layac, 3 Vols., 1963.

Villa, Eduardo W. *Historia del Estado de Sonora*. Hermosillo: Editorial Sonora, 1951.

Villavicencio, E.J. *Vida y Virtudes de el venerable y apostólica Padre Juan de Ugarte de la Compañía de Jesús, misionero de las islas Californias, y uno de sus primeros conquistadores*. México, D.F. 1954.

Von Oppolzer, T.H. *Canon der Finsternisse*. Wien: Gerold, 1887; reprinted New York: Dover, 1962.

Wagner, H.R. *The Geography of the Northwest Coast of America to the Year 1800*. Berkeley: University of California Press, 2 Vols., 1937.

Weber, Francis J. *The Missions and Missionaries of Baja California*. Los Angeles: Dawson, 1968.

Wheelock, Walt and Howard E. Gulick. *Baja California Guidebook.* Glendale: Clark, 3rd edition, 1975.

Williams, Anita A. *Travelers Among the Cucupa.* Los Angeles: Dawson, 1975.

Zapata, J. Ortiz, S.J. *Relación de las Misiones que la Compañía de Jesús Tiene en el Reino y Provincia de la Nueva Vizcaya en la Nueva España, Hecho en el Año de 1768,* Archivo General de la Nación, *Misiones,* Vol. 26, folios 241-269. Printed version in *Documentos Para la Historia de Mexico,* Cuarta Seria, Mexico, D. F.: Garcia Torres, 1857.

Zevallos, Francisco, S.J. *Carta del Padre Provincial, Francisco Zevallos, Sobre la Apostólica Vida y Virtudes del P. Fernando Konsag, S.J., Insigne Misionero de la California.* México, D.F.: College of San Ildefonso, 1764.

Acapulco, 34, 42
Adak, see San Borja, 50, 51
Adventurer, ship, 3
Agiabampo Bay, 29
Agua Caliente, 9; arroyo BCN 53, 75
Agua Dulce BCN, 74
Aguierre, Juan Bautista, pilot, 13
Aguilar, Francisco Javier, 126-127, 131
Alamos, 157
Alava, Spain, 40
Aleutians, 71
Algarve, Portugal, 39
Algodones Dunes, 10, 21, 23
Almaza, Guadalupe, 124
Alta California, occupation of, 71
Altar, presidio of Santa Gertrudis, 7, 15,
    18, 21, 24, 158, 161-188, 213
Alvarado, Francisco Javier, 144-145
Amador, Pedro, 118, 124-125, 144-145
amonites, 49
Anaheim, 85
Andrés, baptized Indian, 135
Angel de la Guarda, island, 44, 51-53
Anian, Straits of, 44
Año Nuevo, bay BCS, 32-33
antiscorbutics, 41, 89, 93
Antonio, José, 208
Anza, Juan Bautista de, 2, 4 ftn. 12 (vita);
    diary 192; expedition description, 9,
    11, 13, 126, 205 n. 1; second expedi-
    tion, 8, 24, 127, 157, 169; trail 162
Apache, raids, 62-63
Arbizu, Manuel Antonio, 208, 214
Areche, José Antonio de, 115-116
Arguello, José Dário, 16, 213
Arias Caballero, Andrés, lieutenant, 213
Aribaipa, 21
Arillaga, José Joaquín, 214
Arizonác, 2
Arizpe, 18, 102, 163, 168, 210, 215
Armona, Matías, governor, 95-100, 102-
    103, 150
Arnes, P. Victoriano, SJ, 51 ftn. 10 (vita),
    55
Arroyo Seco, 85
Arze, Sebastián de, 124

Atondo y Antillón, Admiral Isidro, 27-37
Ayala, Juan Manuel de, 13
Ayvar, P. José, OP, 140-142
Baegert, P. Johann Jakob, SJ, 25, 58
Bahía de Año Nuevo, see Año Nuevo
Bahía de Humos, 85
Bahía de Los Angeles, 50-52; photo 52
Bahía San Luis Gonzaga, 50, 57, 71-74,
    98, 107, 116, 125-126, 143, 156,
    212, 215; photo 70
Bailen, Spain, 209
Bailón, Pascual, 17
Baker, Charles D., 216
Ballenas, canal, 51
Balthasar, P. Juan Antonio, SJ, 49
Barraneche, P. Juan, OFM, 16, 20, 208
Barrett Resevoir, 175
Barri, Felipe, governor, 103-104, 111-
    117, 122, 150, 210
Basterra, P. Dionisio, OFM, 102
Bautista Canyon, 6
bears, 86, meat, 106
bells, mission, 158
Benitez, María Josefa, 208
Bernal, Manuel, 120
Bernasconi Hot Springs, 6
Bicuñer, 16, 20, 157, 164-166, 213
bitumen, 97
Blackwater (AZ), 6
Bocana del Rosario, 111
Bolton, Prof. Herbert Eugene, 217
Bonilla, Antonio, 7
Borja, Doña Maríana, Duquesa de Béjar y
    Gandia, 51
Borrego Flats, 6
Bow Willow Trail, 180
Branciforte, 90
Bratton Valley, 175
Briones, José Antonio, 124
Bucareli, Antonio María, 7, 14, 112-118,
    138-140, 211
Buenavista, 19
Caballada, arroyo, 173
Caballero, P. Felix, OFM, 178
Cabo San Lucas, 41, 72, 98
Caborca, 5, 7, 21, 44, 161